Guide to

Ethnic

London

Ian McAuley

Immel also publishes the Discovery Guide travel books and a wide range of other titles. Please send for a complete list to 20 Berkeley Street, London W1X 5AE.

Guide to Ethnic London, second edition, completely revised.

Photography by Paul Trevor. Additional Pictures: wash-drawing and engravings courtesy of Holborn Library, photograph of Italian London c 1920 by Pino Maestri, photograph inside Cypriot church by David McAuley, all other photographs by Ian McAuley.

British Library Cataloguing-in-Publication Data
A catalogue record for this book is available from the British Library.

ISBN 1898162204

Cover design by Johan Hofsteenge.
Typesetting by Johan Hofsteenge, Galway, Ireland.

Printed in Great Britain by Butler and Tanner Ltd., Frome, Somerset.

IMMEL Publishing Limited, 20 Berkeley Street, London W1X 5AE
Tel: 071 491 1799
Fax: 071 493 5524

To my parents.

CONTENTS

INTRODUCTION

London has always been a cosmopolitan city. It was founded by the Romans, overrun by the Anglo-Saxons and conquered by the Normans. Over the last few centuries it has become the adopted home of many foreign immigrants, some fleeing religious or political persecution, but most simply in search of a better way of life.

Yet if there is a long history of foreign settlement in London, it is the period following the Second World War which stands out as *the* age of immigration, both in the numbers involved and the variety of countries from which they came. In the 19th C Benjamin Disraeli called London 'a nation, not a city'; today that is almost an understatement.

This guidebook is an introduction for the general public to an increasingly important aspect of London life. It focuses on those ethnic groups that have had the greatest impact on the city, but such is London today that there is hardly any part of the world that has not sent at least a small community to live in it.

If you are living or staying in London, the world is on your doorstep. This fully updated edition aims to make the task of exploring it that much easier.

Ian McAuley

CHINESE LONDON

HISTORY

The first Chinese immigrants to Britain were seamen who came to London in the late 18th C and early 19th C on the ships of the East India Company. They settled near the docks in the East End and by the late 19th C the district of Limehouse had a small but busy Chinatown, with a population that made much of its living from catering to the needs of a shifting population of Chinese seamen. By the First World War the Limehouse Chinatown contained over 30 shops and restaurants in the streets of Limehouse Causeway and Pennyfields, E14.

The years leading up to the First World War were a time of tension between British and Chinese seamen in several British ports. British seamen claimed that the Chinese were undercutting their wage rates and that many were falsely claiming to have been born in the British colony of Hong Kong so as to avoid the English language qualification that was compulsory for foreign seamen. The employers retorted that the Chinese were better disciplined and less likely to get drunk than British seamen. The most serious of the clashes that occurred in London were in May 1908 when huge crowds of British seamen repeatedly prevented Chinese crews from signing on at the Board of Trade offices at the East India Dock, East India Dock Road, E14. Feelings ran so high that the Chinese had to be escorted home by the police.

Limehouse was re-created in Hollywood for the hugely successful film *Broken Blossoms* (1919), which portrays the relationship between an innocent young English girl and an idealistic Chinese poet who comes to Britain during the First World War to 'bring the peace of the Buddha to the warring West'. The Chinese man's principles are tested by the girl's sadistic father, who murders his daughter and is in turn killed by the poet, who then commits suicide.

Broken Blossoms was a sympathetic portrayal of the Chinese by the standards of the time. The English author Sax Rohmer (real name Arthur Ward) made his reputation through his creation of the Chinese arch-criminal Fu Manchu, a character that Rohmer said was inspired by a chance view of a well-dressed, unusually tall Chinese man getting into a limousine in Limehouse Causeway on a foggy night in 1911. Fu Manchu first saw the light of day in the novel *The Mystery of Doctor Fu Manchu* (1913), and reappeared in numerous further stories by Rohmer, many of which have been made into films.

The sinister impression of the Chinese given by such material prompted L Wagner, the author of *London Saunterings* (1928), to write: 'We feel in duty bound . . . to say that the Chinese colony "Down East" may be visited with the utmost personal safety . . . Due perhaps to our insular prejudices, John Chinaman has been very much maligned. In novels and plays he is set forth as a trickster and villain of the deepest dye'.

The Limehouse Chinatown was badly hit by bombing in the Second World War, and after the war new Seaman's Union rules on the employment of non-British seamen discouraged further settlement of Chinese seamen. The final blow came in the 1950s when almost all of the buildings in Limehouse Causeway and Pennyfields were demolished to make way for council housing. Today there is little trace of the old Chinatown, though the trade with China that spawned it is remembered in the names of several nearby streets - Ming Street, Canton Street, Peking Street and Nankin Street.

Up until the 1950s the principal trade followed by the Chinese in Britain was in running 'Chinese laundries'. It was the catering business, however, that ushered in the next, and much larger, phase of Chinese immigration to Britain in the 1950s and 1960s. Most of the immigrants were from the New Territories, a large rural area that forms part of the British colony of Hong Kong. With few employment opportunities in poor communities, men were drawn to Britain by prospects in the expanding Chinese restaurant and take-away trade and, once settled here, were then joined by their families.

Today there are an estimated 140,000 people of Chinese origin in Britain, of whom about 55,000 live in London. Although patterns of employment are slowly changing, the catering trade remains by far the major source of employment amongst the Chinese community.

'Inside Out'

Interview with David, a Chinese journalist in his 40s . . .

"Older Chinese people, most of whom work in catering, find it difficult and awkward to be integrated into British society, even though in their work they cater for all classes of British society. A lot of Chinese parents don't want their children when grown up to take over their catering business because it's a hard trade and is not part of the mainstream of British society. So a lot of British-born Chinese children when they grow up are encouraged to do well in schools and universities, and they end up doing things like pharmacy, accountancy, engineering, medicine, computers and that sort of stuff. Even so, these children have a great difficulty in identifying themselves with any culture. They end up wandering in a grey cultural area."

CHINATOWN, SOHO

Neatly tucked in between Shaftesbury Avenue and Leicester Square in Soho is the district known to the Chinese as 'Tong Yan Kai' (literally, 'Chinese Street'), and to everyone else simply as 'Chinatown'. Its few narrow streets are lined with Chinese restaurants and shops, and although few Chinese people actually live here it is always busy, particularly at weekends when the Chinese come from across the whole of the South of England to meet people, do their shopping, see films, eat in the restaurants and above all just *be* Chinese.

Chinatown's roots could be said to lie in the Second World War, when Chinese restaurants were first opened in Soho in response to the demands of British soldiers (who had acquired a taste for Chinese food overseas), and of American soldiers (who were already familiar with it). It was not until the late 1960s however that Chinatown began to develop around the nucleus of a few Chinese restaurants and food stores in Gerrard Street. Taking advantage of cheap property in what was then one of the shabbiest areas of

Soho, the Chinese rapidly expanded their activities in the 1970s to make this the commercial, social and cultural centre for London's Chinese community.

The local council has entered into the spirit of Chinatown by helping to emphasise its Chinese character. Massive oriental arches have been erected at each end of Gerrard Street, and Chinese-style telephone kiosks and street signs with Chinese characters have also been set up in the area.

As you stroll around Chinatown, make sure to take a look in the windows of the Chinese herbal medicine shops at 24a Lisle Street and 15 Little Newport Street. Here you can see animal, mineral and plant products being weighed out for customers on hand-held scales. Some of the more unusual medicinal products they deal in include dried seahorses (which are used for treating coughs) and snakeskins (used as a nutritional supplement for the weak).

During your visit, spare a moment to reflect on the curious sequence of events by which Soho's Chinatown was able to come into being. The story begins with the British taste for tea, a Chinese drink which by the late 18th C had become an indispensable part of British life. This created a trading deficit for Britain with its supplier, China, which led to the British promoting the import of opium into China to try and balance their books. When the outraged Chinese Government attempted to stop the import of opium the British went to war over the issue, ostensibly to protect the principle of free trade. After China's defeat in the Opium War of 1840-2, Hong Kong became a British colony, and as a result, while Communist China was closed to the world in the 1950s and 1960s, the Hong Kong Chinese were free to come to Britain and to create their own corner of China in London.

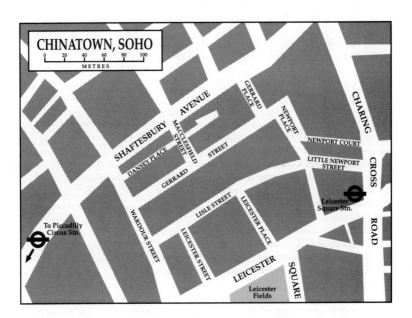

'Inside Out'

Interview with Victor, a retired Chinese civil servant, about London's 'Chinatown' . . .

"To most of the Chinese in London and even in Europe, Chinatown is the focal point of their social life. Otherwise they are just scattered all over London and the country. They come to Chinatown to eat, to shop, they have their wedding receptions here, their birthdays, their Christening parties.

Just imagine when you operate a take-away out in the suburbs all on your own and feeling rather isolated. On Sunday afternoons when all your friends and family come here to Chinatown, they feel so much at home. They come here on Sunday afternoons because this is when English people have the most important meal of the week, so there's no business for the Chinese caterers, and they all come out with their families.

On Sunday afternoons in Chinatown the dim sum restaurants in particular are packed with Chinese families. Making dim sum is very complicated and there are so many different varieties so this is something which people don't make at home. It's simpler to come here, to Chinatown.

What makes Chinatown is the people, of course, who have worked very hard to build up what it is today."

CHINATOWN: SHOPPING

Chinatown is an excellent hunting-ground for that elusive Christmas or birthday present. As a gift for the person who has everything, how about a four-foot long paper fan, a book of poetry by Chairman Mao or martial-arts rice flails painted with the pattern of the Union Jack? Whatever you've got your eye on, the standard of English spoken by the shopkeepers is often rather basic, so don't expect to be able to ask too much about what you are buying - what you see is what you get.

Arts and crafts. The combination of cheap labour and the Chinese talent for intricate work with delicate materials has produced an unbeatable array of attractive and reasonably-priced handmade goods from the Far East. Cork is carved into miniature Chinese gardens that are encased in glass. Pictures are made out of shells, straws, feathers and silk. The sap of the lacquer tree is applied onto jewellery boxes, vases and screens, and carved into exquisite patterns. Paper is transformed into parasols, fans, lanterns, kites and intricate paper cuts of flowers, animals and landscapes. Many such items sport beautiful hand-painted designs, though these are seldom the work of individual craftsmen - each colour will probably have been painted on by a different hand as the object was passed down a manual production line.

Ceramics. A veritable army of statuettes of Buddhas, Taoist deities and characters from Chinese history and legend stand massed on the shelves of the shops of Chinatown. Some of these figures are purely decorative; others are used in the Buddhist and Taoist shrines found in some Chinese homes. Also available are beautiful decorative tea sets and a wide selection of basic kitchenware.

Games. Ma-jong and Chinese chess sets are available in a couple of shops, though bear in mind that English-language instructions are not always enclosed. Ma-jong, which was once common in upper-class British homes, is a popular gambling game amongst the Chinese in Britain. Played by four people, it can best be described as a cross between bridge, gin rummy and dominoes. Chinese chess (hsiang-ch'i) is fairly similar to Western chess, though the military parallels are more overt.

Books and Newspapers. Literature owes a great debt to the Chinese, who invented both paper and printing. In Chinese book shops look out for copies of the *Sayings of Confucius,* the book of oracles *I Ching,* and the Taoist scripture *Tao Te Ching,* all of which are ancient Chinese literary classics that are widely available in English translation. *Quotations from Chairman Mao Tsetung* ('The Little Red Book'), in which Mao interprets Marxist-Leninism from a distinctly Chinese perspective, is a modern Chinese classic. It was much brandished aloft by revolutionary students in the 1960s, both in China and in Britain. Chinatown's book shops also sell *Sing Tao,* a Chinese language daily newspaper which is published in Britain.

'Inside Out'

Interview with Billy, who works in a Chinese newsagents in Soho . . .

"I came over with my parents when I was 3 years old in 1972, and I actually didn't even meet any Chinese people until I went to Polytechnic because where I was brought up up north, I was the only Chinese guy in town. It's only since I've been working here that I've really mixed with Chinese people.

In my house, with my parents, I am very Chinese. I rarely speak English with them, but outside it's different. I think really deep down I'm as English as everyone else. I was so young when I came here, I was naturally accepted by everyone where I grew up, and I think they saw me as just another English person but looking Chinese. I didn't have any racial bother or anything like that, fortunately for me.

Our shops is one of the major importers of Chinese newspapers here. Yesterday's news in Hong Kong is today's news in Britain. People see I am Chinese and they naturally assume I can read and write it but that's totally untrue. My parents sent me to a Chinese evening school when I was ten or twelve but by that age you're rebellious and I just didn't like it at all. Now I need to read the title of the newspapers in Chinese, and yes, it is a handicap. I had a view when I was younger that I was going to get a job in an English company and I wouldn't need to read or write Chinese. Now I'm working in the Chinese community and I regret not learning."

The following shops are within Chinatown itself, or within five minutes' walk of it.

Shaolin Way, 10 Little Newport Street, WC2 (071-734 6391). Open from 1am to 7pm Monday to Sunday. Chinese martial-arts equipment and clothing, and associated English-language books and magazines. The shop is named after the Songshang Shaolin Temple, which was central to the development of the martial arts in China, and still survives, complete with martial monks.

Guanghwa Company, 7 Newport Place, WC2 (071-437 3737). Open from 10.30am to 7pm, Monday to Saturday, 11am to 7pm Sunday. Books, arts and crafts. The large English language book section has an excellent collection of children's picture books, most of which illustrate traditional Chinese stories. The selection of arts and crafts includes paper cuts, Chinese games, equipment for Chinese calligraphy and painting, and traditional Chinese music on cassette.

China Arts and Crafts, 12 Newport Place, WC2 (071-734 1321). Open from 10.30 am to 7pm Monday to Sunday. A wide variety of Chinese artefacts including pottery, ornaments, festive decorations and parasols.

Hong Kong Cultural Services, 46 Gerrard Street, W1 (071-734 5037). Open from 11am to 7pm Monday to Sunday. Arts and crafts. Wooden and paper lanterns, paper kites, Christmas and New Year cards, teapots. Also music on CD and cassette.

Chinese Bonsai Shop, 15a Gerrard Street, W1 (071-287 0369). Open from 12 noon to 8pm Monday to Sunday. Bonsai trees - which the Chinese claim to have developed long before the Japanese.

Ying Hwa, 14 Gerrard Street, W1 (071-439 8825). Open from 11am to 7.30pm Monday to Sunday. Arts and crafts. Notable for masks which display the traditional forms of make-up used in the Chinese opera to denote the various stock characters; even that humble figure the civil servant has his allotted place in this drama. Also music on cassette.

Sound of China, 6 Gerrard Street, W1(071-734 1970). Open from 12 noon to 8pm Monday to Sunday. Large selection of popular and traditional music on CD and cassette.

Tung Po Overseas, 2 Gerrard Place, W1 (071-437 0305). Open from 11am to 8pm Monday to Sunday. Chinese-language books.

Asia Collection, 122 Shaftesbury Avenue, W1 (071-437 3352). Open from 10.30am to 7.30pm Monday to Sunday. Arts and crafts including artificial flowers, vases and porcelain.

Video Sino, 114 Shaftesbury Avenue, W1 (071-437 8802). Open from 11am to 7pm Monday to Sunday. Rentals of unsubtitled videos of TV programmes and films from Hong Kong.

Singalong, 110 Shaftesbury Avenue, W1 (071-437 8789). Open from 11am to 7pm Monday to Saturday, 11am to 8pm Sunday. Music on cassette is the shop's speciality, but traditional clothing, books and souvenirs are also available.

Lucky House, 80 Shaftesbury Avenue, W1 (071-287 1419). Open from 11am to 8pm Monday to Sunday. Arts and crafts, including lacquered bird cages and mirrors.

Welcome Supermarket, 31-37 Wardour Street, W1 (071-437 7963). Open from 11am to 8pm Monday to Sunday. Deals mainly in foodstuffs, but also stocks ceramics and kitchenware.

Lee Fook Electric, 25 Wardour Street, W1 (071-437 7541). Open from 12 noon to 7pm Monday to Sunday. Arts and crafts, rice cookers and china.

Man Cheong Jeweller and Goldsmith, 17 Lisle Street, W1 (071-439 6536). Open from 12 noon to 8pm Monday to Sunday. Earrings, pendants, rings and necklaces in distinctive Chinese designs. Silver and a lot of jade.

Wen Tai Sun Chinese News Agency, 80 Dean Street, W1 (071-437 8234/5188). Open from 11am to 7pm Monday to Sunday. Arts and crafts, music on cassette. Chinese newspapers.

Ray Man Eastern Musical Instruments, 64 Neal Street, WC2 (071-240

1776). Open from 10am to 6pm Monday to Saturday. Oriental musical instruments for sale or hire. Stocks a wide range of bamboo flutes and a fascinating array of percussion instruments: bells, drums, cymbals, rattles, scrapers, shakers, clappers, woodblocks and gongs. Ray Man, the owner of the shop, gives lessons on how to play the Chinese dulcimers, zithers, lutes, mandolins and banjos which are on sale. The shop also stocks sheet music in Chinese and in Western notation, traditional music on CD and cassette, and paper-mache lion heads as used in Chinese New Year lion dances.

Neal Street East, 5 Neal Street, WC2 (071-240 0135/6). Open from 10am to 7pm Monday to Saturday (except opens 10.30am Friday), 12 noon to 6pm Sunday. Arts and crafts, books, furniture. The shop is firmly orientated towards Western tastes in things Chinese, but what it lacks in atmosphere in comparison with the Chinatown shops, it makes up for with its enormous stock of well-chosen goods which are displayed on four levels. There are particularly good selections of artificial flowers, jewellery, books and toys.

Guanghwa Company, 32 Parker Street, WC 2 (071-831 5888). Open from 10am to 6pm Monday to Saturday. Books, arts and crafts. Specialises in materials for Chinese painting and calligraphy, and puts on a variety of Chinese art exhibitions throughout the year.

CHINATOWN: FOOD AND DRINK

Shopping
There are several large food stores in Chinatown, and much that is worth buying even if you are not an expert Chinese cook. An excellent place to start is the *Loon Fung Supermarket,* 42-44 Gerrard Street, W1 (071-437 7332), which is open from 10am to 8.30pm Monday to Sunday. Alongside an abundance of packets of rice and noodles, you can also find tinned shark's fin soup, frozen ready-to-steam dim sum snacks, ready-to-eat savoury snacks (how about some dried cuttlefish?), tinned fruits (loquats, arbutus and winter melon), glutinous rice and confectionery. Almost all of the packaged products are labelled in Chinese and English, and many also feature cooking instructions in English. For something to drink, try Tsing Tao, a popular brand of Chinese beer.

The Chinese sweet tooth is satisfied not in restaurants but in cake shops, of which there are several in Gerrard Street. Try the cake shop at the front of the *Far East Chinese Restaurant,* 13 Gerrard Street, W1 (071-437 6148), which is open from 10.30am to midnight Monday to Sunday. You can buy egg custard tarts and crisp prawn crackers if you want to play safe, or melon paste cakes and lotus seed cakes if you fancy being more adventurous. Savoury buns filled with chicken, barbecued pork or beef curry are also available.

Wet fish is to be found at *Wings Seafood,* 3 Lisle Street, W1 (071-434 0377), which is open from 11am to 7.30pm Monday to Sunday. Live lobsters and crabs are always available, together with fish such as sea bass. A live fish-tank is featured at the *Chinatown Fish and Meat Market,* 14 Newport Place, W1 (071-437 0712), which is open from 11am to 7pm Monday to Sunday. Quails eggs are also stocked.

Many Far Eastern fruits and vegetables are available at *Golden Gate,* 16 Newport Place WC2 (071-437 6266), which is open from 10am to 7.45pm Monday to Sunday. Lotus roots, water chestnuts, mooli and durian are Chinese specialities on offer.

Chinese New Year: waiting for the lion in Gerrard Street, Soho.

Eating Out

One of the great pleasures of eating out in Chinatown is the sheer density of restaurants in the vicinity, which means that you can wander around checking out the menus and peering in the windows of various establishments before making your choice. Any restaurant with a fair number of Chinese customers is a good bet.

For further information on the restaurants in Chinatown see *page 18.*

CHINATOWN:
CHINESE NEW YEAR CELEBRATIONS

The Chinese New Year's Day, which is set according to the lunar calendar, usually falls in late January or early February. For the Chinese this period of the year is a time to clear debts, buy new clothes and visit friends and relatives. New Year's Day is a special time in particular for children, who are given gifts of 'lucky money' in red envelopes (red is considered a lucky colour), and are allowed to stuff themselves with sweets.

Chinese New Year celebrations are traditionally spread out over several weeks, but in Britain they tend to be condensed into the Sunday nearest to New Year's Day. Street celebrations are held annually on this day in Chinatown; you can find out what that date is each year from the London Tourist Board on 071-730 3488 between 9am and 5.30pm Monday to Friday.

On 'New Year Sunday' the streets of Chinatown are festooned with decorations. Stalls sell Chinese food and gifts, the restaurants are crowded with families eating the customarily large New Year meals, and the Chinese greet each other with the Cantonese New Year saying 'Gung Hei Faat Choi' (wishing you prosperity).

You will probably see badges on sale depicting the particular animal associated with the New Year. This is taken from the Chinese zodiac, which is composed of the Rat, Ox, Tiger, Hare, Dragon, Serpent, Horse, Sheep, Monkey, Chicken, Dog and Pig. Each animal gives its name to one year in a never-ending twelve-year cycle. Thus 1993 is the Year of the Chicken, 1994 the Year of the Dog, 1995 the Year of the Pig and so on. The title of each year is thought to affect its character. For example, the Year of the Dragon is considered auspicious for business people, and the Year of the Ox is reckoned to demand hard work from everybody.

The traditional lion dances, which are performed to scare away evil spirits and bring luck for the New Year, form the centrepiece of the street celebrations that last from 12 noon to mid-afternoon. Groups of dancers move the ferocious-looking cloth and paper-mache lions through the streets to collect donations of money pinned to the strings which are hung down from the upper windows of Chinese business premises. On the end of each string is a lettuce, which is 'eaten' by the lion before the money is lowered into its mouth.

Since their inception in 1973, Chinatown's New Year celebrations have become a big tourist attraction. If you want to actually see the lion dance rather than the backs of people's heads, your best bet is to position yourself at a good vantage point close to a hanging lettuce well in advance of the lion dancers, and then defend your position against all-comers. Children perched up on their parents shoulders usually get the best views of the afternoon's proceedings.

The lion dancers.

OTHER PLACES TO VISIT

Percival David Foundation of Chinese Art, 53 Gordon Square, WC1 (071-387 3909). Open from 10.30am to 5pm Monday to Friday. Admission free. A museum dedicated solely to Chinese ceramics? Many might think this one of the least enticing attractions on the London museum scene, yet it was really quite busy when I visited it on a weekday. Anyone who does think it worth a look will certainly be impressed by the beauty and variety of the Chinese ceramics which are on display here.

Victoria and Albert Museum, Cromwell Road, SW7 (071-938 8500). Open from 10am to 5.50pm Tuesday to Sunday, 12 noon to 5.50pm Monday. Admission free, although there is considerable pressure to make a 'donation'. The museum contains a large collection of Chinese antiquities, as does the **British Museum,** Great Russell Street, WC1 (071-636 1555-8), which is open from 10am to 5pm Monday to Saturday, 2.30 to 6pm Sunday, admission free. The Chinese political leader Sun Yat Sen (see *page 22*) studied here in the British Library Reading Room.

Eastern Art Gallery, 40 Bloomsbury Way, WC1 (071-430 1072). Open from 10.30am to 5.30pm Tuesday to Saturday. Art gallery. Original modern and contemporary works of art mostly from mainland China, principally water-colours on scrolls. You will need at least £150 to buy a painting, but their wood-block prints and stone rubbings are much cheaper and you should feel free to take a look round.

The Royal Botanic Gardens, Kew Road, Richmond. Open from 10am to Sunset (about 4pm in midwinter and 8pm in midsummer) Monday to Sunday. Admission charge.

An elegant Chinese-style pagoda, 164 feet high and visible for miles around, is one of the most surprising and charming features of the 288-acre Botanic Gardens at Kew. The pagoda was built in 1761 for Augusta, the Dowager Princess of Wales, when Kew was still a Royal estate and things Chinese were all the rage. Many other Chinese-style buildings were also erected on the estate at that time; a ruined archway, the orangery and some of the temples are still standing.

Chinese visitors apparently find the pagoda rather amusing, and not terribly Chinese - they say the style of the windows looks particularly inauthentic. Access to the building is no longer permitted as the structure is too weak to withstand large numbers of visitors.

There is no Chinese botanical section as such in Kew Gardens, but China's rich flora is well represented. China has been the source of many of Britain's best known garden plants, including varieties of chrysanthemums, rhododendrons, lilies and peonies.

Chinese Graves, The East London Cemetery, Grange Road, E13 (071-476 5109). Open from 8am to 4.30pm Monday to Saturday, 2.30 to 4.30pm Sunday.

The pre-war Chinese presence in the East End is commemorated in the western section of the cemetery by a large stone cross, erected in 1927, which is inscribed in English with 'In memory of the Chinese who have died in England', and in Chinese with 'In memory of Chinese friends'. Clustered around the cross are a number of Chinese graves, the headstones marked in both English and Chinese characters. Most of the headstones are old and worn, but others mark quite recent burials.

The majority of immigrants in the earlier days of Chinese settlement were men, and many married British women. This is evident in the inscriptions on several of the headstones, as for example: 'In memory of a dear dad Wong Bing (1881-1962) and mum Ivy Bing (1915-1973)'.

SHOPPING OUTSIDE CHINATOWN ──────

East Asia Company, 103 Camden High Street, NW1 (071-388 5783). Open from 10am to 5.30pm Monday to Saturday. Large stock of English-language books about China. Good coverage of the arts and a large selection of language-learning material. Also stocks paper cuts, prints and other arts and crafts.

Acu Medic Company, 101 Camden High Street, NW1 (071-388 5783/6704). Open from 9.30am to 5.30pm Monday to Saturday. Stocks acupuncture equipment, books about acupuncture and other 'alternative' medicines, and Chinese herbal remedies such as herb-impregnated arthritis plasters.

Magpie, 82 Westbourne Grove, W2 (071-299 1691). Open from 10.30am to 5.30pm Monday to Saturday. Handicrafts, furniture and silk clothing are imported from China. Particularly attractive and good value are the men's silk pyjamas.

Liberty, Regent Street, W1 (071-734 1234). Open from 9.30am to 6pm Monday to Saturday. The oriental department of this fairly exclusive department store stocks many reasonably-priced items amongst its more expensive goods. Look out for the ornate chopsticks, cloisonné (enamelled metal) boxes, lacquer screens, and the basketware rabbits, swans and cranes which make great presents for children. Pricier items include 19th C antique vases, antique clothes collected by Europeans in pre-revolutionary days, and the rolls of silk fabric for which Liberty has long been famous.

FOOD AND DRINK ──────────────

Take-away food has introduced millions of people to Chinese cuisine, but to the Chinese themselves it is 'lupsup', a Cantonese word for 'mish-mash'. The standard Chinese take-away menu has evolved over many years into a ragbag of cheap and easy-to-prepare dishes that are known to be acceptable to Westerners. The spring roll, a northern Chinese snack brought here by pre-war immigrants, is still sold in British take-aways even though it is not a customary part of the diet of the southern Chinese who now manage these establishments. Chop Suey is a Chinese-American invention, which was supposedly developed when Chinese railway labourers tried to make a Chinese equivalent to the Irish stew eaten by fellow Irish workers. Barbecued spare ribs as we know them are also of Chinese-American origin. In China spare ribs are taken from a completely different cut of meat and, unlike in Britain, are always cut into short lengths before being served so that they can be popped into the mouth and stripped with the tongue.

Anyone familiar only with take-away food should find Chinese restaurants a revelation. Yet even in the restaurants some aspects of authentic Chinese cuisine can be elusive, as many menus will list some dishes only in Chinese. To an extent this is just a realistic judgement of differing tastes - yellow duck's feet, for example, have limited appeal to non-Chinese, as does 'steamed congealed chicken's blood', the Chinese equivalent of black pudding. Yet many of these dishes, such as 'frogs legs with black bean sauce and chilli', are unfamiliar rather than unpalatable. Happily, an increasing number of restaurants are now putting such lesser-known specialities on their English-language menu.

There are many regional variants of Chinese food, of which Cantonese, Szechuan and Peking are the best known in Britain. Most of the Chinese in Britain eat Cantonese food at home, and it is this style which is normally served in restaurants. Cantonese specialities include sweet and sour pork, shark's fin soup and dim sum. The latter are steamed or deep-fried dumplings, buns and rolls filled with savoury or sweet fillings. Dim sum are served only at lunch time and make an ideal light meal. Szechuan cuisine is noted for its hotly spiced dishes, such as fried spicy shrimps, and for its smoked, pickled and salted foods. Peking cuisine, which is regarded as the *haute cuisine* of China, places the emphasis less on rice than on steamed wheat rolls, dumplings and noodles.

Sweets are not a strong point of Chinese restaurants since the Chinese regard them as snacks which should be eaten between meals. Few restaurants provide anything more adventurous than lychees and ice cream. For drink try Mow Tai, a strong, clear, vodka-like drink made from grain and often wrongly described as a wine. At their historic détente meeting President Nixon and Mao Tsetung began the proceedings with a Mow Tai toast.

The customary method of ordering a meal is to choose a number of dishes which are placed in the middle of the table and shared by all. This makes for greater variety and avoids the problem of one person being lumbered with a bad choice. You can ask for a knife and fork instead of chopsticks, but where is the fun in that? Eating with chopsticks becomes much easier if you bear in mind that as far as the Chinese are concerned, not only is it acceptable to hold the bowl up to your mouth when eating, it is actually considered the proper thing to do.

If you're interested in cooking for yourself, Chinatown is the best place to buy all food products.

'Inside Out'

Interview with Teresa, a student whose parents run a Chinese restaurant . . .

"Catering just isn't for me. I just don't think I could handle it. Having lived all my life above a restaurant, there's more out there in life for me. I want to get into fashion, but on the P.R. side of it - photography, journalism, P.R.

My parents aren't strict at all. They're very easy on us. Which can be a bad thing because it's up to us when our curfews are - often we are out till five in the morning and no hassle. Most of my friends all work in restaurants, so I don't really go out that much in the evening. You go out afterwards and then come home at five in the morning.

I think it's good my parents have given us freedom. I respect them more. A lot of my friends they say of their parents, I hate them, because they keep arguing with their parents, but it's because their parents are so strict with them.

A friend called me 'banana' one day because they said I was yellow on the outside and white on the inside. It is true to say that I am only Chinese on the outside really. I know no better. I can't speak Chinese. I'm more European than anything else."

Interview with Teresa's father about his children . . .

"Discipline is the most important value to teach your children. We teach our children that when they come into the house, they've got to greet us, they've got to respect us. It is a bit difficult for children born in this country. You've got to reason with them. It won't work if you just try to drum it in. I find it all quite difficult.

If any of my children fall in love with somebody, whether that person is Chinese or English, it's their life, it's their choice. After all, they are doing the marrying, not me. Of course you've got to invite that person round to see if they've made the right choice, and you can still advise them."

FOOD AND DRINK: RESTAURANTS

Chinatown

New Diamond Restaurant, 23 Lisle Street, WC2 (071-437 2517/7221). Open from 12 noon to 3am Monday to Sunday. Cantonese food. Air-conditioned. Medium price.

Mr Kong, 21 Lisle Street, WC2 (071-437 7341). Open from 12 noon to 2am Monday to Sunday. Cantonese. Good selection of unusual dishes including sautéed venison in ginger wine and frog's legs in black bean sauce.

Poons, 4 Leicester Street, WC2 (071-437 1528). Open from 12 noon to 11.30pm Monday to Sunday. Cantonese. Specialises in wind-dried food. Moderately-priced.

Jade Garden, 15 Wardour Street, Wl (071-439 7851, 437 5065). Open from 12 noon to 11.30pm Monday to Sunday. Cantonese. Specialises in dim sum, excellent seafood menu. Large, lively, open-plan restaurant on two floors. Medium-priced.

Chuen Cheng Ku Restaurant, 17 Wardour Street, Wl (071-437 1398, 734 3281/3509). Open from 11am to midnight Monday to Sunday. Cantonese. Huge unpretentious restaurant on two floors, with lively Chinese music and the bustling atmosphere of Hong Kong. Specialises in dim sum until 6pm. Excellent seafood menu. Moderately-priced.

Wong Kei, 41-43 Wardour Street, W1, no telephone bookings. Open from 12 noon to 11.30pm Monday to Sunday. Cantonese. Outside fast-food establishments, this is probably one of London's cheapest restaurantSs The noodle dishes and soups are particularly good value.

Ley-On's, 56-58 Wardour Street, Wl (071-437 6465, 734 2769). Open from 12 noon to midnight Monday to Sunday (last orders 10.30pm). Cantonese. Specialises in dim sum. Spacious restaurant situated on the northern side of Shaftesbury Avenue. Moderately-priced.

Canton Chinese Restaurant, 11 Newport Place, WC2 (071-437 6220). Open 24 hours Monday to Sunday. Cantonese. Cafe atmosphere and prices to match. Recommended by a Soho dustman for the cleanliness of its kitchens. Cheap.

Eating out in Chinatown.

Lok Ho Fook, 4-5 Gerrard Street, W1 (071-437 2001). Open from 12 noon to 11.45pm daily. This air-conditioned Cantonese restaurant is notable for offering 50 different types of dim sum dishes.

The Dragon Gate Restaurant, 7 Gerrard Street, W1 (071-734 5154). Open from 12 noon to 11.30pm Monday to Sunday. Szechuan food. The hotly spiced dishes are noted on the menu. Moderately-priced.

Dragon Inn, 12 Gerrard Street, W1 (071-494 0870). Open from 12 noon to 11.45pm Monday to Thursday, 12 noon to 12.30am Friday and Saturday. Cantonese. Dim sum daily from noon to 4.45pm.

Lee Ho Fook, 15-16 Gerrard Street, W1 (071-734 9578). Open from 12 noon to 11.30pm Monday to Sunday. Cantonese. Moderately priced seafood is the main attraction here.

Dumpling Inn, 15a Gerrard Street (071-437 2567). Open from 11.45am to 11.45pm Monday to Sunday. One of Soho's first Peking-style restaurants, Dumpling Inn offers six dumpling dishes. Grilling, frying and baking are more popular than steaming in Pekinese cuisine.

Luxuriance, 40 Gerrard Street, W1 (071-437 4125). Open from 12 noon to midnight Monday to Sunday. Pekinese and Shanghai dishes are served in this smart, air-conditioned restaurant. Jellyfish in wine sauce is an unusual speciality.

Dragon's Nest, 58-60 Shaftesbury Avenue, W1 (071-437 3119). Open from 12 noon to 2.45pm, 5pm to 11pm Monday to Sunday. One of London's most authentic Szechuan restaurants. Szechuan duck is a popular speciality.

Mayflower Chinese Restaurant, 68-70 Shaftesbury Avenue, W1 (071-734 9207). Open from 5pm to 4am Monday to Sunday. Cantonese. A favourite for hungry late-night revellers. The Mayflower's menu offers 200 dishes, all moderately-priced.

Young Cheng, 76 Shaftesbury Avenue, W1 (071-437 0237). Open from 12 noon to 11.45pm Sunday to Thursday, 12 noon to 12.45am Friday and

Saturday. Cantonese. A small restaurant with cooking carried out in full view of passers-by. Very popular with Chinese diners. Moderately-priced.

West London

Ken Lo's Memories of China, 67/69 Ebury Street, SWI (071-730 7734/4276). Open from 12 noon to 3pm, 7 to midnight Monday to Saturday. In contrast to the regionalism of most Chinese restaurants, this restaurant provides authentic dishes from all over China. The proprietor, Ken Lo, is the author of over 30 books on Chinese cooking and was formerly a Chinese food inspector for the Egon Ronay guide. The restaurant has proved very popular with visiting delegations from mainland China. Expensive.

Ken Lo's Memories of China, Chelsea Harbour Yard, Chelsea Harbour, SW10 (071-352 4953). Open from 12 noon to 3pm, 7 to midnight Monday to Saturday, 12.30pm to 12 midnight Sunday. Same menu as above.

Zen Central, 20-22 Queen Street, W1 (071-629 8098). Open from 12 noon to 2.30pm, 6pm to 11.30pm Monday to Sunday. The advertised theme of Zen is health-oriented Chinese nouvelle cuisine, but in practice it is not so austere as it sounds. The minimalist décor is relieved by exotic plants.

Queensway

Royal China, 13 Queensway, W2 (071-221 2533, 792 1981). Open from 12 noon to 11.15pm Monday to Sunday. Cantonese dim sum from 12 noon to 5pm.

Mandarin Kitchen, 14-16 Queensway, W2 (071-727 9012/9468). Open from 12 noon to 11.30pm Monday to Sunday. Cantonese, plus some Singapore dishes.

Jade Cottage, 48 Queensway, W2 (071-229 8624). Open from 12 noon to 11.30pm Monday to Sunday. Cantonese, Pekinese and Malaysian cuisine are all featured on the long menu.

New Kam Tom, 59-63 Queensway, W2 (071-229 6065). Open from 12 noon to 11.15pm Monday to Sunday. Cantonese cuisine. Moderately-priced.

FOOD AND DRINK: SHOPPING
Soho's Chinatown is the best place to buy Chinese food products. See page 11.

THE CHINESE MARTIAL ARTS ———

The Chinese martial arts are known in Britain by both their Cantonese name, Kung Fu, and their Mandarin name, Wu Shu. Interest in the Chinese martial arts in Britain outside the Chinese community took off in the mid-1970s with the popularity of Kung Fu films, particularly those in which Bruce Lee starred - *The Big Boss, Fist of Fury, Way of the Dragon* and *Enter the Dragon.*

At that time many teachers of non-Chinese martial arts, such as Karate or Taekwondo, cashed in on the boom by setting themselves up as teachers of Kung Fu after having done little more than watch the films and read a few books on the subject. Some of these teachers also tried to remodel Kung Fu for Western consumption by changing it into a competitive sport complete with belts. Traditionally it is understood as a fighting art, in which the grading of fighters into belts is as inappropriate as classifying Picasso or

Beethoven as black belts in their respective arts. By tradition, a proper teacher of Kung Fu should be able to show a pedigree reaching back to accepted masters.

Kung Fu encompasses a wide variety of martial arts styles. The Praying Mantis is a typical 'street-fighting' style which fits into the popular image of what most British people think Kung Fu should be. At the opposite extreme of Kung Fu, and proving very popular in Britain, is the gentle, graceful style of Ta'i Chi. All styles of Kung Fu are both physical and mental disciplines, but in Ta'i Chi the emphasis is placed firmly on the use of the mind to channel energy so as to utilise it more efficiently. Ta'i Chi is a particularly valuable discipline for the elderly and for those recovering from illness.

If you're interested in the Chinese Martial Arts, you should look for lessons through the normal sporting channels, but be careful who you take lessons from if you're looking for the authentic style.

ACUPUNCTURE & TRADITIONAL MEDICINE

Acupuncture originated in China several thousand years ago. It is an almost pain-free medical treatment that involves the insertion of fine needles into the skin at specific points that are often a good distance from the apparent site of the problem. Putting a needle into an earlobe to treat asthma may seem bizarre, but Western doctors have been forced to admit that acupuncture can be effective, particularly in some of the fields of treatment in which Western medicine is weak, such as migraine, back pain, asthma, rheumatism and arthritis.

Why does it work? The traditional explanation is that energy flows through the body around a system of pathways called meridians and that the insertion of the needles acts to harmonise disturbances in that flow. Various theories are under investigation to find an explanation which fits in with Western medical science, but none has yet proved adequate to the task.

Acupuncture became widely known in the West during the 1970s through direct contacts with China - although there were Chinese acupuncturists in Britain well before that time who were catering to their own community. Today, the majority of both acupuncturists and patients in Britain are non-Chinese.

There is some disagreement amongst practitioners about the precise effectiveness of acupuncture. Many of the Western doctors who practise it believe that traditionally trained practitioners are over-optimistic about what acupuncture can achieve and that at least some of what they do has no medical effect at all. The traditionalists retort that if their critics cannot see the effectiveness of certain treatments it is because they do not understand acupuncture properly.

Caution should be exercised in seeking acupuncture treatment as there is no licensing system and there are some real dangers involved. If you are extra sceptical or ultra-cautious, a referral from your doctor would be the best path. Even if they don't know of an acupuncturist themselves, they can make contact with the *British Medical Acupuncture Society,* 69 Chancery Lane, WC2, whose members are all doctors. Only letters are accepted, accompanied by a G.P.'s written approval.

There are however few doctors who practise acupuncture and fewer still on the National Health Service. Your other option is to contact a trained lay acupuncturist through the **British Acupuncture Association and Register,** whose members have all passed the BAAR exams or equivalent. The BAAR can be contacted at 34 Alderney Street, SWI (071-834 6229).

Chinese herbal medicines are gradually attracting a following outside of the Chinese community, although language can still be a barrier in discussing treatment at many places. One place that is easy to deal with is *The Centre for Traditional Chinese Medicine,* 78 Haverstock Hill, NW3 (071-284 2898). As well as Chinese herbal medicine, it also deals with traditional massage and acupuncture.

PEOPLE

Sun Yat Sen, the 'Father of the Chinese Republic', fled from China in 1895 following his involvement in an unsuccessful rebellion against the Imperial Government of the Manchu dynasty. He arrived in London in 1896 and took lodgings at 4 Gray's Inn Place, WC1 (another building now stands on the site, which is marked by a plaque). It was while Sun was staying at this address that he became embroiled in an affair that scandalised London and brought him international renown. The events are described at length in his book *Kidnapped in London* (1897).

Sun spent his first week in London looking around the sights of the city he called 'the very centre of the universe'. While out walking alone one day he met some Chinese men who pressed him to come back to their lodgings for a chat. On passing through an innocent-looking door, Sun suddenly found himself a prisoner inside the Chinese Embassy at 49 Portland Place, Wl. It emerged that Sun's capture had been ordered personally by the Emperor of China, and that the Embassy planned to smuggle Sun, bound and gagged, on to a steamer at London's docks and thence back to China. What would follow, Sun was certain, would be the 'customary exquisite torture' to force him to reveal the names of his accomplices in the rebellion, and then death.

Sun was imprisoned in the Embassy for almost a week before he managed to persuade a British servant to take out a message to one of Sun's British friends. In the best traditions of Victorian melodrama, his message concluded: 'I am certain to be beheaded. Oh! Woe is me'.

For several days the British authorities were reluctant to accept that Sun had been kidnapped, whilst the Chinese Embassy denied all knowledge of his whereabouts. Eventually the *Globe* newspaper broke the 'Startling Story !' to the public and the next day the Chinese Embassy released Sun after pressure from the British Government.

In the ensuing press debate a leader writer in *The Times* commented that the whole affair would have been 'comic opera' if it hadn't been so serious. This view was echoed by *The Speaker,* which stated: 'It's impossible to pass number 49 Portland Place without a romantic shudder. That middle-class dwelling is now a Bastille *pour rire,* and excites the mirth of tradesmen's boys'. The building was demolished in 1980 and a new Chinese Embassy has now been constructed on the same site.

After his release, Sun sent an open letter of thanks to the British Government and Britain's newspapers, in which he wrote: 'If anything were needed to convince me of the generous public spirit which pervades Great

Britain, and the love of justice which distinguishes its people, the recent acts of the last few days have conclusively done so . . . Knowing and feeling more keenly than ever what constitutional government and an enlightened people mean, I am promoted still more actively to pursue the cause of advancement, education and civilisation in my own well-beloved but oppressed country'.

After many travels around the world, Sun eventually returned to China following the overthrow of the Manchu dynasty in 1911. He became president of the new republic for a brief period, founded the Nationalist Party in 1912, and after being recalled as president of China in 1923, saw through a merger between the Nationalist Party and the Communist Party before his death in 1925. The suppression of the Communists by Sun's successor Chiang Kai-Shek led to a civil war that ended only with the Communist victory in 1947. Both the Communists and the Nationalists (who still control Taiwan) now lay claim to being the legitimate heirs to Sun's political legacy.

It is interesting to note that Sun was a member of a Triad, one of many such secret societies existing at the time. All of the Triads started off as revolutionary organisations but, over time, most gradually degenerated into criminal gangs. The latter are very powerful in Hong Kong and Taiwan, and exist too in Britain, where they are much feared by the Chinese community.

LITERATURE

Sour Sweet by Timothy Mo (1982). A tragi-comic tale set in London in the 1960s, following Mr Chen, a Chinese waiter, and his family, as they start out in their own take-away business. But Mrs Chen still finds it impossible to understand the British way of life, and Mr Chen cannot escape from his entanglement with the Triads. It was made into a feature film of the same name, released in 1988. Adapted by the writer Ian McEwan, it starred Sylvia Chang, a famous Taiwanese actress. *Recommended.

Sikh in a Southall street with a 'kirpan' in his belt (see page 34).

ASIAN LONDON

HISTORY

The first Briton known to have set foot in India was a Jesuit missionary called Thomas Stephens in 1579. By that time, there were already some 10,000 people of Indian origin in England; they were the Romany gypsies, the descendants of nomadic tribes from Northwest India. The Romanies are thought to have first reached Britain in the I5th C, bringing with them much of their ancestral culture. They spoke Romany, which is of recognisably Indian origin; they worked as entertainers, animal dealers, metal workers, herbalists and astrologers, the same trades that had been followed by their low caste Indian ancestors; and they adhered strictly to the concept of caste, whereby anyone who married outside their community was deemed 'unclean' and expelled from it.

Direct trading links between Britain and India were opened up in the 17th C, but whereas numerous Britons were soon travelling to India, it was not until the 18th C, when Britain's East India Company took control of large parts of India, that there was any appreciable movement of Indians in the opposite direction. Many of the earliest Indian visitors were nannies and ladies' maids, known as Ayahs, who were employed by ex-colonial families. Most of the others were seamen who came to London on the ships of the East India Company. Between voyages, the seamen are known to have congregated in lodging houses in The Highway, E1. Seamen who had fallen on hard times also probably made up the bulk of the Indian beggars that were found on London's streets until well into the 19th C.

It was not until the late 19th C that Indian princes began to visit Britain, but within a very short time many were sending their sons to British schools and universities. Meanwhile, a good number of the princes' contemporaries from India's middle classes were sending their sons to Britain to study law at London's Inns of Court. It was from this latter group that India's leaders of the future were to emerge, such as Gandhi, Nehru and Jinnah (see *People, page 51*).

However, it was not until the 1920s and 1930s that a settled Indian population became established in Britain. They were a very mixed bunch of people, including doctors, lawyers, seamen and door-to-door peddlers, and were scattered about the country in small groups. In many cases it was groups such as these that provided the nucleus around which larger communities were to develop in the years of mass immigration after the Second World War.

In 1947 British India was partitioned into the independent states of India and of Pakistan (the eastern section of which was later to become Bangladesh). As it was no longer possible to use 'Indian' to describe all the peoples of the Indian sub-continent, the term 'Asian' arose to fulfil that function. This is certainly an unsatisfactory term in that it invites confusion with the Chinese and other peoples of Asia, but there is at present no better word available in common usage - although the American term 'South Asian' is gaining some currency.

Eurasians, who are also known as Anglo-Indians, formed the first wave of post-war Asian immigrants. They were members of a mixed-race (European and Indian) community which in British India formed an administrative class sandwiched between the rulers and the ruled. The Eurasians were Christians, spoke English, had European names and identified (and were identified) strongly with the British. Many chose to leave India when independence came. Figures are hard to come by, but it seems that about 30,000 Eurasians came to Britain between 1947 and 1952, most settling in London. As a community they were, and have remained, committed towards integration to a very high degree, even to the extent of never having formed any kind of organisation to speak up publicly to defend their interests. Concealed within the shadow of the Asian community, they are one of Britain's least known ethnic groups.

Hundreds of thousands of Asians settled in Britain in the 1950s and 1960s. They came from many parts of the Indian sub-continent, but the majority were from just a few particular regions, such as the Punjab and the Sylhet, which had already established strong links with Britain. Most of the immigrants had previously been peasant farmers, but there were also significant numbers of traders and professionals amongst them.

The last major wave of Asian immigrants came from East Africa, where Indians had settled during British rule and prospered as traders, dominating business life. Friction with the native black population after those countries became independent led to a large exodus of Asians from Kenya in 1968, and most dramatically, from Uganda in 1972 when 28,000 Asians expelled by General Idi Amin arrived in Britain within the space of three months. Asians from East Africa now play an important role in Asian business enterprise in Britain.

Today there are about 1,450,000 people of Asian origin in Britain, of whom about 525,000 live in London. What is known as the 'Asian community' actually consists of a very diverse collection of people, some of whom have less in common with each other in linguistic, religious and cultural terms than a Briton would have with a Russian. They come from several nations (India, Pakistan, Bangladesh and Sri Lanka), speak many languages (the principal tongues are Bengali, Gujarati, Hindi, Punjabi, and Urdu), and profess a number of different religions (most are Hindus, Muslims or Sikhs, but there are also significant minorities of Christians and Parsees).

In London, some sections of the Asian community are associated with particular districts, and some with particular professions. Southall is a mainly Punjabi district with a large Sikh community. Bangladeshis are concentrated in the East End and work mainly in the garment and catering trades. Wembley is a mainly Gujarati district, and it is Gujaratis who make up a large proportion of London's Asian shopkeepers.

As for the original Indian immigrants, the Romany gypsies, there are still an estimated 2000 to 3000 families living 'on the road' in Britain. About 500 of these families live in the London region, where they make up about half of its total gypsy population, most of the others being of Irish origin.

SOUTHALL

Southall is London's most remarkable ethnic quarter. At its heart in The Broadway and South Road is a mile-long stretch of Asian shops, snack bars, banks and travel agents, and walking down these streets you will see few except Asian faces.

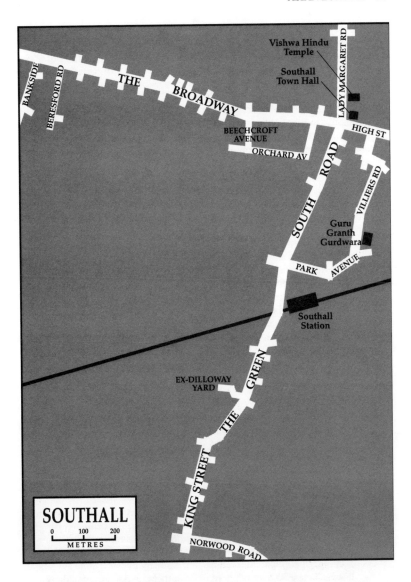

Southall became an Asian district in the late 1950s, when Asians who had been commuting to work in nearby factories began to settle locally. Most of these early immigrants were adult males; it was not until the early 1960s that they were joined by their families. Southall's proximity to Heathrow Airport made it a convenient first port of call for new immigrants and encouraged further growth. Today about 60 percent of the population of Southall is of Asian origin, a figure which rises to about 80 percent in the central area around The Broadway.

The majority of Southall's Asian population is of Punjabi origin. Of those women who wear Asian clothes, most wear the national costume of the Punjab, the salwar kamiz. This consists of a matching tunic and trouser suit which is usually worn with a kind of scarf called a dupatta. The salwar kamiz should not be confused with the better-known saree, which consists of a six yard strip of cloth that is draped around the body and is worn with a tight blouse called a choli. You will see relatively few sarees being worn in Southall. Traditional Punjabi men's' clothing is very similar to the women's except in that it is looser and made in plainer fabrics. The man's shirt is called a kurta, and the trousers are called pyjamas. Far fewer of the men wear Asian clothing in Southall than do the women.

However, where religion is concerned, Southall's Asians are a very mixed group of people, including Hindus, Muslims and Sikhs, reflecting the multi-religious traditions of the Punjab. The Sikhs, however, form the largest religious group in Southall, though that will not be immediately apparent to those people who believe that all male Sikhs can be identified by their turbans - in fact perhaps only about half of male Sikhs wear them. You can often tell if shops are Sikh-owned because they frequently display a picture of Guru Nanak, the founder of Sikhism. The turbaned and white bearded Guru is always depicted holding his palm up towards the viewer in a gesture of blessing and peace.

The **Suman Marriage Bureau**, at 83 South Road, caters for the Indian custom of arranged marriages. A large painting on the glass of its front window depicts the marriage of two Hindu couples. In the centre of the picture is the elephant-headed Ganesh, a Hindu god of prosperity and luck. The swastikas are ancient Indian symbols of good luck, long pre-dating the Nazi swastika, in which the pattern is reversed.

'Inside Out'

Interview with Mumta, a young woman who lives in Southall . . .

"I'm eighteen years old and I've lived in Southall all my life. It's a nice place to be brought-up, but when it comes to opportunities and setting out for the American dream, I think you need to go elsewhere.

My parents expect me to have a nice comfortable life sitting at home and doing the normal girlie stuff - cooking, cleaning, getting married to a nice safe husband that they find for me, and that's not my idea of a good life. I mean, I want to get out and do something exciting.

It's very close-knit round here, so if somebody does something out of line, everyone knows about it. There's loads of gossips around and people really poke their noses in basically. But it's secure as well. If you didn't have all these people worrying about you, it becomes lonely, so I enjoy it in a way, even though I rebel against it.

With girls it's recognised that if you're brought up here, you're not strictly Asian, you are also British in some ways, and some parents expect you to just be Asian. It's hard to hold on to those Asian roots if you've been brought up in Western society, and that's what most youngsters have problems with. I mean you have to compromise. That's what it's all about, compromise."

'Inside Out'

Interview with 'Nik', an Asian D.J. in his early twenties, at a disco he's organised at a Southall venue . . .

"I'm an ex-student, I'm on the dole, that's what I do. I D.J. as a hobby. I'm an outsider here. Normally where I work in South Wales and things I hire out clubs and have like raves going on. The owner of this place phoned me up and said come down here and put a sort of Western influence into Southall, because they need it, especially the youngsters.

I've been in Southall six weeks and I haven't been out until tonight because there's nothing to do here. There is absolutely nothing to do. Asian families don't go out much.

To get this evening going, I managed to get hold of a few girls round here and I said, 'look, could you turn up?'. They said only on the condition that it starts early and finishes early and that's the reason we're doing it from 8 in the evening. The girls are only allowed out between certain hours, you know. Probably their parents think that nightlife's a swearword or something.

When I came here I was going to put on a black dance night, because Asian people like black music. But I was told by a lot of people to just put a bit of bhangra in because the youngsters love it, and they do."

SOUTHALL: SHOPPING

Southall is by far the largest Asian shopping centre in the London region. The Broadway and South Road are the main shopping streets.

Gifts, Music, Books

Southall's shops are particularly good for Asian music on CD, record and cassette, providing everything from religious devotionals and film music from India to *bhangra* music from British Asian groups.

'Inside Out'

Interview with Channi, lead singer of pioneering bhangra group Alaap, at his Southall home . . .

"My career started from here and the people of Southall have always pushed me towards my career . . . I started in the temple singing hymns. Our group started in 1977 and as we grew up we started performing where no Asian band had ever performed, like the Royal Albert Hall, and then we expanded to the world and we've played alongside Robert Palmer, Peter Gabriel, UB40.

People have told me I should move out of Southall to a bigger house somewhere else, but this is where I live and I don't want to leave our people here. I think you've got to live among your own people to really be able to enjoy your culture. But the same people who say to me, don't live in Southall, they come from a 40 or 50 mile radius to shop in Southall. They can't stay away."

IHR, 70 South Road, Middlesex (081-571 1306). Open from 10.30am to 7pm Monday to Saturday. Large selection of popular and classical music from India and Pakistan in Hindi, Gujarati, Tamil, and Punjabi. Also magazines and newspapers.

IHR, 41 The Broadway, Middx (081-574 4739). Open from 10.30am to 7pm Monday to Sunday. Popular and classical music in Hindi, Gujarati, Tamil and Punjabi. Also stocks Islamic prints, prayer mats, magazines, newspapers and some Urdu-language books.

Metro Music, 55 The Broadway (081-574 4765). Open from 10am to 8pm Monday to Sunday. Indian audio cassettes, magazines and videos.

Atlantic Video, 78 The Broadway (081-843 2223). Open from 3 to 9pm Wednesday to Monday. Indian film and videos.

ABC Music Shop, 7 The Broadway (081-574 1319). Open from 10.30am to 7pm Monday to Saturday, I to 7pm Sunday. Large selection of popular and classical music in Hindi, Gujarati, Bengali and South Indian languages. Also stocks newspapers and magazines, posters of Indian film stars and a wide range of Islamic, Hindu and Sikh religious books in Urdu, Hindi and Punjabi, plus a few in English translation.

Virdee's, 26 South Road (081-571 4870). Open from 10am to 7pm Monday to Saturday, I to 7pm Sunday. Popular and classical music from India and Pakistan in Hindi, Punjabi and Gujarati. Also stocks magazines, newspapers and a limited selection of Hindu and Sikh religious books in Punjabi and Hindi.

Virdee Brothers, 102 The Green (081-574 4765). Open from 11.30am to 7.30pm Monday to Saturday, 2 to 7.30pm Sunday. Popular and classical music in Hindi, Punjabi and Gujarati. Books in Punjabi, Hindi, Gujarati and Urdu.

J S Discount Jewellery, Unit 7, Liberty Shopping Centre, South Road (081-571 3188). Open from 10am to 7pm Monday to Saturday, 11am to 6pm Sunday. Large selection of Indian-design fashion jewellery. Bangles, earrings, Indian wedding jewellery.

Oberoi's, 101 The Broadway (081-574 0611). Open from 10am to 7pm Monday to Saturday (except to 5pm Wednesday). Gifts, fashion jewellery, religious requisites. Large stock includes bangles, paper garlands, Hindu home shrines and Hindu and Sikh statues, prints and wedding items.

Kumar's, 48 High Street 081-(843 0844). Open from 10am to 7pm Monday to Saturday. Principally a second-hand shop dealing in a variety of general goods, it also stocks a small selection of Indian musical instruments (tablas, sitars, harmoniums), and an attractive collection of new and second-hand brass ornamental objects from India.

Chaggar's, 122 The Green (081-574 5551). Open from 10am to 7pm Monday to Saturday, 2-7pm Sunday. Hindu and Sikh posters and paintings are sold as a sideline to the shop's main business of framing pictures and installing shop fronts.

Bina Musicals, 31-33 The Green (081-843 1411). Open from 10.30am to 6.30pm Monday to Saturday, 11.30am to 4.30pm Sunday. Stocks an exceptional range of sitars, tablas, harmoniums, bamboo flutes and other Indian instruments.

Clothing

There are scores of shops in Southall which stock fabrics for Indian clothes, but you will find relatively few ready-made Indian clothes on sale here, for Asian women are traditionally expected to make the clothes up themselves. If you want to have fabrics made up into Indian clothes, or want to buy ready-made clothes, try the following shops:

Gold jewellery in a Southall shop.

Babito, 68 South Road (081-571 3224). Open from 11.30am to 7.30pm Monday to Sunday. Ready-made salwar kamiz and 'high fashion' for women.

Red Rose, 25 King Street (081-843 1001). Open from 10.30am to 7pm Monday to Sunday. Makes up salwar kamiz.

Century Emporium, 4-6 The Broadway (081-574 9113). Open from 10.30am to 7pm Monday to Saturday, Sunday 1pm to 7pm. Women's fashion. All clothes are imported from the Far East and include many silks.

Salwar kamiz and sarees are traditionally worn with sandals. The following shops specialise in fashion sandals for Asians, displaying a fascinating variety of women's sandals in fancy styles (many in gold and silver), and some matching handbags.

Ajanta Footwear, 116 The Broadway (081-574 3220). Open from 9.30am to 6.30pm Monday to Saturday.

Ajanta Footwear, 80 Broadway (no telephone). Open from 9.30am to 6.30pm Monday to Saturday.

Gold Jewellery

Southall's jewellers stock a wide range of 22-carat gold jewellery of Indian design. All shops are locked and the bell must be rung to gain entry.

Hayes Jewellers, 103 The Broadway (081-571 3813/2452). Open from 10am to 7.30pm Monday to Saturday.

Ruby Jewellers, 127 The Broadway (081-574 4221). Open from 10am to 6.30pm Monday to Saturday.

Ramesh Jewellers, 104 The Broadway (081-574 1917, 571 3875). Open from 10.30am to 7pm Monday to Saturday.

Ram Parkash Sunderdass and Sons, 20 The Broadway (081-571 4451). Open from 9.30am to 7pm Monday to Saturday.

Ramesh Jewellers, 57 The Broadway (081-571 5314). Open from 10.30am to 6.30pm Monday to Saturday.

Ram Parkash Sunderdass and Sons, 2b King Street (081-574 6599). Open from 9.30am to 7pm Monday to Saturday.

SOUTHALL: FOOD AND DRINK

Shopping

Everything you could ever require for making Indian food is available in Southall's grocers and greengrocers. Here you will find packets of Basmati rice (the most highly regarded Indian variety), tins of ghee (clarified butter used for cooking) and a huge number of different chutneys, pickles, herbs and spices.

Dokal and Sons, 133/5 The Broadway (081-574 1647). Open from 9am to 8pm Monday to Sunday. Grocers specialising in cash and carry.

Asian Meat Market, 114 The Broadway (081-574 8945). Open from 8am to 7pm Monday to Saturday. Asian butchers which sells goat's meat, lamb and chicken, but no beef (offensive to Orthodox Hindus) or pork (offensive to Muslims).

Liberty Fresh Fish, Unit 57, Liberty Shopping Centre, South Road. Open from 10am to 7pm Monday to Saturday. Exotic tropical fish.

Sira, 43 South Road (081-571 4529). Open from 9am to 9pm Monday to Sunday. Grocers and greengrocers.

Eating Out

There are many cheap café/restaurants along the Broadway that serve Indian sweets at a counter at the front of the shop and good, basic North Indian food at the tables at the back. These are the best places to eat if you want to get a real flavour of Southall.

Most such places serve very similar food, but one place notable for its excellent vegetarian food is *A Sweet*, 106 The Broadway (081-574 2821), which is open from Tuesday to Sunday, 9am to 7pm.

If you want to eat in a formal restaurant, try the following:-

Maharajah, 171-173 The Broadway (081-574 4564/843 1796). Open from 12.30pm to 2.30am Monday to Sunday. Standard North Indian food. Moderately-priced.

Shahee Tandoori, 241 The Broadway, Southall, Middlesex (081-574 9203). Open from 12 noon to 3pm, 6 to 12 midnight Monday to Sunday. Standard North Indian food. Moderately-priced.

Brilliant Restaurant, 72-74 Western Road (081-574 1928). Open from 12 noon to 3pm, 6pm to 11pm Tuesday to Sunday (except no lunch Saturday and Sunday). A little off the beaten track, this is Southall's best-known and most highly regarded restaurant. North Indian food.

SOUTHALL: SIKHISM & THE GURU GRANTH GURDWARA

Sikhism was founded by Guru ('teacher') Nanak in the Punjab in the early 16th C AD. It sprang largely from Hinduism, though there is a strong influence too from Islam in its monotheistic doctrine and its emphasis on the equality of all before God. That equality is symbolised by the use of the name Singh ('lion') by almost all male Sikhs, and the name Kaur ('Princess') by the women. In Britain these are usually used as middle names.

Guests at a Sikh wedding in Southall pose with their presents for the video recording of the event.

Funeral of a leading 'Khalistani' (a Sikh who actively supports the foundation of an independent Sikh state in Indian territory).

Sikhs are divided into two religious categories: the baptised amritdharis, who are required to follow a strict code of conduct, and the unbaptised saihajdharis, who are not. On baptism, Sikhs join the order of the Khalsa ('the pure ones'), and must wear the 'five K's: Kesha (uncut hair), Kangha (comb), Kara (steel bracelet), Kirpan (a small sword or dagger or a symbolic model of one) and Kachha (a shorts-like undergarment). Turbans are not a specific requirement of this code, but have become the customary means by which the uncut hair and beard are kept neat.

The five K's emphasise both cleanliness and a readiness to do battle. The latter provision arose through necessity in the turbulent conditions that prevailed during the development of Sikhism, and became a lasting tenet of faith. The Sikh military spirit has manifested itself in many ways over the centuries. Since the annexation of the Punjab by the British in 1849, Sikh military talents have been employed by the Indian Army in an unparalleled tradition of service. Another face of that same military spirit has been in evidence in the violent conflict that has shaken the Punjab in recent years as militant Sikhs have fought for an independent Sikh state which they have called 'Khalistan'.

Sikhism is still inextricably bound up with the language, culture and history of the Punjab. Sikhs may have settled all over India, and been amongst the most ambitious of Indian emigrants, yet over 90 per cent still live in the Punjab and the neighbouring state of Haryana. The Sikhs' high profile in Britain, where they are the largest religious group of Indian origin, might give a deceptive impression of their position in India, where they in fact form only a tiny minority of the population, outnumbered even by Christians.

The **Guru Granth Gurdwara** in Villiers Road is a small and welcoming Sikh temple housed in what was once a Methodist church. On the front of the building is a stone relief depicting the khanda, a double edged sword representing freedom and justice, and the swastika, a symbol of good luck. Over the building flies the yellow and black Sikh flag.

If you want to go inside, phone 081-574 7700/5609/0037 to arrange a convenient time to make a visit. Once inside the temple, you will be asked to remove your shoes and cover your head before entering the main hall. The hall is empty apart from a brightly coloured canopy on the dais and a few Christmas-style decorations draped around the chamber. The canopy houses the Holy Book of Sikhism, the Granth Sahib, which is always covered with an ornate fabric when it is not in use.

On entering the main hall, Sikh worshippers always walk straight up to the canopy and kneel in front of it, pressing their heads to the floor. On rising, they place a donation of money in the collection box in front of the canopy (it would be polite if you were to give a donation yourself before leaving), and a priest then gives them a portion of sanctified food (prasad), which is normally a thick, mushy looking substance made out of semolina, sugar and butter. During services worshippers sit on the carpeted floor, men on one side of the hall and women and children on the other.

'Inside Out'

An interview with Amarjit, a British-born Sikh in his 30s, on a visit to his Gurdwara . . .

"I left home ten years ago and moved to London and I'm sort of finding Sikhism interests me more now. I've been coming to the gurdwara much more in the last couple of years. I'll be honest, when they're reciting from the Granth Sahib, I can't follow all of it because they're using really pure Punjabi words, but I'm hoping the more I come, the more I'll pick it up.

I can't say I'm an orthodox Sikh because half the things I don't do - like wearing a turban, growing my beard and things like that. The only thing I do wear is my kara, my bangle.

Sikhism is a modern religion, it's only 500 years old, and I don't think it's very complicated. I mean we don't have any rituals, it's the way you live your life, in honesty, truth and helping your neighbour. I think that's why I like Sikhism - things like that.

I get strength from my religion. It sort of cleanses me coming here every week. It's just like say instead of going to gym and doing a heavy workout, I come here and I pray to God and say, 'look help me, am I going the right path?' . . . and it just sort of relaxes me, brings me down to earth."

SOUTHALL: HINDUISM & THE VISHWA HINDU TEMPLE

Hinduism, the religion of about 85 percent of the Indian population, is not easy to define. The modern meaning of the word was established by the British to describe the religious beliefs of those Indians who weren't Muslims, Sikhs, Parsees, Christians or Jews, and it encompasses a fantastically varied range of sects, beliefs and practices.

There is no central scripture in Hinduism equivalent to the Granth Sahib for Sikhism, or the Bible for Christianity. It does have a shared literary tradition in the ancient scriptures of the Vedas and the Puranas, but even then various Hindu sects draw from and interpret these scriptures in many different ways.

Shrines in the Vishwa Hindu Temple, Southall.

Hindus worship many gods, who are viewed as incarnations and aspects of one Absolute Truth. In mainstream Hindu belief, the principal aspects of this Absolute are assigned to three gods: Brahma the Creator, Vishnu the Preserver and Siva the destroyer. Vishnu and Siva are the most commonly worshipped, although some Hindus worship only Vishnu, some only Siva, and others both. The powers of Vishnu and Siva are further delegated to other deities; Vishnu has ten incarnations, of whom the most widely revered are Rama and Krishna.

Most Hindus believe in the doctrine of cause and effect known as karma whereby the behaviour of a person in one life determines how they will be reincarnated in the next. Orthodox Hindus believe that people are born into different stratas of society, known as castes, in accordance with their conduct in previous lives. Listed in descending order of 'merit', these castes are: Brahmins (the priestly caste), Kshatirya (the warrior and ruling caste), Vaishya (the caste of farmers, merchant and craftsmen) and Shudra (the servant caste). Below these castes are the untouchables, who are allotted the jobs that even servants consider beneath them.

Ultra-orthodox Hindus believe that there can be no movement between castes within a lifetime, and that members of different castes should not eat with or marry members of another caste, or indeed of another sub-caste. Progressive Hindu opinion militates against the concept of caste, and discrimination on grounds of caste is now illegal in India. Caste nevertheless continues to exert a strong influence on Hindu society, including in Britain, and particularly so where marriage is concerned.

The *Vishwa Hindu Temple,* 2 Lady Margaret Road, (open from 6am to 8pm) is housed in a former social club with its facade remodelled in a traditional Hindu temple style. Once inside the temple, you will be asked to remove your shoes before going into the main hall. Female worshippers usually cover their heads before entering, but female visitors are not obliged to do so. Inside, worshippers kneel or sit on the carpeted floor, facing the striking array of shrines that line the far wall. The wall itself is covered with a mural depicting white clouds drifting against a blue sky, giving the impression that the shrines are located out of doors.

On the shrines stand statues of various gods, including Vishnu, Krishna and Ganesh, who are garlanded with flowers, a traditional mark of respect. The statues were commissioned for the temple from a Jaipur factory. Peacock feathers appear in praise of Krishna, who wore them in his crown. To the right of the shrines is a large model of a mountain range, which represents the Himalayas. From it bubbles a tiny stream of water, representing the sacred river Ganges.

At some point during their stay, Hindu worshippers usually ring the bell in the middle of the hall so as to attract the attention of the gods to their prayers. At the foot of the shrines are collecting boxes for donations of money (to which it would be polite to make a contribution yourself before you leave). Note the food offerings left at the side of the shrines. After prayer, worshippers are given sanctified food by the priest, and a drink of water that not only symbolises Ganges water but actually contains water from the river itself, albeit diluted with London tap water.

SOUTHALL: POLITICAL DISTURBANCES

Although Southall is usually the most peaceable of places, there have been several occasions on which violent conflict on its streets has attracted national attention.

During the general election campaign of 1979, the far-right National Front Party booked a room in Southall Town Hall, High Street (at its junction with Lady Margaret Road), for an election meeting to be held on the evening of Monday 23 April. Despite many protests from Asians about the use of council premises by a party which openly espouses racist policies, the council refused to ban the meeting.

On the Monday afternoon, tension built up as Asian demonstrators gathered around the Town Hall and the police tried to keep the area clear. In the late afternoon the Town Hall was cordoned off by several thousand police, and the protesters, now also several thousand strong, were pushed back along The Broadway, South Road and the High Street.

Clashes soon broke out between the police and the protesters. There were baton charges by the police, missiles thrown from the crowd, many arrests, and injuries on both sides. National Front members arrived at the Town Hall at about 7pm. Some paused on the steps to give Nazi salutes to a token group of demonstrators who had been allowed through the police cordons. The meeting ended about 9.30, and soon afterwards the protesters dispersed.

In the aftermath of these events, there were widespread complaints about brutal and indiscriminate batoning by the police. Blair Peach, a teacher from New Zealand and one of the few non-Asian protesters present, had his skull fractured in an incident near the junction of Beechcroft Road and Orchard Avenue, and later died of his injuries. Witnesses said that Peach was struck by a policeman, but the man responsible has never been identified.

An all-night vigil over Blair Peach's body held at the Dominion Theatre, The Green, was attended by thousands of local Asians. The Dominion Theatre has since been demolished and a community centre called the Dominion Centre has been built on the site. On the opposite side of the road stands the Victory Pub; it was outside here that a young Asian, Gurdip

Singh Chaggar, was stabbed to death by a gang of white youths in 1976. The judge at the trial declared that there was no racial motive, but there are few Asians locally who saw it that way, and his death marked the beginning of a radical phase in youth politics in Southall.

On Friday 3 July 1981, further rioting occurred in Southall when a skinhead band played a concert at the Hambrough Tavern, The Broadway (at the west end on the stretch between Bankside and Beresford Road). After skinheads caused disturbances in the area, a pitched battle broke out between Asian youths and skinheads and, when police intervened, continued between Asian youths and police. During the clashes the Hambrough Tavern was burnt out. It has since been rebuilt.

Political conflict in India itself has had repercussions in Southall. Sikh militants in favour of an independent state have murdered a number of their opponents in Britain over the last ten years. On 23rd July 1984, the premises of an anti-Khalistan Punjabi newspaper in ex-Dilloway Yard, Southall, was firebombed and the assistant editor killed, and on 16th January 1986, a leading anti-Khalistan Sikh politician was shot dead in an off-licence in The Broadway.

SPITALFIELDS

Indian seamen have been living in the East End since the late 18th C. Amongst them from at least the late 19th C were Bengali-speakers from the Sylhet (a rural district of what is now Bangladesh), and it was this group that laid the foundations for the large Bengali community that developed in the East End in the 1960s.

The heartland of the Bengali settlement is in the area around Brick Lane in Spitalfields, a district which has been noted for its immigrant population for over 300 years. The Bengalis are only the most recent arrivals in a long line that includes Huguenots (French Protestants), Irish Catholics, and Jews. These successive waves of immigration are reflected in the history of the building on the corner of Fournier Street and Brick Lane. Constructed in 1744 as a Huguenot church, and used as a synagogue from 1898 to 1975, it is now a mosque, the London Jamme Masjid, catering to the predominantly Muslim Bengalis.

In Brick Lane, and in particular in the vicinity of the mosque, you will see Bengali men wearing the white cotton skull caps or oval fur hats that are characteristic of Asian Muslims. The more religiously orthodox of Bengali Muslims keep their heads covered all the time, and most Bengali men will do so when they visit a mosque.

Spitalfields has been associated with the garment trade since the 16th C. In their time the Huguenots, Irish and Jews have all played a prominent role in this line of business, and today the manufacture of Western-design clothes is the most important source of employment for East End Bengalis. The workshops, which are scattered all over Spitalfields and Whitechapel, are particularly numerous in the northern area of Brick Lane. Here, through workshop windows, you can see the steam rising from the presses under the glare of fluorescent strip lighting.

On one of my visits to Spitalfields, I happened to glance through an open workshop door and catch sight of a Bengali child hard at work. This is of course illegal, but apparently not uncommon in this very poor community.

As a local Bengali told me, some Bengali parents reason that since their children will work in the garment industry when they leave school anyway, they might as well learn the trade beforehand and earn some much-needed money for their families.

The most serious anti-Semitic disturbances in Britain during the 1930s took place in the East End. So too, since the 1970s it has been the scene of some of the worst racist violence in the country, though the victims now are Bengalis. On 11 June 1978 about 150 to 200 white youths rampaged down Brick Lane, attacking Bengalis, smashing windows and damaging cars. Arson and other forms of violence and intimidation have frequently been used to keep Bengalis from moving into white housing estates.

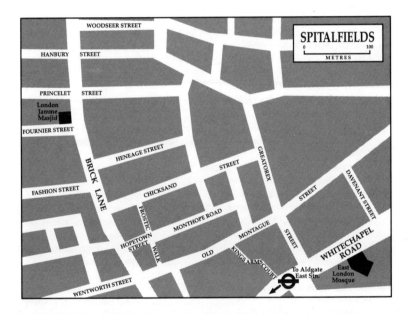

An Indian assassin named Udham Singh once lodged in Spitalfields in the loft of 15 Artillery Passage, E1. Singh came to London in 1937 to avenge the infamous massacre at Amritsar in the Punjab of 1919, when hundreds of Indians were killed after a British officer ordered his soldiers to open fire without warning on an unarmed crowd.

Singh blamed Sir Michael O'Dwyer (Lieutenant-Governor of the region at the time of the massacre), and tracked him down to London. After obtaining employment from O'Dwyer as a chauffeur, he shot and killed him at a public meeting in Caxton Hall, Caxton Street, SW1. Singh was found guilty of murder after a trial at the Central Criminal Courts, Old Bailey, EC4, and was hanged at Pentonville Prison, Caledonian Road, N7, on 31 July 1940. His remains were exhumed in 1974 and flown back to New Delhi, India, where they were given a martyr's welcome from Indira Gandhi, then the Prime Minister of India.

SPITALFIELDS: SHOPPING (incl. Food and Drink)

Shops which cater to the Bengali population are concentrated on the stretch of Brick Lane between Hopetown Street in the south and Woodseer Street in the north. Snack bars serve Indian sweets and savoury snacks, and shops stock Asian groceries, clothes-fabrics and music cassettes. *Halal* butchers deal only in meat that is permitted under Islamic law. Newsagents sell Bengali newspapers and magazines. Brick Lane is only a local shopping centre however, and its shops are no match for those of Southall in West London.

Ambala Sweet Centre, 55 Brick Lane, E1 (071-247 8569). Open from 10am to 8pm Monday to Saturday, 9.30am to 7.30pm Sunday. Indian sweets.

Modern Saree Centre, 67 Brick Lane, E1 (081-247 3308). Open from 9.30am to 7pm Monday to Saturday, 10am to 6.30pm Sunday. Fabrics for sarees.

Brick Lane Music House, 74 Brick Lane, E1 (071-247 3308). Open from 10.30am to 9pm Monday to Sunday. Indian and Bengali music on cassette and CD, magazines.

Sangeela, 75 Brick Lane, E1 (071-247 3393). Open from 10am to 9pm Monday to Saturday. Books, magazines and music cassettes.

Music Lovers, 77 Brick Lane, EC1 (071-247 8150). Open from 10am to 9pm Monday to Sunday. Indian and Bengali music on cassette, videos and men's clothing.

Sargarn, 84 Brick Lane, E1 (no telephone). Open from 11am to 11pm Monday to Sunday. Indian and Bengali music on cassette, magazines and newspapers.

Bilash Saree Centre, 100 Brick Lane, E1 (071-247 6308). Open from 10am to 7pm Monday to Sunday. Fabrics for sarees.

Taj Stores, 112 Brick Lane, E1 (071-377 0061). Open from 9am to 9pm Monday to Sunday. Food supermarket with large selection of frozen fish.

Clifton Sweetmart, 118 Brick Lane, E1 (071-247 5811). Open from 10am to 11pm Monday to Sunday. Indian sweets.

Titash Saree Palace, 138 Brick Lane, E1 (071-247 1511). Open from 10am to 6.30pm Monday to Sunday. Fabrics for sarees, children's clothing.

SPITALFIELDS: EATING OUT

In amidst the shabbiness of Spitalfields are some surprisingly smart restaurants, several of which are clustered together on Brick Lane on the stretch between Banbury Street and Woodseer Street. Disappointingly, the food they serve is of the standard North Indian style, and not authentic Bengali cuisine, which is based around fish dishes.

The Shampan, 79 Brick Lane, E1 (071-375 0475). Open from 12 noon to 3pm, 6pm to midnight Monday to Sunday. A high standard restaurant which caters principally to City businessmen.

The Clifton, 126 Brick Lane, E1 (071-247 2364,377 9402). Open from 12 noon to 1am Monday to Sunday. Cheerful and smart restaurant which is justly renowned for its murals depicting alluring women in scenes from Indian history and legend. Menu includes a few Bengali fish dishes. Moderately-priced.

Clifton Sweetmart, 118 Brick Lane, E1 (071-247 5811). Open from 10am to 11pm Monday to Friday. Café/restaurant. Prices are low, and Tandoori dishes are cooked in a genuine clay oven.

Minaret of the East London Mosque, Whitechapel Road.

'Allah' inscribed over the main entrance of the mosque.

SPITALFIELDS: ISLAM &
THE EAST LONDON MOSQUE

The religion of Islam, whose adherents are called Muslims, was founded by the prophet Mohammed in the 7th C AD. There are probably about 800,000 Muslims in Britain, mostly of Asian origin but also including Turkish Cypriots, Iranians, Arabs and East Africans. Although it is regularly stated in British newspapers that there are between 1.5 and 2 million Muslims in Britain, these figures are over-enthusiastic guestimates that originate from Islamic organisations.

Islam rests on three basic beliefs. *Tawhid* (Oneness of Allah): there is only one God, whose proper name is Allah. *Risalah* (Prophet-hood): Allah guides man's conduct through messengers and prophets, who are ordinary men of flesh and blood. Following in the same prophetic line as Adam, Noah, Abraham, Moses and Jesus, Mohammed was the last and greatest prophet. *Akhirah* (Life after death): every person's actions will be judged by Allah in the hereafter.

Every Muslim should perform the five duties known as the pillars of Islam. *Ash-shahadah:* stating the declaration of the faith - 'There is no God but Allah, and Mohammed is his prophet'. *Salah:* daily prayers made in the direction of Mecca. *Zakah:* compulsory payment of alms for welfare purposes. *Sawm*: during Ramadan, the ninth month of the Islamic year, a Muslim must abstain from food, drink, sex and smoking, from dawn until sunset every day. *Hajj:* every Muslim who can afford to do so must undertake a pilgrimage to Mecca at least once in their lifetime.

Muslims are also required to follow a strict dietary code. Eating the meat of certain animals, such as pigs, is completely forbidden. Animals whose meat may be eaten must be killed in a prescribed manner and the blood drained off before the meat can be consumed. Meat permitted by Islamic law is called halal.

The *East London Mosque* at 84-92 Whitechapel Road, E1 makes a striking sight on the skyline of the East End. Opened in 1985 with the assistance of a one million pound donation from the Saudi Arabian Government, it is a successful architectural fusion of clean-lined modern design with that of a traditional oriental-style mosque. Three minarets rise over the domed brick building; a crescent moon, a symbol of Islam, stands on the top of the tallest. The word 'Allah' is inscribed in Arabic script over the main entrance of the mosque.

If you want to go inside, telephone 071-247 1357 to arrange a convenient time for a visit. Women visitors should be modestly dressed and wear a head covering. Male visitors are not obliged to wear a head covering, though it is usual for Muslims to do so. On entering the Mosque you will be asked to remove your shoes.

The interior of the building is austere. The main hall is a huge, empty chamber. There are no religious pictures or statues; these are forbidden in Islam. Apart from the patterned carpet, the only colour comes from the small stained-glass windows located in the south eastern wall towards which the worshippers pray, facing Mecca. Women worship separately from the men, confined behind a translucent curtain on a balcony which overlooks the main hall.

OTHER PLACES TO VISIT ──────────

Victoria and Albert Museum, Cromwell Road, SW7 (071-938 8500). Open from 10am to 5.50pm Tuesday to Sunday. Admission is free, but there is very strong pressure to make a 'donation'. The Indian gallery contains a large collection of Indian art and antiquities.

British Museum, Great Russell Street, WC1 (071-636 1555). Open from 10am to 5pm Monday to Saturday, 2.30 to 6pm Sunday. Admission free. Indian art and antiquities, particularly Hindu and Buddhist sculpture.

The Commonwealth Institute, Kensington High Street, W8 (071-603 4535). Open from 10am to 5.30pm Monday to Saturday, 2 to 5pm Sunday. Admission free. Exhibitions and cultural events of Asian interest are often held here.

Bharatiya Vidya Bhavan/Institute of Indian Culture, 4a Castletown Road, W14 (071-381 3086). A well established centre for Indian classical culture which presents regular performances of music and dance.

See also **Imperial India:** *National Army Museum, page 60.*

SHOPPING ──────────────

Southall is by far the best place to shop for Asian goods in the London region. Other Asian shopping centres include Upper Tooting Road, SW17; Brick Lane, E1; Drummond Street, NW1; Green Street, E7, and Ealing Road, Wembley, Middlesex. Most of the shops listed in this section are located in central London.

Shops

Donis, 23 Carnaby Street (071-734 1104). Open from 9am to 7pm Monday to Saturday. Ethnic-look clothes.

Fifth Dimension, 8a Great Russell Street, WC1 (071-580 6389). Open from 10am to 6pm Monday to Saturday. Ethnic-look clothes. Also batik prints, jewellery, traditional paintings, statuettes and embroideries.

House of Sarees, 169 Tottenham Court Road, W1 (071-388 3917). Open from 9am to 6pm, Monday to Saturday. Fabrics for sarees. Also shawls, women's sandals.

Liberty, Regent Street, W1 (071-734 1234). Open from 9.30am to 6pm Monday to Saturday (closes 7.30pm Thursday). *Basement Floor. Oriental Department.* An attractive selection of Indian arts and crafts, including modern paintings executed in the Mogul style, statuettes and antique furniture. *Third Floor. Shyam Ahuja* (extension 2337). The Indian dhurrie rug, which is characteristically patterned with stripes and arrowheads, is traditionally a cheap floor covering woven in bright cotton fibres. The dhurries sold at this outlet are hand-woven in India on traditional looms, and are made in quality wools, cottons and silks. Shyam Ahuja also stocks hand-woven cotton and silk fabrics sold by the metre, and cotton rag rugs.

The Conran Shop, 81 Fulham Road, SW3 (071-589 7401). Open from 9.30am to 6pm (except 10am to 6pm Tuesday and 2-5pm Sunday). One section of the shop stocks hand-woven Indian fabrics which are sold by the metre for upholstery, curtains and cushions. Some of these fabrics are of traditional design, others are adapted to Western tastes. Dhurries and cushion covers are also available.

Ambros Tradeways, 50-51 Berwick Street, Wl (071-439 6819). Open from 10.30am to 6.30pm Monday to Friday, 12 noon to 6pm Saturday. The northern end of Berwick Street is known for its numerous costume jewellery shops. At Ambros they specialise in Indian costume jewellery, particularly bangles and necklaces. They also stock jade, red garnet and rice-pearl Indian jewellery, plus Indian clothes, leather hand-bags and arts and crafts.

Books From India, 45 Museum Street, WC 1(071-405 7226/3784). Open from 10am to 5.30pm Monday to Friday, 10am to 5pm Saturday. Extensive range of books about (and mainly from) India, Pakistan and Bangladesh. Excellent English language stock, plus Hindi, Gujarati, Bengali, Urdu, Punjabi and Tamil. Also supplies posters on Indian subjects, and Indian classical music on record and cassette.

Asian Book Shop, 45 Grafton Way, Wl (071-387 5747). Open from 10am to 6pm Monday to Friday. Books from India, Pakistan and Bangladesh, in Hindi, Urdu, Gujarati, Bengali, Punjabi, and a few in English. Pulp paperback thrillers and romances in Hindi. Also stocks tape cassettes of children's stories.

Islamic Book Centre, 120 Drummond Street, NW1 (071-3880710). Open from 10am to 6pm Monday to Saturday, 11am to 7pm Sunday. Good selection of Islamic books, mostly English language, some Urdu. Also stocks tape cassettes of readings from the Koran in English and Urdu.

Ruposhi Bangla, 220 Tooting High Street, SW17 (081-672 7843/1718). Open from 10am to 5.30pm Monday to Saturday. Books from and about Bangladesh and the adjoining Indian region of Bengal. Mostly Bengali-language, some English. Also Bangladeshi documentary videos, maps, arts and crafts and computer software..

Soma Books, 38 Kennington Lane, SE11(081-735 2101). Open from 9.30am to 5.30pm, Monday to Friday. Books from and about India. Large collection of children's books in English and in Indic languages.

Quest Bookshop, 12 Bury Place, WC1 (071-405 2309). Open from 10am to 6pm Monday to Friday, 10am to 4pm Saturday. Bookshop managed by the Theosophical Society (see *Annie Besant, page 61).* Amongst much else on 'religious and esoteric subjects', they stock books on yoga, meditation, and the Indian mystic Jiddu Krishnamurti.

Garecha, 6 Park Walk, SW10 (071-352 8972). Open from 12 noon to 7pm Monday to Sunday. Arts and crafts from India and south-east Asia.

Andrew Martin, 200 Walton Street, SW3 (071-584 4290). Open from 9.30am to 5.30pm Monday to Friday, 10.30am to 4.30pm Saturday. Furnishing fabrics include silks from India and the Far East.

Andrew Martin, 11 Sheen Road, Richmond, Surrey (081-940 5432). Open from 10am to 5pm Tuesday to Saturday. Similar stock to the Walton Street shop.

Ganesha, 6 Park Walk, off Fulham Road, SW10 (071-352 8972). Open from 10am to 11pm Monday to Sunday. Indian arts and crafts.

Asian shops: a short history

Over the last 20 years non-Asian Londoners have looked on in amazement at the phenomenal growth of Asian-owned shops in the capital, many of them grocery stores and newsagents. London's first Asian-owned shops opened up in the 1950s to cater for those members of the then predominantly male Asian community who were unable to shop during the day. It was because of this that Asian shops didn't specialise, unlike other local shops of the period, but sold everything under one roof, from groceries to vegetables. Asian shopkeepers quickly recognised the commercial advantages of late night and Sunday opening for selling a full range of food to the general public, and exploited those advantages to the full, unaware of or unrestrained by local custom and rarely enforced by-laws.

The immigration to Britain of Asians from traditional trading families has also been an important factor in business expansion. Few non-Asians realise that a large percentage of Asian businessmen come from particular communities - such as the Gujarati community - and that what is commonly viewed as an 'instinctive' Asian talent for business is in many cases the expression of long-established family traditions. In short, it is not a culture shared by all Asians.

The pioneering example of Asian shopkeepers has been crucial in opening up the political debate concerning the removal of many of the legal restrictions placed on shop opening hours. Ironically, however, over the last few years many Asian-run shops have started closing earlier and also on Sundays. Having established themselves, many shopkeepers are no longer willing to tolerate the long hours they once worked.

The rise of the Asian shopkeeper has been presented uncritically as a great success story, and of course, in many ways it is. However, it was only the gradual decline of the local high street shops in the 1970s that made it possible for Asians to move into the trade in such large numbers. In some ways, Asian shopkeepers provided a boost to a declining trade by making it more convenient to shop locally. On the other hand, by selling a wide range of foods, they helped to accelerate the decline of the traditional specialist local shops that had already been set in motion by the development of large supermarkets and shopping malls.

The Asian local shopkeeper today is often far from the brilliant success that is commonly assumed. The turnover is steadily on the decline, hours are long, returns are often poor, and shopkeepers are not infrequently the victims of robberies. On the whole it is those shopkeepers who used grocery stores and newsagents as a springboard into other business ventures that have been really successful.

FOOD AND DRINK

RESTAURANTS

Indian food first appeared on London menus back in the 18th C, when it was served in the select coffee houses that catered for the 'nabobs' (see *Imperial India*). It was to remain very much a minority interest until the 1960s, when restaurants providing cheap, good quality Indian food for the general public were pioneered in Britain by the Sylhetis from Bangladesh, who continue to dominate the field.

The success of the Sylhetis has its roots in the 19th C when Sylheti seamen acquired a near monopoly on work as cooks and galley hands on Indian ships. The move to quayside catering was an obvious step, especially after they found themselves barred from many ports following the partition of India in 1947. Sylheti cooks were accustomed to providing a generalised North Indian cuisine to suit the varied regional tastes of all the Indian seamen, and with a few adaptations, this cuisine was to prove perfect for the British palate.

Indian restaurants are now such an integral part of the London food scene that non-Asian Londoners have been known to complain, in all seriousness, that the trouble about taking holidays on the Continent is that you can't get a decent curry! Many Indian restaurants in London do not even feel it necessary to provide the most basic of translations on their menu. For the uninitiated (where have you been?), the following are a few of the dishes you will find on most menus:

Tandoori. A kind of Indian barbecue. Chicken, lamb or prawns are marinated in a mild sauce and cooked in a clay oven (tandoor). A good choice for anyone who doesn't like their food too hotly spiced.

Pillao rice. Yellow-coloured fried rice cooked with spices.

Biriani. Pillao rice mixed with vegetables, egg and pieces of chicken or lamb. This is a dry dish; you may want to order a vegetable curry in addition to provide some sauce to mix with it.

Samosa. Triangular pasties filled with meat or vegetables.

Dhal. Lentils.

Gosht. Lamb.

Bindi. Okra/ladies fingers.

Murgh. Chicken.

Bombay duck. Not duck at all but pungent sun-dried fish.

Popadam. Disc-shaped wafers usually made out of lentil flour.

Chappati. Heavy, disc-shaped bread made from unleavened wheat flour.

Paratha. Buttered disc-shaped bread made from unleavened wholemeal wheat flour and shallow-fried until crisp. Often stuffed with vegetables.

Nan. Oval-shaped bread made from leavened white refined wheat flour. Similar to pitta bread in texture.

Kulfi. Indian ice-cream. Hard and rich.

A kind of shorthand has evolved on the standard London menu to indicate how hotly spiced some of the dishes are. 'Korma' means very mild (though strictly speaking it should be used to describe a rich, creamy sauce), 'Madras' means hot (food is customarily hotter in South India, where the city of Madras is located), and 'Vindaloo' means very hot (though in India it means a Goan dish made of pork, vinegar and potatoes).

Standard Restaurants

Indian restaurants which serve standard North Indian fare of a good quality and at a moderate price can be found on practically every high street in London. However, they are becoming increasingly rare in Central London. The following are both centrally located.

Neel Akash, 2 Hanway Street, W1 (071-580 9767). Open from 12 noon to 3pm, 5.45pm to 12 midnight, Monday to Saturday. Good cheap food.

Passage to India, 5 Old Compton Street, W1 (071-734 1057). Open from 12 noon to 12 midnight, Sunday to Thursday, 12 noon to 1am Friday and Saturday.

'New Wave' Restaurants

During the 1980s a whole new wave of Indian restaurants have opened up in response to Londoners' increasingly sophisticated appreciation of Indian food, a move largely inspired by the Bangladeshi entrepreneur Amin Ali. The dishes they serve are strongly influenced by luxury North Indian food (mughlai cuisine), with its subtle spicing, rich, creamy sauces and Middle-Eastern influences. In many respects this cuisine is more authentic than the standard Indian fare, as, for example, in the appearance of regional specialities. However, they have also been influenced by European 'haute cuisine'. None of these restaurants worry much about authenticity where alcohol is concerned however, and supply a wide range of Western-style cocktails, many with jokey Indianised names such as 'Raj Rascal' or 'Khyber Pass-Out'.

The 'new wave' restaurants are typically spacious, air-conditioned and tastefully decorated in pinks, greens and purples, with elegant Mogul-style prints hanging up on the walls. A reception area for meeting friends is a welcome innovation. These restaurants may be more expensive than the average Indian restaurant, but they are very reasonably priced for what they provide when compared with restaurants which serve similar quality food of other national cuisines.

Bombay Palace, 50 Connaught Street, W2 (071-723 8855/0673). Open from 12 noon to 3pm, 6 to 11pm Monday to Sunday. Good range of vegetarian specialities. Moderately-priced.

The Red Fort, 77 Dean Street, W1 (071-437 2525/2115). Open from 12 noon to 3pm, 6 to 11.30pm Monday to Sunday. One of London's best-known Indian restaurants, and justly so. Good food in attractive surroundings. Moderately-priced for the standard of food it serves.

The Bombay Brasserie, 14 Courtfield Close, SW7 (071-370 4040). Open from 12.30pm to 3pm, 7pm to 11.45pm Monday to Sunday. Luxurious premises, incorporating a beautiful conservatory. Emphasis on regional specialities. Expensive.

Lal Qila, 117 Tottenham Court Road, W1 (071-387 4570/5332). Open from 12am to 3pm, 6 to 11.15pm Monday to Sunday. Moderately priced. A set price buffet is served at lunchtime.

Salloo, 62-64 Kinnerton Street, SW1 (071-235 4444). Open from 12 noon to 3pm, 7pm to Midnight Monday to Saturday. High-class Pakistani cuisine. Expensive.

Vegetarian Restaurants

The number of Indian vegetarian restaurants in London has increased markedly over the last few years. The food is usually cheap and the decor simple - some feature stripped-pine furniture to give that 'wholemeal' look.

There are two styles of vegetarian cuisine found in London - South Indian, and Gujarati. Gujarati is much closer in style to standard North Indian food, but tends to sweetness, even in savoury dishes. The Gujarati restaurants often include South Indian dishes on their menu, but you'd be much better off going to a South Indian restaurant for these dishes. South Indian food is well worth exploration, though bear in mind that it is sometimes very hotly spiced. Typical dishes include steamed rice cakes and pancakes filled with various mixtures of chick peas, onions, nuts and lentils. It is quite distinct from the type of North Indian vegetarian dishes found in the standard Indian restaurant.

Diwana Bhel-Poori 121-123 Drummond Street, NW1 (071-387 5556) . Open from 12 noon to 11.30pm Monday to Sunday. Gujarati and South Indian food. Lunch buffet. Cheap.

Chutneys, 124 Drummond Street, NW1 (071-388 0604). Open from 12 noon to 2.45pm, 6pm to 11.30pm Monday to Saturday, 12 noon to 10.30pm Sunday. Vegetarian food from various regions of India.

Ravi Shankar, 133-135 Drummond Street, NW1 (071-388 6458). Open from 12 noon to 11pm Monday to Sunday. Gujarati and South Indian. Moderately-priced.

Diwana Bhel-Poori House, 50 Westbourne Grove, W2 (071-221 0721). Open from 12 noon to 3pm, 6pm to 11pm Tuesday to Friday, 12 noon to 11pm Saturday and Sunday. Gujarati and South Indian. Moderately priced.

Mandeer, 21 Hanway Place, W1 (071-323 0660, 580 3470). Open from 12 noon to 3pm, 5.30pm to 10pm Monday to Saturday. Gujarati and South Indian. The self-service section (open from 12 noon to 3pm) is severely functional and rather gloomy, but the adjacent waiter-service room is pleasant enough. Moderately priced.

Harekrishna Curry House, I Hanway Street, W1 (071-636 5262). Open from 12 noon to 11pm Monday to Saturday. Gujarati. Moderately priced.

Woodlands Restaurant, 77 Marylebone Lane, W1 (071-486 3862). Open from 12 noon to 2.45pm, 6 to 10.45pm Monday to Sunday. South Indian. Smarter decor than is usual for a vegetarian restaurant. Moderately-priced.

Sree Krishna, 192-194 Tooting High Street, SW17 (071-672 4250/6903). Open from 12 noon to 3pm, 6 to 11pm Sunday to Thursday, 6 to 12pm Friday to Saturday. This is not a solely vegetarian restaurant, but it does serve a wide range of excellent vegetarian South Indian dishes. Moderately-priced.

Other Restaurants

Veeraswamy, 99-101 Regent Street, W1 (071-734 1401). Open from 12 noon to 2.30pm, 6pm to 11.30pm Monday to Saturday. The oldest of London's Indian restaurants is tastefully decorated in a distinctive 'Raj' style. Food from various regions of India is beautifully presented and elegantly served by sari-clad waitresses, but the set buffet lunch is less than inspiring.

Ragam, 57 Cleveland Street, W1 (071-636 9098). South Indian. Regional specialities from the Kerala region.

Khan's, 13-15 Westbourne Grove, W2 (071-727 5420). Open from 12 noon to 3pm, 6pm to 12 midnight Monday to Sunday. A place you either love or hate. Attractive and unusual decor - tall metal pillars in the form of palm trees hold up the ceilings, and the walls and ceilings are done out in 'trompe d'oeil' sky and clouds. It's cheap and popular, but the food is indifferent, it's very noisy and the service is poor.

Royals, 7 Bow Street, WC2 (071-379 1099). Open from 12 noon to 2.30pm, 5.30pm to 11.30pm Monday to Saturday. A very smart restaurant, reflecting its proximity to the Royal Opera House and Drury Lane Theatre.

Neel Kamal, 36 Percy Street, W1 (071-636 6971/580 6125). Open from 12 noon to 3pm, 6pm to midnight Monday to Saturday, 6pm to midnight Sunday. Hidden in the basement, prices are surprisingly moderate for central London and the quality of the North Indian food is high.

Haandi, 161 Drummond Street, NW1 (071-383 4557). Open from 12 noon to 2.30pm, 6pm to 11.30pm Monday to Sunday (last orders midnight Friday and Saturday). Specialises in fish dishes.

Prince of Ceylon, 39 Watford Way, NW4 (081-202 5967). Open from 12 noon to midnight Monday to Sunday. Sri Lankan cuisine, dishes tend to be hot.

Spice of India, 29 Church Lane, E11 (081-539 7337). Open from 5pm to 12 midnight Monday to Sunday. Serves some Bengali fish dishes alongside a standard North Indian menu.

See also **Southall: Eating Out,** *page 33* and **Spittalfields: Eating Out,** *page 40.*

SWEET AND SAVOURY SNACKS

Indian sweets deserve to be more widely appreciated, but at present they are usually available only in the snack bars and specialist sweet shops that are located in Asian districts.

The following are some of the commonest types of Indian sweets:

Halva. Usually square, and made out of corn flour or vegetables. Often jelly like. Should not be confused with the 'halva' sweets found in Mediterranean and Middle Eastern countries.

Ladoo. Round, usually made from powdered lentils.

Barfi. Thick and crumbly, made from milk solids. Westerners often find some Indian sweets too sickly for their tastes, but barfi will provide an easy introduction.

Indian savoury snacks are usually sold alongside Indian sweets, and are also available in many Asian-owned grocers. These snacks are made up of mixes of ingredients such as cashew nuts, chick peas, lentils, rice and sultanas.

Ambala Sweet Centre, 112 Drummond Street, NWI (071-387 7886/3521). Open from 10am to 8.30pm Monday to Sunday. High quality sweets and savoury snacks, plus excellent vegetarian and non-vegetarian samosas.

Gupta Confectioners, 100 Drummond Street, NW1 (071-380 1590). Open from 11am to 7pm Monday to Sunday. Indian sweets.

Savera Balcony, 129 Drummond Street, NW1 (071-380 0290). Open from 10am to 8pm Tuesday to Sunday. Savoury snacks and Indian breads.

See also **Southall: Shopping,** *page 29.*

TEA AND COFFEE

China was Britain's major supplier of tea until the 19th C, when Indian and Ceylonese imports took a lead which they have never lost. Darjeeling, which is grown in the Himalayan foothills, is the most highly regarded Indian tea.

Whittards of Chelsea, The Conran Shop, 81 Fulham Road, SW3 (071-589 4261). Open from 9.30am to 5pm Monday to Saturday, 12 noon to 5pm Sunday. Specialists in teas and coffees from all over the world. Supplies many brands of Darjeeling, Assam and Nilgiri teas, which are sold both loose or in tea bags. Also stocks Indian Mysore coffee, which is sold as green beans, roast beans or ground to order.

MUSIC ————————————————————————

The Indian sub-continent has rich classical and folk music traditions, but it is the modern songs from Indian films that are the standard listening fare for the majority of the older generation of Asians. *Filmi* music, as it is known, can be heard on community radio stations in London such as *Spectrum Radio* or *Sunrise Radio.*

The best introductions to *filmi* music are the LP/CD compilations *'Golden Voices From The Silver Screen'*, which are available on Globestyle Records through general record shops. There are now three volumes available, covering a full range of *filmi* music from the 1950s through to the 1970s.

Asian musicians in Britain have had little impact on mainstream music, but they have created a style of music all their own, called *bhangra.*

Modern bhangra has developed out of a traditional Punjabi folk music which accompanied a lively Punjabi folk dance. Both the dance and the music are known as bhangra, or as it is often termed today, traditional bhangra. This music was played in Britain mainly by amateur groups of Punjabi musicians at weddings.

In the mid-1980s, former wedding groups such as *Alaap* and *Heera* created a Western pop/Punjabi folk fusion that started a whole musical movement in Britain. Although the music came out of Punjabi culture, it was adopted enthusiastically by Asian youth from all communities, and bhangra groups were soon playing to huge crowds of Asian youths in dance halls across Britain.

One feature of the 'bhangra' boom was that dances were held during the day, enabling Asian boys and girls to meet without their parents necessarily being aware. In this way those with stricter parents could mix with those whose parents were more liberal.

The bhangra boom played an important role in bringing Asian youths together from all communities and in creating a genuinely British-Asian culture. The music lost its momentum in the early nineties, but fresh influences from black music - particularly 'house' and ragga - is now taking place.

Bhangra music can be found in any Asian music shop, although Southall in by far the best place to shop. *Diamonds from Heera* by Heera and *Alaap* by Alaap are both good introductory albums.

Bhangra dance lesson in a Southall backyard.

PEOPLE

Mohandas Gandhi, the founding father of independent India, was born into a Hindu family in 1869, the son of the Prime Minister of a tiny princely state in Gujarat. At the age of 18 Gandhi was keen to go and train as a barrister in England, which he then admired as 'the land of philosophers and poets, the very centre of civilisation'. This scheme was opposed by the leaders of his caste, who insisted that it would be impossible for him to fulfil his religious obligations in Britain. Gandhi took a solemn vow to abstain from wine, women and meat while he was abroad, but despite this he was expelled from his caste when he went ahead with his plans.

Gandhi arrived at Tilbury Docks on 29 September 1881, and spent his first night in London at the Victoria Hotel (now called Northumberland House), Northumberland Avenue, WC2. He subsequently lived at numerous other addresses around London. At first he was not happy: 'Everything was strange, the people, their ways and even their dwellings . . . England I could not bear, but to return to India was not to be thought of. Now that I had come, I must finish the three years'.

He became a student of law at the Inner Temple, EC4, and set about trying to adapt to his new social circumstances by donning fashionable clothing and taking lessons in elocution, dancing and playing the violin. He soon tired of his lessons, though he continued to dress in a dandyish style. A friend at that time remembers how he once saw Gandhi 'wearing a high silk top hat, polished bright, a stiff starched collar, a flashy tie of all the colours of the rainbow under which was a fine-striped silk shirt . . . He had leather gloves and a silver topped cane and was at the very height of fashion for a young man about town'.

Gandhi's vegetarianism caused him considerable difficulties until he discovered The Central, a vegetarian restaurant in Saint Bride's Street, EC4 (the building has since been demolished), where he had his first hearty meal since his arrival. Through the restaurant Gandhi made contact with the London Vegetarian Society, of which he became an active member, and was eventually elected onto the executive committee.

Gandhi qualified as a barrister in 1891, and 'not without deep regret' left 'Dear London' for India. His stay in London had been an important formative experience. Through his commitment to vegetarianism Gandhi had come into contact with all manner of unconventional Victorians whose wide-ranging ethical, religious, political and social beliefs had made a considerable impact on him. For example, he first read the *Bhagavad-gita*, a Hindu scripture that was later to take a central place in his personal philosophy, when it was introduced to him in English translation by British friends in London. And of course Gandhi had gained a deeper understanding of the country that ruled his own, a knowledge that he was to utilise with uncommon skill when he later pitted himself against British rule in India.

Back in India, Gandhi met with little success in the legal profession, and in 1893 he went to South Africa, a British colony which was the adopted home of a large number of Indian settlers. Shocked at the humiliating treatment he received from South African whites, Gandhi was soon at the forefront of a powerful and imaginative campaign against racial injustice that made his name celebrated amongst Indians throughout the world.

It was in South Africa that Gandhi developed the tactics of *Satyagraha*, which is usually translated as 'passive resistance', though its literal meaning is closer to 'truth persuasion'. Gandhi believed that his campaign had to be moral in its methods if it was to be true to its moral aims, and therefore that any protest he led had to be non-violent, even when violence was used to suppress it. At the end of the day, he insisted, 'the strongest physical force bends before moral force when it is used in the defence of truth'.

Gandhi visited London in 1906 and 1909 to further his campaign for Indian rights in South Africa. On both his visits Gandhi observed the activities of the women's suffrage movement, and he met the suffragette leader Emmaline Pankhurst during his visit in 1909. Although Gandhi took inspiration from the suffragettes' peaceful protests, he condemned the militants who were prepared to use violence.

By 1909 Gandhi's views on the benefits of Western civilisation had changed radically since his own days as a student in London. He was now of the opinion 'that it is altogether undesirable for anyone to come and live here'. Nevertheless, immediately after leaving South Africa for good in 1914, he made one further visit to London, where he helped to raise volunteers for war service in an Indian Ambulance Corps before returning to India in 1915.

After the war Gandhi rapidly emerged as the pre-eminent Indian nationalist leader, directing the struggle against the British through demonstrations and boycotts organised in accordance with his ideas about non-violent resistance. Gandhi also spent a great deal of his time campaigning for social justice within Indian society, for he believed that India had to demonstrate that it was morally ready for independence. Through his identification and work with ordinary Indians, he was instrumental in transforming the Indian National Congress (usually known simply as Congress) from a middle-class party into a mass organisation, and became universally known amongst Indians by the title Mahatma ('great soul').

His last visit to London was in 1931 as the sole representative of Congress at the Round Table Conference on India's future. By now he was a world-famous figure, and conspicuously clad in traditional Indian clothes, was surrounded everywhere he went by reporters, photographers and crowds of onlookers. It was a busy three-month trip. He spoke at numerous public meetings, had talks with the Prime Minister, Ramsay MacDonald, at 10 Downing Street, had a much-publicised meeting with Charlie Chaplin, and sipped tea with King George V and Queen Mary at Buckingham Palace.

During his visit Gandhi stayed at Kingsley Hall, 21 Powis Road, E3 (marked by a plaque), a welfare centre for the East End poor. His hostess at Kingsley Hall, a social worker called Muriel Lester, gave this description of his visit to a nearby East End slum street:

'This street Mr Gandhi chose to explore early one morning in November. His movements always created excitement. A large crowd was very soon accompanying us as we crossed Bruce Road and made our way to Eagling Road [a short stretch of Eagling Road survives off Bruce Road, E3, but most of the old road is now covered by a housing estate]. In and out of the houses he went, on both sides of the street. The women were inordinately proud. They had no idea he was coming . . . but all were ready to display every corner of their little domain for him to inspect, to ask about and to admire . . . Upstairs they took him and out into their backyards. They showed him their pets, their rabbits and their chickens; occasionally there was a piano to be proud of . . . Mr Gandhi enjoyed that morning more than any other spent in London, and those whose homes he visited will hold it always memorable'.

From Gandhi's point of view the Round Table Conference itself achieved little. Nevertheless, his visit was a great success - with the British public. On the day on which he arrived back in India in December 1931 he stated: 'I am not conscious of a single experience throughout my three months' stay in England and Europe that made me feel that after all East is East and West is West. On the contrary, I have been convinced more than ever that human nature is much the same no matter under what clime it flourishes, and that if you approached people with trust and affection you would have ten-fold trust and thousand-fold affection returned to you'. Such sentiments were entirely lost on the British authorities in India, who arrested him shortly afterwards.

Gandhi and Congress had always campaigned for a united, independent India, but by 1946, when the British announced their intention to withdraw, the demand for a separate Islamic state was too strong to be ignored. In 1947 British India was partitioned into the independent states of India and Pakistan, an event attended by violence between the several religious communities that claimed hundreds of thousands of lives. It was anger at Gandhi's remarkable achievements in bringing about reconciliation in the aftermath of partition that led to his assassination by a Hindu extremist on 30 January 1948.

The following day, an article in the *Manchester Guardian* declared: 'A leader who shows perfect courage, perfect honesty and absolute freedom from envy, hatred, malice and all uncharitableness does not live in vain. To India, Mr Gandhi gave a new standard of courage and virtue in public life. To the West he is the man who revived and refreshed our sense of the meaning and value of religion'.

Gandhi has continued to be an inspiration to the West. His philosophy of peaceful protest influenced both the black American civil rights movement led by Martin Luther King and the Campaign for Nuclear Disarmament in Britain. The film *Gandhi* (GB/India 1982) introduced him to a new generation.

A statue of Gandhi in the centre of the park in Tavistock Square, WC1, was unveiled in 1968 by the Prime Minister, Harold Wilson. Sculpted by Fredda Brilliant, it is a worthy memorial. Gandhi, who looks weary, yet strong and composed, sits cross-legged over a hollow-fronted base which is designed to accommodate bunches of flowers. For those who are that way inclined, the park is an ideal place in which to meditate on Gandhi's philosophy of non-violence - perhaps whilst sitting under the very copper beech tree that was planted by Nehru (see *page 57* for details).

'Inside Out'

Interview with Indian tourist visiting Gandhi's statue in Tavistock Square . . .

"This is the first time we have visited London. We've just come from India, and we're just going around the shows in London, so we stopped here first. It's a great feeling when you come to a city like London and you find that there's a statue of the father of your own nation, the person who fought against British rule in India. You feel great about it, you really feel that his contribution has been recognised all over the world and especially in a country where he lived and he fought against that country's rule, so I am feeling very delighted.

Gandhi meant something to the entire world. He's still very relevant to the nations that are fighting, where there are turbulences. If people just try and follow what Gandhi said and did, I think that peace can be achieved through non-violent means.

We're proud of him. Really proud of what he did for our country. I mean, we all owe everything to him really."

Mohammed Ali Jinnah, the founding father of Pakistan, was born into a Muslim family in Karachi in 1876. After education at a Christian mission school in India, he came to London in 1892 to train as a barrister. Of his arrival in Britain, Jinnah said: 'I found a strange country and unfamiliar surroundings. I did not know a soul, and the fogs and winter in London upset me a great deal, but I soon settled down and was quite happy'.

Jinnah later said that he chose to study at Lincoln's Inn, WC2, because he had noticed while on an exploratory visit to the place that the prophet Mohammed was featured in a fresco in its Great Hall which depicts the 'great law-givers of the world'. During his stay in London Jinnah is known to have spent some time living at 35 Russell Road, W14 (marked by a plaque), to have studied at the British Library in the British Museum and to have made frequent visits to the Houses of Parliament, where he listened with great interest to debates on Irish Home Rule and heard the maiden speech of Britain's first Indian MP, Dadabhai Naoroji (see *page 57*).

By the time Jinnah returned to India as a qualified barrister in 1896, English had become his first language (he was noted for the reprimand: 'My dear fellow, you do not understand'), and he had adopted Western dress. In the 1920s the wife of a British officer wrote of Jinnah: 'He talks the most beautiful English. He models his manners and clothes on Du Maurier, the actor, and his English on Burke's speeches' . A Muslim League worker who was asked in the 1930s about his image of Jinnah replied: 'We had all heard stories of his Western clothes; that he was very English'.

Following a successful career as a lawyer in Bombay, Jinnah entered politics in 1906 as a member of Congress, the majority of whose members were Hindus. It was not until 1913 that he joined the Muslim League, which had been established in 1906 to safeguard Muslim interests. Even then, and as President of the League in 1916 and 1920, Jinnah worked to promote joint action between the League and Congress. However, in 1921 he finally cut his connections with Congress because he felt it did not give enough consideration to Muslim concerns.

Jinnah returned to London several times in the 1920s, both for holidays and on political business. He was back again in 1930 and 1931 to attend the Round Table Conferences on India's future. They were not happy experiences:

'I received the shock of my life at the meetings of the Round Table Conference. In the face of danger, the Hindu sentiment, the Hindu mind, the Hindu attitude, led me to the conclusion that there was no hope of unity. . .I began to feel that neither could I help India, nor change the Hindu mentality; nor could I make the Mussalmans [Muslims] realise that precarious position. I felt so disappointed and so depressed that I decided to settle down in London. Not that I did not love India, but I felt so utterly helpless'.

Jinnah bought a house (since demolished) in West Heath Road, NW3, in September 1931, and set up a law practice in chambers at Kings' Bench Walk, EC4, in the Inner Temple, EC4. He quickly settled into the routine of his new life, spending his leisure time socialising with other lawyers in their London clubs, and at weekends taking long walks across Hampstead Heath, NW3. He was roused out of his political slumber in July 1933 by a visit from Liaquat Ali Khan, a Muslim politician, who appealed to him to return to politics for the sake of India's Muslims.

Jinnah returned to India, where in 1934 he became the permanent president of the Muslim League and rapidly established himself as the undisputed leader of the movement for a separate Muslim state. Although Congress believed that Muslim interests would be safeguarded within a united India, Jinnah and the League were adamant that such an outcome would result in Hindu oppression of the Muslim minority.

On 3 December 1946, Jinnah arrived in London with Jawaharlal Nehru (see below) and other Indian politicians for talks with the British Government about the shape of Indian independence. After the talks broke down, Jinnah stayed on to speak to a Muslim League meeting on 14 December in Kingsway Hall, 70 Great Queen Street, WC2. In his address to the packed hall he said: 'Is Britain going to stand by with its bayonets and hand over authority to the Hindu majority? If that happens, you will have lost every cent of honour, integrity and fair play . . . There is no other way but to divide India. Give Muslims their homeland and give Hindus Hindustan'.

Congress eventually felt it had no choice but to agree to the partition of British India, and on 15 August 1947 the Muslim state of Pakistan was born. Jinnah was its Governor-General until his death from tuberculosis in Karachi on 11 September 1948.

Jawaharlal Nehru was second in importance only to Gandhi in India's struggle for independence. Born into a Hindu family in Allahabad in 1889, his father was a wealthy lawyer of liberal views. Nehru was brought up by British governesses and tutors, and in 1905 was sent to Britain for a public school education at Harrow School, High Street, Harrow.

His housemaster at Harrow later described him as 'a very nice boy, quiet and very refined. He was not demonstrative but one felt there was a great strength of character. I should doubt if he told many boys what his opinions were, or the masters with whom he had a good name, as he worked well and seldom (almost never) gave trouble'. Looking back, Nehru said: 'Always I had a feeling that I was not one of them'. He kept to himself, and in private followed Indian political developments with great interest.

After two years at Harrow Nehru went to Trinity College, Cambridge, where he took a degree in natural sciences and found life a great deal more enjoyable. After graduation he returned to London to study law at the Inner Temple, EC4, and to spend two rather wild years living the high life in London - gambling, drinking and going on spending sprees - before qualifying as a barrister in 1912 and then returning to India.

After seven years in England, Nehru admitted: 'I had imbibed most of the prejudices of Harrow and Cambridge and in my likes and dislikes I was perhaps more an Englishman than an Indian. I looked upon the world from an Englishman's stand-point. And so I returned to India as much prejudiced in favour of England and the English as it was possible for an Indian to be'.

Notwithstanding this pro-British prejudice, after the First World War Nehru threw himself into full-time politics as a member of Congress. In 1921 he was imprisoned by the British authorities for his political activities. It was the first of the nine terms and a total of nine years in jail.

By the mid-1930s Nehru was a close associate of Gandhi and widely seen as his natural successor. They were very different men. Nehru was an agnostic socialist who firmly believed in industrial progress, whereas Gandhi stressed the spiritual aspects of the struggle and rejected the idea of Western material advances. In combination Nehru and Gandhi managed to hold together a broad alliance of interests within Congress and thus to maintain it as the principal voice of Indian nationalism.

Nehru visited London several times in the 1920s and 1930s, and in 1946 he was back again for negotiations on the shape of Indian independence at which he opposed the plans put forward by Jinnah (see *page 55*) for the creation of an independent Muslim state. The London talks broke down without agreement, but Nehru eventually conceded to the partition of British India.

As Prime Minister of India from Independence in 1947 until his death in New Delhi in 1964, Nehru laid the foundations of the modern Indian state. During that period he made numerous visits to London, and on a visit in 1953 planted a copper beech tree (marked by a plaque) in Tavistock Square, WC1, to mark the allocation of a site there for a statue of Gandhi. The tree, now a healthy 30 feet high, stands next to the central path to the south of Gandhi's statue.

Three Indians were elected to the House of commons during British rule in India, all representing London constituencies. All three were Parsees, a small religious community in India of Persian descent, who are settled mainly in Bombay. They dominated trade during the development of Bombay and worked closely with the British as a favoured minority.

Dadabhai Naoroji came to Britain in 1855 as a partner in Cama and Company, the first Indian business firm to be established in Britain. Elected to Parliament as the Liberal candidate for Central Finsbury in 1892, he won the seat after a recount with a majority of five votes. In his maiden speech at the House of Commons he praised 'the love of justice and freedom in British instincts which has produced this extraordinary result', and asserted that 'Central Finsbury has earned the everlasting gratitude of the millions of India . . . Its name will never be forgotten by India'.

Naoroji was defeated in the 1895 general election but remained active in British politics. Following a general trend in Indian opinion, Naoroji's enthusiasm for British 'freedom and justice' waned considerably over the following years. 'All our sufferings of the past centuries demand before God and men reparation', was his message to India as President of Congress in 1906. Known as 'The Grand Old Man of India', and its first great statesman, he died in Bombay in 1917.

Sir Mancherjee Bhownagree qualified as a lawyer at Lincoln's Inn, WC2, in 1885. A wealthy man, he was elected to Parliament in 1895 and 1900 as the Conservative candidate for Bethnal Green North East, but lost his seat in 1906. He remained active in British politics, lobbying on behalf of the Indians in South Africa and liaising with Gandhi during his visits to London in 1906 and 1909. Bhownagree died in London in 1933. The Bhownagree Gallery at the Commonwealth Institute is named after him.

Shapurji Saklatvala came to Britain in 1905 to work in the London office of the Indian iron and steel company, Tata. In 1921 he joined the Communist Party of Great Britain, and in 1922, when it was still possible to hold joint membership of the Labour and Communist parties, he won Battersea North as a Labour candidate. He lost his seat in 1923, regained it as a Communist candidate in 1924, and lost it again in 1929.

Saklatvala was constantly in the news, and at various times was banned from entry into Belgium, the United States and India itself. He was the first person to be arrested in the general strike of 1926, following a speech in Hyde Park, W2, in which he appealed to soldiers not to fire on striking workers. Convicted of sedition, Saklatvala spent two months in prison at Wormwood Scrubs, Du Cane Road, W12. He died in London in 1936.

Many other Indians of note have lived in and visited London over the centuries. Here follows a brief selection:

Rammohan Roy (1772-1833) has been called 'The Father of Modern India'. A scholar, educationalist and religious reformer, he campaigned vigorously against the practice of suttee - the burning of widows alive on the funeral pyres of their husbands. Roy came to London in 1830 as the first ambassador to Britain of the Mogul Emperor, and lived at 49 Bedford Square, SW1 (marked by a plaque). He died in Bristol in 1833.

Maharajah Dhuleep Singh (1838-93), the son and heir of the Sikh ruler Ranjit Singh (1780-1839), had his dominions annexed by the British when he was 12 years old. Adopting Christianity, he came to Britain where he lived in great style on a British Government pension. Dhuleep married a German woman and Queen Victoria became the godmother of their first born son. To sustain his spendthrift lifestyle Dhuleep asked for an increase in his pension, and when this was not forthcoming, demanded the return of the Koh-i-noor diamond (see *page 60),* announced his return to Sikhism and travelled to Russia to appeal for help from the Tsar to restore him to his throne in the Punjab. The Tsar gave him little encouragement and Dhuleep was eventually obliged to meet Queen Victoria and beg her forgiveness. Part of his pension was restored and he died a wealthy man in France in 1893 shortly after a second marriage, which was to an English woman. The golden chair of state from the palace of Dhuleep's father is on display at the Victoria and Albert Museum.

Abdul Karim (1863-1909) was appointed as a servant to Queen Victoria in 1887 and quickly rose to a privileged position. He gave her lessons in Urdu, cooked her curried meals and worked as her private secretary on Indian affairs. The Queen, who described Karim in her diary as 'a perfect gentleman', commissioned his portrait in oils and left instructions that he be given a place of honour in her funeral procession. Karim served the Queen until her death in 1901, and then returned to India.

Prince Ranjitsinhji (1872-1933), later the Maharajah Jam Sahib of Nawanagar, was the first Indian to play cricket for the English national team. He played in 15 tests, and captained Sussex from 1899 to 1904. Under the nickname of 'Ranji', he was the first Indian in Britain to become a household name.

Rabindranath Tagore (1861-1941), philosopher, educationalist, composer and poet, was India's model 'Renaissance man'. His first stay in Britain was from 1878 to 1880, when he studied at the University of London which was then located at Burlington Gardens, Wl, in the building now occupied by the Museum of Mankind. He visited London again in 1912, when he stayed at 3 Villas on the Heath, Vale of Heath NW3 (marked by a plaque). On this visit he met the poets Ezra Pound and WB Yeats, who assisted him in the publication of his book of poetry *Gitanjali* (Song of Offerings) in English translation. This book earned Tagore the Nobel Prize for Literature of 1913, an award which brought him world renown. He subsequently travelled widely on lecture tours and made several more visits to Britain. He received a knighthood in 1915 but renounced it after the Amritsar Massacre of 1919, when hundreds of Indians were shot dead in India after a British officer ordered his soldiers to open fire on an unarmed crowd. The national anthems of India and of Bangladesh were both written by Tagore.

V K Krishna Menon (1896-1974) studied at the London School of Economics, Houghton Street, WC2, and then at the Middle Temple, EC4, where he qualified as a lawyer. He became a tireless campaigner in London for the cause of Indian independence, and a well-known figure at Speaker's Corner (which is situated at the north-east corner of Hyde Park, W2). Menon was a St Pancras Labour Party borough councillor from 1934 to 1957 and served the Indian Government as the first High Commissioner for India, as the Indian representative at the United Nations, and as Minister of Defence. He lived at 57 Camden Square, NW1 (marked by a plaque), from 1924 to 1947.

IMPERIAL INDIA ———————————————

'If civilisation is to become an article of trade between the two countries I am convinced that this country will gain by the import cargo.' – Thomas Munro, the Governor of Madras, in a statement made in 1813 to the House of Commons.

Between the early 17th C and Indian independence in 1947, hundreds of thousands of British soldiers, administrators, traders and their dependants lived in India. It was through these people that Indian culture was to make a remarkable impact on Britain long before there was any appreciable direct Indian immigration to these shores.

Clothes and Fabrics. Textiles were the most important imports from India during the first two centuries of trade with Britain. The largest shipments were of painted and resist-dyed cottons known as chintzes, which were much superior to European dyed fabrics. Some indication of the impact of Indian textiles on the British garment trade can be gauged by the words of Indian derivation that are still in use today, such as chintz, cashmere, calico, dungaree, mull and seersucker.

Indian fabric design has had a tremendous impact on Britain and the West. One of the chief means by which it was introduced to Britain was by way of the humble Indian shawl, which was first worn in Britain at the end of the 18th C and became very fashionable in the 19th C. The designs on the shawls were soon widely copied onto other fabrics; the classic Paisley pattern acquired its name from Paisley, in Scotland, at a time when shawls bearing that pattern were being manufactured there in large numbers. Indian influence is still apparent in British floral fabric designs.

The Nabobs. The word nabob is a corruption of the Hindu word nawab, the title of certain Indian officials who worked in the service of the Mogul Empire in India. These men were renowned for acquiring great wealth, giving rise to an English phrase, 'rich as a nabob'. In the 18th C this phrase was applied to those Britons who returned home after acquiring a large fortune in India. Notorious for their ostentatious show of wealth, the nabobs were a familiar figure of fun in contemporary satire; one element amongst them attracted much ridicule for their practice of parading up and down fashionable Jermyn Street, SWI, wearing fancy Indian-made coats and a tastelessly extravagant display of jewellery.

Robert Clive, the most famous nabob of all, was born in Shropshire in 1725. He went out to India to work for the East India Company as a lowly member of the civil service, but after joining the army rapidly made his name there as a soldier. In defiance of the company's policy, which looked for peaceful trade rather than territorial gains, Clive established control of Bengal at the Battle of Plassey in 1757 and in so doing laid the foundations of British rule in India. In 1766 Clive retired to Britain, where he lived at 45 Berkeley Square, W1 (marked by a plaque). In 1773 he was censured by an enquiry into his conduct in India, and the following year he shot and killed himself at his Mayfair home. A statue of Clive stands at the west end of King Charles Street, SW1 .

The Indian Army. Throughout British rule in India it was Indians themselves who made up the majority of the troops in the Indian Army, where they served under British officers and alongside a smaller number of British troops. The history of a shared military tradition that lasted from 1746 to 1947 is presented in the *National Army Museum,* Royal Hospital Road, SW3 (071-730 0717), alongside the history of the British Army. Open from 10am to 5.30pm Monday to Saturday, 2 to 5.30pm Sunday. Admission is free.

The museum's extensive displays on the Indian Army feature weaponry, uniforms, photographs, paintings and full-size tableaux such as a mess scene complete with regimental silver and models of officers. Amongst the many relics of the Indian Army Mutiny of 1857 is a shirt worn in the siege of Lucknow and a telegram which states: 'Yes go on and join the column in pursuit of the mutineers, 50Rs for every head and musket, 20Rs for every head alone'.

The involvement of the Indian Army in 20th C conflicts is not neglected. During the First World War over a million Indians served overseas, and in the Second World War almost three million Indians enlisted, creating the largest volunteer army the world has ever seen. The museum's coverage of the Indian Army stops at Independence, though for those Gurkha regiments who decided to continue serving under British command, the story continues.

The *Museum Bookshop* stocks a large selection of books on the Indian Army.

There is a *Memorial to the Indian Army* in the north aisle of St Paul's Cathedral, EC4. Unveiled in 1971, the memorial commemorates '201 years of faithful service given by British, Indian and Gurkha soldiers, who, as comrades, served in the Indian Army . . . In the two centuries of service here commemorated this was a volunteer army.'

Polo. Polo was introduced to Britain from India by the British military. Matches can be viewed every Sunday afternoon between May and September at the *Ham Polo Club* (081-940 2020), off Petersham Road, Richmond, Surrey.

The Koh-i-noor Diamond. The Koh-i-noor (Mountain of Light) diamond, which is now fitted in the Crown of Queen Elizabeth, was in Indian hands until the British annexed the Punjab in 1849. In addition to the abdication of the 12-year old Maharajah Dhuleep Singh (*see page 58*) the British demanded that the legendary diamond be given as a 'voluntary' gift to Queen Victoria. On its arrival in Britain the diamond was felt to be lacking in refinement and was reduced from 187 to 109 carats by Dutch master cutters, without, it is said, any apparent improvement. The Koh-i-noor diamond can be seen together with the rest of the Crown Jewels in the Jewel House at the Tower of London.

Tippoo's Tiger. *The Victoria and Albert Museum* features the prize curiosity 'Tippoo's Tiger', a large wooden model of a British East India Company officer being mauled by a tiger. Inside the tiger are a bellows and a miniature organ keyboard which can simulate the groans of a dying man - though unfortunately this is not demonstrated. 'Tippoo's Tiger' was found in the town of Seringapatam after it was stormed in 1799 by British troops in an action against Tippoo, the Sultan of Mysore, who was killed in the battle. Also on display are Tippoo's watch, brooch, telescope and sword.

Literature. India has been a constant source of inspiration to British writers, whether in the pulp adventure tales for young boys found in 19th C comics such as *Boys of the Empire,* in the comedy of Edward Lear's nonsense poem *The Akond of Swat* or in more serious literature such as E M Forster's *Passage to India.*

Rudyard Kipling is the most celebrated writer of British India. Born in Bombay to British parents in 1865, he attended school in Britain between the ages of five and 16 and then returned to India, where he became a journalist. In September 1889 he came back to Britain and took lodgings at 43 Villiers Street, WC2 (marked by a plaque), where he lived until 1891. He had enjoyed a limited success as a writer of fiction prior to his return to Britain, but it was while he was living at this address that he became famous.

Most of Kipling's best works were about India, and classic works such as *The Man Who Would Be King* (from *The Phantom Ricksaw,* 1888), *The Jungle Books* (1894-5) and *Kim* (1901), continue to attract a large readership today.

After living abroad for several years Kipling returned to Britain in 1896 and settled in Sussex. In 1907 he was awarded the Nobel Prize for Literature. He died in Middlesex Hospital, Mortimer Street, Wl, in 1936, and was buried in Westminster Abbey, SW1.

Annie Besant, Theosophy and Astrology. Born in London in 1847, *Annie Besant* was brought up in Harrow as a staunch Anglican. In 1873 she left her husband, the Vicar of Sibsey in Lincolnshire, and returned to live in London where she became nationally known as a social reformer, trade union organiser and militant atheist. In 1874 she lived at 39 Colby Road, SE19 (marked by a plaque). In 1889 she announced her conversion to Theosophy, a mystical movement marrying Eastern and Western philosophies which had been founded in the United States in 1875. In 1893 Besant settled in India, where the Theosophists had their headquarters, and where she believed that she had been born three times in previous incarnations. She was president of the Theosophical Society in India from 1907 until her death in Madras in 1933.

Besant played an influential role in the radicalisation of Indian politics between 1916 and 1920. A founder member of the Home Rule League, Besant was interned by the British authorities in 1917. She was President of Congress in 1918.

Theosophy was an important force in the popularisation of Indian religious thought in the West, and the interest that this helped to generate in Indian traditional culture produced a much greater awareness of the Indian approach to astrology. The European tradition of astrology had been badly shaken by the discovery of new planets, whereas for Indian astrology they had posed no problems. As Indian astrology became better known in the West, European astrologers drew heavily from it to revitalise their own practices. The outcome was a huge popular revival of astrology in the West. Today it seems hard to believe that the first astrological prediction in a British newspaper was printed only in 1930.

An Indian astrologer who is well respected both within and outside of the Asian community is Meera Gandhi (appointments on 081-951 3828). She is based in Stanmore, Middlesex, but also visits clients.

See also *Quest Bookshop, page 45.*

Food and Drink. The British experience in India brought several additions to British cuisine. These include kedgeree (a dish of rice, fish and eggs, which is different but not dissimilar to its Indian progenitor), chutney (brought back to Britain by the Prince of Wales's chef after the Prince's visit to India during 1875 and 1876), mulligatawny soup (which was adapted by Indian cooks from an Indian sauce when they were asked to provide soup for their British employers) and the drink punch (whose name is derived from the Marathi word for five, the original number of ingredients - sugar, limejuice, spices, water and a local spirit called arrack).

Words. Some of the following words were taken directly from Indian languages, whilst others evolved out of the British experience in India. Several of them were brought back to Britain as soldiers' slang, and a few, such as pepper, were being used in Britain long before any Briton had even set foot in India: bangle, Blighty (Britain), bungalow, candy, cashmere, choky (jail), chutney, cot, curry, cushy, dekko (look), dinghy, dungaree, ginger, gymkhana, jodhpurs, juggernaut, kedgeree, khaki, loot, nirvana, opal, pariah, pepper, polo, posh, punch (the drink), pundit, pyjamas, shampoo, shawl, sugar, swastika, yoga.

LITERATURE ——————————————————

East End at Your Feet by Farrukh Dhondy (1976). A collection of short stories about Asian teenagers in the East End of London. Deals with a wide variety of subjects and themes: school, parents, boyfriends/girlfriends, careers, politics, racial and cultural conflicts. *Recommended.

The Nowhere Man by Kamala Markandaya (1973). Srinivas, a Brahmin Hindu, leaves India in the 1920s to settle in London after his family's involvement in Nationalist politics has blighted his career prospects there. He sets up a spice importing business, but following the death of his wife soon afterwards, he feels lonely and adrift. His life perks up when he takes up with an Englishwoman of his own age, and she moves into his South London home, but their relationship develops against the backdrop of growing racial tensions in 1960s Britain. When Srinivas finds he has leprosy and is forced to evict his tenants, his English neighbours turn viciously upon him. *Recommended.

A Wicked Old Woman by Ravinder Randhawa (1987). Kulwant is a middle-aged woman who surveys the unhappy state of her life, and her family, in a string of personal encounters. The cost of moving from India to London, and having to live with two cultures, has been a high one, but life must go on . . .

The Buddha Of Suburbia by Hanif Kureishi (1990). As a football commentator might say, 'a book of two halves'. Part one is a very funny, and sometimes very rude, send-up of life in the South London suburbs in the 1970s. The hero, Karim Amir, is of mixed race parentage, and is bisexual. When his father, a lapsed Muslim, becomes a spiritual guru who is taken up by a trendy English crowd, Karim gets a chance to experience some of the excitement he craves. In part two Karim goes to live in Central London and becomes a successful actor, but the energy of the novel sags once the suburbs are left behind. *Half-recommended.

The Red Box by Farhana Sheikh (1991). Set in the mid 1980s, a middle-class Muslim woman is doing research in an East End school into questions of identity in adolescent girls of Pakistani extraction. Against a background of bitter racial conflict between white and Asian school pupils, the researcher gradually learns about the tensions, fears and realities of life for young Muslim girls growing up in London.

Transmission by Atima Srivastava (1992). Angellie is an Asian woman fresh out of University and discovering the moral dilemmas to be faced in her job as a researcher for a TV documentary about Aids. The story switches between her home-life with her Hindu parents in North London and life in the fast lane in the TV business. A strong storyline, in which Angellie falls for a man who is HIV-positive, plus a strong feel of life in modern London, together make this a very readable book. *Recommended.

Memories of Rain by Sunetra Gupta (1992). A Bengali woman looks back on her ten years of marriage to an Englishman, who brought her over from Calcutta to live in London. It's a sad tale, in which memories of Calcutta intermingle with the story of her husband's infidelity.

Polish Air Force Memorial, Middlesex.

POLISH LONDON

HISTORY

The Polish presence in Britain has been determined for the most part by the push of political events in Poland rather than the pull of economic opportunity in Britain. Unsuccessful rebellions against the rule of Russia, Prussia and Austria, who in 1795 had completely divided Poland amongst them, brought several waves of Polish exiles to Britain, where by 1870 they formed a community that numbered about 1500.

These political exiles were joined in the late 19th C and early 20th C by a steady trickle of labourers and artisans in search of a better standard of life. Large numbers of Jewish Poles also came to Britain in this latter period, but as they invariably integrated into the Jewish community they have not been discussed any further in the Polish section of this book. By the 1930s there were about 5000 Christian Poles in Britain, with a London community that was centred on the Polish Roman Catholic church in Devonia Road, N1.

Following the German invasion of Poland in September 1939, many Poles fled their country to continue the battle on other fronts. In 1940 about 33,000 military and civilian personnel of the Polish Armed Forces and the Polish Government-in-Exile arrived in Britain, where they set up a state within a state whose heart was in Mayfair, Belgravia and South Kensington.

The Poles were quickly into the fray. Polish pilots shot down one in seven of all German planes destroyed in the Battle of Britain of 1940, a vital contribution in such a closely fought battle. Polish forces subsequently fought on land, sea and air in many theatres of war, from Narvik to Tobruk, from Monte Cassino to Arnhem.

After the war and the Soviet occupation of Poland, the British Government pledged that any of the 250,000 Poles who fought under British command could settle with their families in Britain. Those who did were joined here by other Poles who had been displaced by the war, including survivors of the Warsaw Uprising against the Germans in 1944, and people who had been unwillingly conscripted into the German Labour Force. In all over 150,000 Poles settled in Britain.

The political and military background to their settlement gave the Polish community some unusual characteristics. There was a disproportionately large middle-class element, including numerous doctors, dentists, chemists, engineers, teachers, civil servants, military officers and landowners. Although many of these people were forced to take unskilled jobs due to language problems or because their qualifications were not recognised, it is notable how their children have invariably moved straight back up to the social scale into middle-class occupations. Many immigrant communities contain more men than women, but this was particularly marked amongst the Poles, and as a result a large number of Polish men have married British women.

The Polish community is respected by those who are familiar with it as being exceptionally well organised for its size. *Dziennik Polski*, a Polish-language newspaper, is published daily in Britain. The part-time Polish-language schools, the Polish Boy Scouts and Girl Guides Association, and the Polish sports clubs have all played important roles in keeping Polish culture and language alive in the second generation. The church has also been a focus of community life. The vast majority of Poles are Roman Catholics, and the suppression of Polish nationhood has given Polish Catholicism a strong nationalistic streak.

The Polish population in Britain was at its largest in the late 1940s and early 1950s. Many Poles have since re-emigrated to the United States, Canada, Argentina, Australia and France. There have been relatively few new arrivals from Poland to replace them; most Polish emigrants head for the USA. The census of 1991 recorded 21,823 Polish-born people living in London, and the Polish community can probably be numbered at about 50,000.

Rising post-war property prices after the war drove the Poles out of the West End of London. Many settled in Earls Court in the 1950s and early 1960s, when the Earls Court Road, W8, became known as 'The Polish corridor'. The Polish community has since dispersed further, down south to Balham and Croydon, north to Finchley and Willesden, and out west to Hammersmith and, in particular, Ealing.

The effect of the collapse of communism in Poland on Britain's Polish community is as yet uncertain. Many Polish organisations have had to re-examine their purpose now that they no longer have the focus of opposition to the Polish Government. The integration of the British-born generation into British society and the death of many of the older generation has brought about a strong sense of decline in the Polish community. However, the raising of the Iron Curtain means that Britain is now faced with a new trickle of economic migrants and the future shape of the Polish community will probably depend on them.

'Inside Out'

Interview with Olgierd Opat-Pietrykowski, the editor of The Polish Daily ('Dziennik Polski'), who came to Britain in 1946 ...

"People were very happy when the communists fell and we had an elected government in Poland in 1989. We had wished and hoped and prayed and worked for a free, independent Poland for 45 years and had enormous expectations.

Now, I can't say that people are very happy. The Polish community here is going through a very strange transformation. They realise that they have to stay put, and this is totally unexpected. Back in 1948, 1950, we thought the communist system would last no more than 5, 10, 15 years, and then we would go back, bringing the old values back with us. No-one thought it would last so long. Now people are too old to return, there is no work, and for those Eastern Poles whose old homes are now in Byelorussia and the Ukraine, there is nowhere to go back to anyway, and the Polish Government is doing nothing for them. The Polish Government think it all happened a long time ago and they want to forget about it.

Also, the importance of the Polish community in Britain is now much diminished, I really feel it. Until the fall of communism, London was the main Polish political centre. The Polish Government-in-Exile was here. There were many international conferences here. Now this is no more and many institutions have closed down. The Poles here had considerable influence against the communists. The Polish community have done a lot for Poland, but now the Government just ignores us.

I enjoy my work here on the paper. I started here two years ago. Before that I worked for the BBC World Service. The paper started in 1940, after the defeat of France and the Polish Army coming to Britain. It's still a daily paper and never a day has been missed. Of the old Polish community, the majority buy or read it, but of the generation born here, few read it. It's a problem. I don't think the paper can keep going indefinitely. Perhaps not many years.

Obituaries are an important section of the paper. It is there that people learn of other people's deaths and the details of their funeral so that they can attend. The old Poles realise they are fewer and fewer."

PLACES TO VISIT

The Sikorski Museum, 20 Princes Gate, SW7 (071-589 9249). Open from 2 to 4pm Monday to Friday, 10am to 5pm on the first Saturday of each month. Admission free.

The museum is named after General Sikorski, who was both Prime Minister of the Polish Government-in-exile and the Commander-in-Chief of the Polish Armed Forces from 1939 until his death in a plane crash in 1943. Most of the exhibits on display relate to Second World War Polish military history, but the museum also contains a room dedicated to the history of Polish royalty, and a large collection of paintings of famous Polish historical figures. The staff are helpful, which is just as well considering that there is no guidebook and that many of the exhibits are labelled only in Polish, if at all.

The Enigma machine is a prized exhibition. Prior to the Second World War the Germans invented a system of coding messages that could only be cracked by using a duplicate of their own coding machine. Polish cryptologists built the machine on display here to do exactly that, and it gave the Allies an important intelligence advantage over the Germans when it was brought to Britain shortly before the invasion of Poland.

Two shell casings record the first shots of the Second World War; these were warning shots fired by the Polish Navy at German ships approaching its coast just before the German invasion. Other curiosities on display include a piece of the plane in which Hitler's deputy Rudolf Hess flew to Scotland in 1941, and radios made by Polish prisoners in German camps that were used to broadcast weather reports to Britain so as to assist the Allied bombing campaign.

The Polish Social and Cultural Centre (POSK), 238-246 King Street, W6 (081-741 1940). Open from 8.45am to 11pm Monday to Friday, 10am to 12 midnight Saturday, 10am to 11pm Sunday.

POSK is managed by a Polish charity dedicated to the promotion of Polish culture through education and the arts. This huge purpose-built block, which was completed in 1982, is in itself an impressive monument to the determination of anti-communist exiles in London.

There is much here of interest to the general public. (See *page 71* for details of the *Lowiczanka Restaurant and Cafe,* and see *page 70* for details of the

The Enigma machine at the Sikorski Museum.

bookshop, *PMS Publications*.) The 300-seat auditorium hosts performances of Polish classical music, folk music, opera, dance and drama (sometimes in English), plus fortnightly screenings of Polish films (some English-subtitled). If you are interested in attending any of these events, contact POSK for their bilingual quarterly diary of events. POSK also houses a social club, youth club, the Joseph Conrad study centre, a library of 100,000 Polish books, and the **Pilsudski Institute Museum**, which is open from 3 to 7pm Tuesday and Thursday. Within are displayed memorabilia of Marshal Pilsudski, Prime Minister of Poland 1914-18, who died in 1938. Admission is free.

Polish Hearth Club, Exhibition Road, SW7 (071-589 4635). During the war, this was the Polish Air Force Club, and it was the principal Polish centre until POSK opened. There is a restaurant here (see *page 72*), and various events are held.

Polish Cultural Institute (PCI), 34 Portland Place, W1 (071-636 6032/3). Open from 10am to 4pm Monday to Friday. Admission free. The PCI, which is run by the Polish Embassy, holds about 20 exhibitions a year of work by Polish artists.

Centaur Gallery, 82 Highgate High Street, N6 (081-340 0087). Open from 10am to 6pm Monday to Saturday. Arts and antiques displayed in a cosy, artistically cluttered environment. Prices range from £1 to £10,000. Much of the stock is of Polish origin, the rest British and international. The gallery specialises in Polish folk art: sculpture, wooden toys, paper 'chandeliers', paper cuts and flowers made out of wood shavings. There are frequent exhibitions of painting and sculpture in the garden, by contemporary Polish artists; former pigsties at the back of the building have been gracefully transformed into the main exhibition area.

Drian Galleries, 7 Porchester Place, W2 (071-723 9473). Open from 11am to 4pm Monday to Friday. Art gallery. Occasional exhibitions by contemporary Polish artists. Permanent exhibition upstairs.

Polish Mission and Church, 2 Devonia Road, N1 (071-226 3439). Built in

1844, since 1930 this church has been the headquarters of the Polish Mission. The Polish Resistance convened here during the Second World War and their military leader, General Sikorski, is commemorated within by a monument; his regalia is also displayed.

St Andrew Bobola's Polish Catholic Church, 1 Leysfield Road, W12 (081-743 8848). This is one of several Polish Roman Catholic churches in London. The interior has been extensively remodelled in modern Polish style since the church was taken over by the Poles in 1962. Large stained glass windows dedicated to the exploits of the Polish Armed Forces demonstrate the importance of the Second World War in the minds of the Polish community. The church was given its present name in 1962 and it makes a clear statement to those who understand its significance. St Andrew Bobola was a Pole who was savagely murdered in 1657 by Russian Cossacks after refusing to renounce Catholicism. It was a natural choice of name during Soviet domination of Poland.

The Polish Air Force Memorial stands at the intersection of West End Road and Western Avenue in Northolt, Middlesex, on the edge of Northolt Airport, which was the main base of the Polish Air Force (PAF) in the early part of the Second World War. Unveiled in 1948, this is an impressive and dignified memorial. Behind an ornamental stretch of water an eagle stands poised on the top of a large stone obelisk. Engraved on the obelisk are the names of the four bomber squadrons and ten fighter squadrons of the PAF and the theatres of war in which they saw action. At the back of the memorial there is a curved stone wall inscribed with the names of all the 1241 members of PAF aircrews who died on operational flights. Above the wall is a biblical quotation: 'I have fought a good fight, I have finished my course, I have kept the faith'.

The Katyn Memorial and the *Grave of General Komorowski,* Gunnersbury Cemetery, Gunnersbury Avenue, W3. November, December, January: open from 9am to 4.30pm Monday to Sunday. February, March, October: open from 9am to 5.30pm Monday to Sunday. April to September: open from 9am to 7pm Monday to Friday, 9am to 6pm Sunday.

The brooding, black *Katyn Memorial* stands at the end of the cemetery's central avenue. On the base of the 20-foot high obelisk is the inscription: 'In remembrance of the 14,500 Polish prisoners of war who disappeared in 1940 from camps at Kozielsk, Starobielsk and Ostaszkow of whom 4500 were later identified in mass-graves at Katyn near Smolensk'. This may not mean much to the average Briton, but it speaks volumes to Poles.

The events the memorial records have their origins in the non-aggression pact signed by Germany and the Soviet Union in August 1939. This included a secret clause that divided Polish territory into German and Soviet spheres of influence. One week later, the Germans invaded western Poland, and several weeks after that the Soviets took control of eastern Poland, an area in which Christian Poles were in a minority to Jews, Ukranians and Byelorussians. Fearful of an uprising behind their extended frontier, the Soviets deported millions of their newly acquired subjects to camps within the Soviet Union.

In 1941 the Germans attacked the Soviet Union, and in 1943 their occupation forces at Katyn announced the discovery of the bodies of 4500 Polish military officers in a mass burial ground. These were deportees, the Germans asserted, who had been murdered by the Soviets. Until 1990, the Soviets denied responsibility for the deaths, claiming that it was all a

German plot designed to damage relations between the Allies. When this memorial was first erected, the Poles remained convinced that the Soviets were responsible, but concrete evidence was lacking. That is why the original inscription reads: 'Sumienie Swiata Wola O Swiadectwo Prawdzie' ('The world's conscience asks for a verification of the truth'). Following the Russian admission of guilt, a plaque has recently been added, which reads, in Polish, 'Murdered by the Soviet Secret Police on Stalin's orders 1940. As finally admitted in April 1990, by the USSR, after 50 years'.

The Katyn Memorial has a particular significance for many of the Poles who settled in Britain. Following the German invasion of the Soviet Union, the Soviets allowed General Wladyslaw Anders to raise an army from the Poles held in Soviet camps. The 100,000-strong army so formed fought for the Allies in Italy between 1943 and 1945. At the end of the war a large number of these Poles decided to stay in exile, not only because of their experiences at the hands of the Soviets but also because most of the area in which they had lived had been incorporated into the Soviet Union. Many of them came to live in Britain, where they made up the largest single group amongst Polish immigrants.

The *grave of General Komorowski* is situated about 50 yards from the Katyn Memorial on the border of the cemetery's main southern pathway. Komorowski commanded the Polish Home Army in the Warsaw Uprising of 1944, which is yet another contentious event in the history of Polish-Soviet relations. The uprising began as the Germans were retreating in disorder through Warsaw before the advancing Red Army, but after the Soviet front line came to a halt on the outskirts of the city, the Germans struck back at the insurgents. The Poles held out against the Germans for two months before surrendering, leaving a devastated city and over 200,000 dead.

The Poles accused the Soviets of deliberately holding back their forces so as to allow the defeat of the uprising because such an outcome suited the Soviets' long term plans for the domination of Poland. The Soviets retorted that the rebellion had not been co-ordinated with them in advance and that when it broke out their whole warfront across Europe was coming to a halt because of overstretched lines of communication after an advance of 450 miles in five weeks. Be that as it may, the Soviets were clearly not interested in assisting the rebels and indeed stopped supplies getting through to them in the critical early phase of the uprising by refusing to allow British and American supply planes the use of Soviet airfields.

General Komorowski was captured by the Germans and sent to a prison camp. After being released by Allied forces he came to live in Britain, knowing that he risked imprisonment and perhaps death if he returned to Poland. Sixteen other underground leaders who came out of hiding after the Soviets overran Poland were arrested and put on trial in Moscow, and most were never seen again. Komorowski lived in London until his death in 1966.

SHOPPING

PMS Bookshop, POSK, 238-246 King Street, W6 (081-748 5522). Open from 10am to 6pm Tuesday to Friday, 12 noon to 6pm Saturday. Book shop on the ground floor of the POSK building (see *page 67*). Books from and about Poland, mostly in Polish, a few in English. Also handicrafts, guidebooks and music cassettes.

Orbis, 66 Kenway Road, SW5 (071-370 2210). Open from Monday to Friday 9.30am to 5.30pm, 10am to 4.30pm Saturday. Polish and English-language books from and about Poland alongside literature on other Eastern European countries. Also stocks Polish classical, folk and pop music cassettes, and a small selection of Polish gifts.

Veritas Foundation Bookshop, 63 Jeddo Road, W12 (081-749 4957). Open from 8am to 6pm Monday to Friday. Polish-language books, mostly of Roman Catholic interest.

FOOD AND DRINK

RESTAURANTS

Restaurants listed in this section mix Polish specialities with other dishes from central and eastern Europe. Look out for the following Polish dishes:

Bigos. Sauerkraut and mixed meat stew. The Polish National dish.

Golabki. Cabbage leaves stuffed with savoury fillings.

Pierogi. Dumplings stuffed with savoury fillings.

Kielbasa. Ground beef and pork sausage flavoured with garlic.

Sledz w smietanie. Herring in cream.

Flaki. Tripe.

Barszcz (Polish for borsch). Beetroot soup.

Grzyby lesne. Wild mushrooms.

Nalesniki. Savoury pancakes.

Kotlet mielony. Spicy pork cutlets.

With your meal make sure to try some Polish vodka, which is highly regarded by connoisseurs. Zubrowska vodka is the luxury liquor of Eastern Europe, and Polish plain spirit, at 98 percent proof, is the strongest vodka in the world. Polish vodkas are produced not only in the familiar clear form but also coloured red, yellow and green.

Lowiczanka Restaurant, 238-246 King Street, W6 (081-741 3225). Open daily from 12 noon to 3pm and from 6pm. Closes Sunday and Monday 11pm, Tuesday to Thursday 11pm, Friday 11.30pm and Saturday 12 midnight. An elegant restaurant on the first floor of the POSK building (see *page 67).* Large menu and a good range of Polish specialities. Moderately-priced.

Lowiczanka Cafe, address as above but on the ground floor. Open from 9am to 10pm Monday to Sunday. Serves cakes, teas and some hot meals - bigos, tripe, pierogi. Cheap.

Daquise Restaurant/Cafe, 20 Thurloe Street, SW7 (071-589 6117). Open from 10am to 11.30pm Monday to Sunday. Meals served from 12 noon to 12 midnight. Cosy and homely, equally pleasant for daytime snacks and evening meals. There is a greater emphasis here on Russian food than at the Lowiczanka Restaurant. Cheap.

Wódka, 12 St. Alban's Grove, W8 (071-937 6513). Open from 12.15pm to 2.30pm, 7pm to 11pm Monday to Saturday (no lunch Saturday). Less 'ethnic' in atmosphere than most other Polish restaurants. As may be expected, there is a wide range of Polish vodkas.

Café la Yolla, 114 Pitshanger Lane, W5 (081-991 9814). Open from 10am to 5pm, 7pm to 10pm Monday to Saturday, 10am to 4pm Sunday. Polish and East European food.

Polka Continental Restaurant, 20A Lower Addiscombe Road, East Croydon, Surrey (081-686 2633). Open 6pm to 11pm Monday to Sunday.

Navigator Restaurant, Klub Lotników, 14 Collingham Gardens, SW5 (071-370 1229). Open from 12 noon to 3pm, 6pm to 11pm Tuesday to Sunday. Reasonably priced Polish food. Most diners are club members but others are welcome.

Ognisko Polskie, Polish Hearth Club, 55 Princes Gate (071-589 4635). Open from 12.30pm to 3pm, 6pm to 10pm Monday to Sunday. Reasonably priced Polish food. Many diners are club members but others are welcome.

Adam and Agusia, 258 King Street, W6 (081-741 8268). Open from 8am to 10pm Monday to Friday, 10am to 10pm Saturday, 11am to 8pm Sunday. Informal café with good cheap food and lively atmosphere.

'Inside Out'

Interview with Agusia, a teenager whose parents run the 'Adam and Agusia' Polish delicatessen/café in Ealing . . .

"I just feel Polish, even though I was born here. I was brought up with Polish people, speaking Polish, eating Polish food. I only learnt English when I was 4 or 5 and went to school, so it was my second language.

I went to Polish school on Saturdays from the age of five, and Polish girl scouts till I was about eight. All my friends at the moment are Polish. I met them at the Polish school and now we're all at college together. Living in Ealing, that happens because Ealing's really Polish. My parents are friends with their parents, we all know each other. If someone asks me where I come from, I'll say I was born here, but I'm Polish 100%. I don't feel English.

My father was a builder before he opened this place a couple of years ago. What we serve here is what Polish people eat at home. There aren't any specialities. In the daytime the customers are 50/50 Polish and English but it's Polish mainly in the evenings.

I come in and help in the café on Saturdays and half-term, but mainly I'm studying for my A-levels. As for my future, I don't know, but being bilingual has given me an interest in languages. I want to go to France and study French and take it from there."

SHOPPING

If Londoners wanted something different from British food in the 1950s and 1960s, then they went to an Italian or a Polish delicatessen. The number of Polish delicatessens in London has declined sharply since then; the Polish-born population is now much smaller, and today many shops and supermarkets in London stock a wide range of Continental goods.

In the delicatessens that remain, make sure to check out the breads, patisseries, vodkas and the sausage and cured meat counters, which are always well stocked. Most shops now mix Polish goods with other continental fare, so you have to be discriminating if you're looking for something specifically Polish.

Prima Delicatessen, 192 North End Road, W14 (071-385 2070). Open from 9am to 6.30pm Monday to Saturday.

Acorn Delicatessen, 2 Horn Lane, W3 (081-922 2055). Open from 9am to 6pm Monday to Saturday (closes Wednesday at 1pm, Saturday at 5pm). Polish and German foods.

Adam and Agusia Delicatessen, 258 King Street, W6 (081-741 8268). Open from 8am to 10pm Monday to Friday, 10am to 10pm Saturday, 11am to 8pm Sunday.

Croydon Delicatessen, 11 Surrey Street, Croydon, Surrey (081-688 5421). Open from 8.30am to 5.30pm Monday to Friday, 7.30am to 6.30pm Saturday.

Encafood, 2 Salisbury Pavement, Dawes Road, SW6 (071-385 5762). Open from 7am to 6pm Monday to Friday, 9am to 6pm Saturday.

Eagle Delicatessen, 24 The Avenue, W13 (081-566 8669). Open from 9am to 6pm Monday to Saturday.

Kristine Patisserie, 11 Tamworth Street, SW6 (071-385 3244). Open from 9.30am to 5.30pm Tuesday to Saturday. Polish patisserie and delicatessen.

PEOPLE

The author *Joseph Conrad* was born Jozef Teodor Konrad Korzeniowski in 1857 in the Polish Ukraine, which was then under Russian rule. His father, a literary figure from the Polish landowning nobility, was arrested in the ferment leading up to the unsuccessful Polish rebellion of 1863 and sentenced to exile in Northern Russia. As the son of a political convict, Joseph's future in Poland looked bleak, and in 1874 he emigrated to France, where he took up work as a seaman. In 1878 he moved to London, which was his base for the next 15 years as he sailed around the world. It was in London that he studied for his Board of Trade certificates and eventually qualified as a Master Seaman. He lived at many addresses in the capital, of which only 17 Gillingham Street, SW7, is marked by a plaque.

Conrad gave up his seafaring career in 1893 to concentrate on writing. His first novel, *Almayer's Folly,* was published in 1895. Further work such as *Youth* (1898), *Lord Jim* (1900), *Heart of Darkness* (1902) and *Nostromo* (1904), established Conrad as one of the greatest writers in the English language. In 1896, shortly after his proposal to an English woman, Jessie George, in the National Gallery, Trafalgar Square, the two were married at a registry office in Hanover Square, W1. They settled down together in Kent, where Conrad died in 1924.

Conrad is remembered today for the stories of seafaring and adventure around the globe that form the bulk of his literary output. He wrote comparatively little about life in Britain. Perhaps his best British-based work is the novel *The Secret Agent* (1907), which is set in London. This book concerns an attempt by anarchists to blow up the Greenwich Observatory, a storyline inspired by an actual attempt in 1894. In his introduction to *The Secret Agent* Conrad referred to the loneliness of his early days in London: 'I had to fight to keep at arm's length the memories of my solitary and nocturnal walks . . . lest they should rush in and overwhelm every page'.

In *Heart of Darkness* (which is set mainly in Africa), Conrad's description of the river Thames reveals the depth of his feelings for Britain and its seafaring history:

'The air was dark above Gravesend, and farther back still seemed condensed into a mournful gloom, brooding motionless over the biggest, and the greatest, town on earth . . . The old river in its broad reach unruffled at the decline of day, after ages of good service done to the race that peopled its banks, spread out in the tranquil dignity of a waterway leading to the uttermost ends of the earth. We looked at the venerable stream not in the vivid flush of a short day that comes and departs for ever, but in the august light of abiding memories. And indeed nothing is easier for a man who has, as the phrase goes, "followed the sea" with reverence and affection, than to evoke the great spirit of the past upon the lower reaches of the Thames. The tidal current runs to and fro in its unceasing service, crowded with memories of men and ships it had borne to the rest of home or to the battles of the sea. It has known and served all the men of whom the nation is proud . . . the adventure and the settlers . . . hunters for gold or pursuers of fame, they had all gone out on that stream, bearing the sword, and often the torch, messengers of the might within the land, bearers of the spark from the sacred fire. What greatness had not floated on the ebb of that river into the mystery of an unknown earth ... The dreams of men, the seed of commonwealths, the germs of empires.'

Conrad worked hard to adjust and fit in socially with the British way of life, but in his writing he allowed himself more latitude. In 1914 he told a Polish interviewer: 'The English critics – and indeed I am an English writer – when speaking of me always add that there is in my work something incomprehensible, unfathomable, elusive. Only you can grasp this elusiveness, understand the incomprehensible. It is Polishness'.

In his fictional work Conrad wrote only in English and nothing about life in Poland. This angered a few of his countrymen, who denounced him for having abandoned country, culture, language and, indeed, his own name. Conrad responded: 'I have no way disavowed my nationality or . . . name . . . for the sake of success. It is widely known that I am a Pole and that Jozef Konrad are my two Christian names, the latter being used by me as a surname so that foreign mouths do not distort my real surname. It does not seem to me that I have been unfaithful to my country by having proved to the English that a gentleman from the Ukraine can be as good a sailor as they, and has something to tell them in their own language'. Most Poles agreed.

Conrad's feelings about Poland had ready echoes amongst Poles in Britain during their anti-communist exile. For Conrad Poland was 'that country which demands to be loved as no other country had ever been loved, with the mournful affection one bears to the unforgotten dead and with the unextinguishable fire of a hopeless passion'. Conrad despaired of his homeland ever gaining its independence: 'I cannot think about Poland too frequently – it's painful, bitter, heart-breaking. I could not live if I did'.

Conrad's gloom about Poland's future left him at the outbreak of the First World War. At last there was hope of change, and Poland did indeed establish its independence at the end of the war. Conrad's last visit to London before his death was to attend a luncheon in his honour at the Polish Legation. A similar pleasure has been experienced in the last few years as Polish exiles have at last been able to return to Poland, and many war heroes have for the first time received the honour they were due.

Frederic Chopin, the pianist and composer, was born near Warsaw in 1810. He left his homeland when he was about 20 and lived in Paris for most of the rest of his life. After the disappointment of a broken marriage engagement, Chopin made a brief visit to London in 1837 with the intention of relaxing and enjoying himself. He wrote of the visit: 'One can have a moderately good time in London if one doesn't stay too long. There are extraordinary things: Imposing toilets too narrow to turn round in. And the English! And the horses! And the palaces! And the pomp, and the carriages! Everything, from the soap to the razors, is extraordinary'.

In 1848, although he was suffering badly from tuberculosis, Chopin went on a concert tour of Britain. This visit is commemorated by plaques at 99 Eaton Place, SW1, where he gave his first London concert, and at 4 St James's Place, SW1, which marks the house from which he left to give his last ever public performance – a concert at the Guildhall, Guildhall Yard, EC2. Fittingly, this latter concert was in aid of Polish exiles from the rebellion of 1848. Chopin died in Paris in 1849.

Adam Kossowski (1905-1986). A sculptor and artist who was educated at the Kraków and Warsaw academies of art. During the war he was held prisoner in a Russian labour camp from 1939 to 1942, and after the war, he settled in Britain. Here he became well-known for his religious art, working mainly in churches and other religious buildings all over Britain. However, his major work in London is the huge Old Kent Road mural on the outside of the North Peckham Civic Centre and library. In this he recreated the history of the old Kent road in a mural 24 metres long and made up of 2,000 panels.

LITERATURE

Future to Let by Jerzy Peterkiewicz (1958). A hapless Englishman inherits a house in Earls Court which comes complete with a vivacious Polish tenant. Through her he is drawn into the world of Polish émigré politics – a baffling web of intrigue featuring Communist plots, defectors and endless disputes between competing Polish factions. A light comedy with some serious overtones.

Italian Procession, Clerkenwell.

ITALIAN LONDON

HISTORY

Roman rule in Britain began in AD 43 when Aulus Plautius landed in Kent at the head of a Roman army. In the course of their initial campaign to subdue the British, the Romans built a bridge across the Thames in the area in which London Bridge stands today. A settlement soon grew up alongside it on the north bank of the river in the area now occupied by Lombard Street and Gracechurch Street, EC3. Londinium, as the Romans called it, grew rapidly into the largest city in Roman Britain, of which it was probably the capital by the end of the 1st C AD.

Yet few Italians ever lived in Roman London. Most of the soldiers in the invading army were Romanised Gauls, and although soldiers and administrators were subsequently sent to Britain from many places across the Roman Empire, they seldom came from Italy itself.

Roman Britain disintegrated in the 5th C under the pressure of raiding Picts, Scots and Saxons, and in the process Christianity was swept aside from much of the country. In AD 597 Pope Gregory sent the Italian St Augustine and 40 other monks as missionaries to England, where they played an important part in the re-establishment of Christianity. They converted the Saxon King Ethelbert of Kent, and founded a cathedral at Canterbury, where Augustine became the first Archbishop.

The next major phase of Italian involvement in British affairs was between the 13th C and the 16th C, when Italian bankers and merchants played a prominent role in finance and commerce in London. They lived and worked in Lombard Street, EC3, which is so named because many of the early Italian bankers came from Lombardy.

It was the Italian bankers who gave us the word bankrupt, derived from the Italian 'banca rotta' (broken bench), which itself refers to the Italian tradition of breaking the working benches of insolvent bankers. The Italians also gave us the pawnbroking symbol of the three golden balls, which is derived from the coat of arms of the Medici family, one of the richest of the Italian merchant bankers.

The economic and religious importance of the Italians in Britain declined in the 16th C with Britain's growth as an economic power and Henry VIII's break with the Roman Catholic Church. However, the cultural and scientific developments of the Italian Renaissance had already forged a new kind of link with Britain. Italy had the culture, Britain had the patrons, and from the late I5th C through to the 19th C, Britain attracted a steady stream of Italian scholars, artists, architects, scientists and craftsmen, alongside others such as opera singers, dancing teachers, riding instructors and fencing masters.

Nevertheless, the roots of the Italian community in Britain lie not in this immigrant elite, but in the street vendors, entertainers and other itinerants who first appeared in Britain in the 17th C and 18th C. They were joined in the mid-19th C by many Italian political exiles, and by 1860 the Italian community in Britain was some 5000 strong.

In the late 19th C a surge of immigration from Italy led to the development of the Italian Quarter in Clerkenwell and Holborn. These immigrants were attracted to Britain principally by employment opportunities in the catering trade, though many also worked as street entertainers, street vendors (typically selling ice-cream, chestnuts or plaster statuettes), and as craftsmen or labourers laying mosaics, terrazzo, parquet and asphalt. By 1900 there were about 20,000 Italians living in Britain, of whom about half lived in London.

The rate of immigration declined in the 20th C and virtually ceased after 1927 due to the restrictions on emigration imposed by the fascist Italian Government, which followed a policy of allowing out only those people whom they believed would bring prestige to Italy. The Italian Government was particularly eager to impress the powerful British Government, and assiduously cultivated the Italian community in Britain as their 'ambassadors abroad'. The Italian Embassy gave financial support to an Italian school in Hyde Park Gate, SW7, invited Italians to lavish receptions and gave Christmas presents and free holidays to Italian children.

Such activities led to difficulties for many in the Italian community after Mussolini declared war on Britain on 10 June 1940. The British Government ordered the internment of all adult Italian-born males (including those who had become British nationals), together with those of Italian origin who were judged to be sympathetic to fascism. Many British-Italians had welcomed the support given to their community by the Italian Government without being sympathetic to fascism as such, but this was a distinction which was often difficult for the British authorities to make. A number of prominent figures in the community were unjustly labelled fascists because of their contacts with the Italian Embassy and the organisations which it supported. The policy of the British Government towards women was much more lenient, and only those who were demonstrably committed fascists were interned.

Peppino Leoni, the founder of the Quo Vadis Restaurant *(see page 97)*, recorded his feelings on being interned in his autobiography *I Shall Die on the Carpet* (1966):

'As I walked down the corridor towards the cells I felt a sudden hatred for the police, for the British Government which had issued the instructions for my internment, and for all forms of authority. I had slaved for years, in fact 33 years, because I first came to England in 1907, to establish my restaurant, and a man of my own nationality had destroyed everything in an instant . . . I deeply resented the fact that after 33 years in England with no political or police blemish on my record, I'd be scooped up without proper consideration.'

Most of the Italian internees were taken to camps on the Isle of Man, where they lived in blocks of boarding houses surrounded by barbed wire, while the rest were shipped to camps in Canada and Australia. Disaster struck on 2 July 1940 when the liner *Arandora Star*, which was carrying 1500 Italian and German internees to Canada, was sunk by a German submarine off the west coast of Ireland. Of the 712 Italians on board, 470 were killed, many of them Londoners. The tragedy was compounded by the confusion surrounding internment, for it took months for information to get back to relatives about who had actually been on the ship, who had died, and who had been rescued and reinterned.

Many Italian internees were released soon after the Italian armistice with the Allies was announced in September 1943, although a few were not finally to gain their freedom until 1946. During internment their property had been looked after by relatives or the Custodian of Enemy Property, and life soon resumed in as normal a fashion as was possible in the circumstances. Despite some public hostility, particularly from British people whose relatives or friends had been killed in the North African and Italian campaigns, few British-Italians went back to Italy. Indeed, some of the Italians brought to Britain as prisoners of war from the North African campaign settled down here after the war.

Post-war Italian immigration, which peaked in the mid-1950s and early 1960s, increased the Italian population of Britain manyfold. The service trades, particularly catering, were the main sources of employment. The rate of immigration declined in the 1960s, and by the 1970s more Italians were returning to Italy than were arriving from it. Britain's entry into the EEC in 1973 left the door open for further immigration, but Italy has much improved its standard of living relative to Britain over the last few decades, and as a result the rate of immigration has remained low. The census of

Italian barrel-organist entertaining in Victorian London, by Gustave Doré (London, 1872).

1991 recorded 30,052 Italian-born people living in London, and the Italian community in London can probably be numbered at around 75,000. There has been a significant increase in young Italians coming to London over the past few years, but they have few connections with the old established Italian community in London, and it remains to be seen whether they will settle.

'Inside Out'

Interview with Giuseppe Giacon, now retired, who founded the system of part-time Italian language classes in London for the Italian community . . .

"I arrived here in 1947 and I started work with my father-in-law in an Italian continental store. But my children, they went to University, two are solicitors, one is in business, one a teacher and so on. When all my children were in their positions, I sold out the grocery business.

Life behind the counter is very hard. I remember waking up at 5 o'clock in the morning to go to Smithfield, doing all the buying and coming back to the shop and working till late - 8, 9, 10. I did it because I had a large family, nine children, but if my children can provide for their children without slogging the same way that I did - I'm quite happy about that.

When I came over to England, I noticed that these Italian children going to English schools were forgetting their Italian. So I started Italian classes for the children of Italian immigrants, during the evening or Saturday morning to give them the opportunity of learning Italian as a language to speak or write.

I feel that it was very important work, because if you bring your culture into society, you bring something that can enrich that society. And if you speak the language of your own country, your identity will always be there and you'll be integrated with your own society as well.

The classes are still going strong, and I feel very proud of that. Because people who went to those classes, they say, 'Ah, Mr Giacon, how are you? The Italian classes still going on?', and I say 'yes'.

We have a big family and I love it. Family traditions are very important to me. I think family is the place where society is formed. So if the family goes well, the province, the state, the world goes well. I think the family is something that should be kept - to have parents make that sacrifice for their children, not only for their material benefit, but for their moral benefit."

Interview with Giovanna, Giuseppe Giacon's daughter . . .

"I was brought up in London with Italian food, the Italian language and the whole Italian manner of being together, sharing each other's company. My blood's Italian, but I suppose I'm an Anglo-Italian. I'm neither Italian nor English. My father says 'You're neither fish nor meat'. You're neither, and you're both. I think it's a very positive thing. I've personally never had any problems because I know I'm both and I actually think that's a benefit, rather than a disadvantage. Because you can pick the best of both worlds, hopefully. You can pick the English theatre but Italian opera. You can have English punctuality but Italian flair and style. Also I think more importantly you can always see things from two perspectives. There's always at least two ways of seeing something and that makes you more tolerant of other people and other cultures.

I think the sense of family is the biggest difference between what I consider typical English and typical Italian - and to me it's everything. I mean they're not just family, they're my friends as well. I know that sounds a bit daft, but I spend a lot of time with them and I enjoy their company a lot. We speak English at home but we'll still use certain words in Italian that can't be translated. Like saying someone is 'sympatico'. It's not the same as sympathetic, it's very difficult to explain.

We take our food very seriously. Italians are very fussy. It's all got to be done just right. Food is a big thing in our lives, and family too. The two go together when you eat together.

The Italians of London are the Italians of Italy say 40, 80 years ago, not of Italy today, because we almost stopped in time. And Italy went one way and we went another. A lot of people go back to Italy to retire and there's a great many of them who have difficulties and have to come back because it's not the Italy they left. And so we are different. That's why we're not English and we're not Italian."

THE ITALIAN QUARTER, CLERKENWELL AND HOLBORN ———

Italians first began to settle in Clerkenwell and Holborn in the 1840s, and by the 1890s a distinct Italian Quarter had developed in the triangle bounded by Rosebery Avenue, Farringdon Road and Clerkenwell Road. The core of the settlement was in Back Hill, Eyre Street Hill and Summers Street, in the vicinity of the Italian Church of St Peter's. This area was known to Italian residents as 'The Hill', and to outsiders as 'Little Italy'.

The Italians formed a tightly-knit community that was unembarrassed about displaying its origins. A reporter in the *Daily News* in 1901 observed that the 'vistas of pitiful squalor' which were typical of the district were in the Italian Quarter 'redeemed by the bright clothes of the poor inhabitants. Coloured kerchiefs adorned the heads of all the women, and . . . some of the swarthy, black-moustached men wore bright yellow neckties. Babies sprawling in the pavement were remarkable for earrings and brilliant frocks'.

When the weather was fine, life in the Italian Quarter readily spilled out onto the streets. Tradesmen worked on benches set up on the pavement. Other men sat and smoked their curved reed pipes, played cards or gambled with dice (keeping one eye open for the police). Women sat on chairs in the shade knitting, or washed, ironed and cooked in the Quarter's numerous alleyways and courts, which were regarded by the Italians as their private territory.

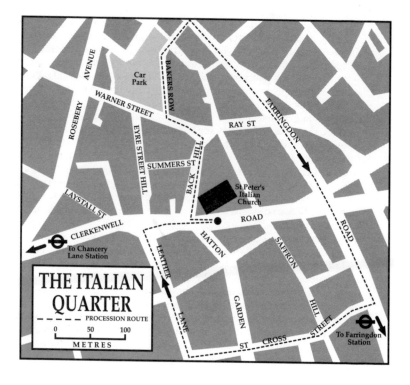

Fine weather or not, the streets of the Italian Quarter were always busy on working mornings as the street vendors prepared their barrows for the day ahead. This was the centre of London's ice-cream trade, and in the morning the ice-cream vendors would sing Italian folk songs as they churned their homemade ice-cream before loading it up onto their brightly-painted barrows. Also to be seen issuing forth from the Quarter each morning were barrel organists with their monkeys and birds, groups of women singers and dancers wearing Italian costume, and the many other colourful and exotic acts that earned their living entertaining on the streets of London.

Living in the Italian Quarter may have had its compensations in a rich community spirit, but it was still a slum, and residents invariably moved out to better areas if they got the chance. The Italian population of the Quarter was at its height between 1900 and 1930, and went into a steep decline thereafter as slum clearance reduced the amount of accommodation available and the Italian Government's restrictions of emigration prevented new blood coming in to replace those who were moving on. The dispersal of the Italian population through internment finally sealed the fate of the Quarter as an Italian residential district.

Today it is hard to recapture the spirit of the old Quarter on a visit to the area. Few Italians now live here, and most of the old houses, courts and alleyways have been demolished and replaced by drab industrial buildings. Yet Clerkenwell remains the focal point of London's Italian community, mainly because of St Peter's. The church is still the customary location for weddings and funerals of London Italians, and Sunday morning mass attracts a large congregation from across the city. The time after mass has become an occasion on which to meet friends and acquaintances, visit local clubs, and to keep in touch by reading British-Italian publications such as the Italian-language *La Voce Italiani* and *London Sera,* or the mixed English and Italian-language magazine *Back Hill,* which features articles on local history alongside news from Italy and results from the Anglo-Italian Football League.

A few Italian businesses survive in the old Quarter. There has been an Italian hairdresser at 10 Laystall Street, and delicatessens at **Gazzano's** and **Terroni's** since before the First World War. Number 10 Laystall Street is particularly rich in historical associations for the Italian community. A plaque on the first floor commemorates the Italian revolutionary Giuseppe Mazzini, who held meetings here in the mid-19th C to raise money and recruit volunteers for his schemes to unify Italy. The name of an organisation he founded, the Italian Operative's Society, can be seen laid out in the mosaic floor in front of the doorway to the upper part of the building. These premises have continued to be used for social events and meetings through to the present day, and you can still get a good Italian haircut from **Frank's Gentleman's Hairdressers** (071-278 6785) on the ground floor, in amidst genuine 1930s decor.

Mazzini (see *page 105*) is also commemorated by a plaque at 5 Hatton Garden, EC1, where he founded an Italian-language school in 1841.

The celebrated clown Joseph Grimaldi (see *page 104*) lived in Exmouth Market, EC1, in 1822, and died in a house in Southampton Street (now Calshot Street, N1). He was buried about half a mile from the Italian Quarter at St James's Chapel, Pentonville Road, N1.

'Inside Out'

Interview with the Gazzano family, who run an Italian delicatessen in Clerkenwell ...

Father (40s): "When people first came to England, the luckiest had a ride, the unluckier had to walk. Some of them came with one shoe on and one shoe off. It was bad in those days because there was no work in Italy, especially in the South. No prospects of anything.

The family opened the business in 1901. It was my grandfather and grandmother who opened it, and I'd like to see the tradition go on. I would hate to think that it would all be wasted. I've got a daughter who works here full-time, she's on holiday now, but she's got it in her blood, she loves it. It takes time before you get that repartee with the customers, but she is very very good at it. My son works part-time and he is getting to the stage where he is beginning to be good."

Son (teenager): "I enjoy working here at weekends, 'cause I like to be with my dad. Before that I never saw him. But to carry on full-time, no, that's not for me. It's not my cup of tea. I want to branch out into other things. I want to go into accounting and also as pastime I enjoy acting, so I want to go into the drama side".

Father: "We all have these ideas when we're young!"

Grandfather: "He's got to learn the delicatessen business anyway, and after that he can do what he likes. You never know what will happen tomorrow. You've got to know a trade."

Father: "After that he can do what he likes. He'll always have something to fall back on. If he goes into acting, instead of waiting for that phone call at home, he can be in here slicing salamis."

Grandfather: "Business today, in a lot of places, everything is money. With us, there is not only the money to collect, there's got to be friendship with the customer."

Father: "What we're here for, and this is where the tradition comes in, is to advise the customer. If people ask we'll help them to choose, to get the right pasta with the right olive oil. Mind you, you can't always get it right. I remember once an Englishwoman came back in and said, 'Oh, that spaghetti was a bit hard'. I said, 'why?'. She said, 'After I took it out of the frying pan it all broke!' I said, 'Well, I'm sorry darling, you have to boil it first!' I don't think that could happen now because the general public are a lot more educated."

THE ITALIAN QUARTER: SHOPPING

George and Graham 3 Back Hill, EC1 (071-278 1770). Open from 7.30am to 7.30pm Monday to Sunday (except 7.30am to 2.30pm Saturday). Newsagents. Stocks *Back Hill, La Voce Italiani* and *London Sera,* plus same-day issue Italian newspapers and a wide range of Italian magazines.

C N T Cucina, 73 Clerkenwell Road, EC1 (071-405 4173). Open from 9.30am to 6.30pm Monday to Friday. Italian kitchen and dining room furniture and fittings.

Carlo Jewellers, 25a Hatton Garden, EC1 (071-242 2407). Open from 10am to 5.30pm Monday to Friday, 10am to 4pm Saturday. About half of their stock consists of 18-carat jewellery made in distinctive Italian designs.

Food and Drink

Ferraro Continental Stores, 90 Leather Lane, EC1 (071-405 9324). Open from 7.30am to 5.30pm Monday to Friday, (closes 6pm Friday), 9am to 1pm Saturday. Delicatessen. Fresh pasta and antipasti.

L Terroni, 138 Clerkenwell Road, EC1 (071-837 1712). Open from 9am to 6pm Monday to Wednesday, 9am to 2pm Thursday, 9am to 3pm Saturday, 10am to 2pm Sunday. Delicatessen. Fresh pasta daily.

G Gazzano, 167-9 Farringdon Road, EC1(071-837 1586).Open from 8am to 6pm Tuesday to Saturday, (closes 5.30pm Saturday) 10.30am to 2pm Sunday. Delicatessen. Established in 1901 and still run by the same family. Arguably the best Italian delicatessen in Britain.

Cantina Augusto, 91-95 Clerkenwell Road, EC1(071-242 3246/7). Open from 9am to 6pm Monday to Thursday, 9am to 6.30pm Friday. Large stock of reasonably-priced Italian wines, including some vintages. In the cellar of the shop is a wine bar which serves wine and food, much of it Italian. It is open from 11.30am to 5.30pm Monday to Friday.

THE ITALIAN QUARTER: EATING OUT

Jazz Bistro, 340 Farringdon Street, EC1 (071-236 8112). Open from 12 noon to 3pm, 6pm to 11pm Monday to Saturday (not for lunch Saturday). Italian dishes are served accompanied, on Wednesday and Thursday evenings, by live jazz.

ST PETER'S ITALIAN CHURCH

St Peter's Church, at 4 Back Hill, was opened in 1863 to serve Italian Roman Catholics in London. It is modelled on the Basilica of St Crisogona in the Trastevere quarter of Rome. The main entrance of the church is on Clerkenwell Road, although due to problems with vandalism the door is usually kept locked between services. Whether locked or not, you can still view the two memorial plaques in the entrance porch. A plaque at the top of the stairs records the names of Italians from the London community who were killed in the First World War after returning to fight in Italy. Immediately above it there is a plaque which commemorates the British-Italians who went down with the liner *Arandora Star* on 2 July 1940 (see *page 78*). A memorial service for those who died is held annually in St Peter's on the Sunday nearest that date.

If you want to look around inside the church, telephone 071-837 1528 to check when it would be convenient to make a visit. In the interior, note the bronze statue of St Peter situated to the left of the main altar. This is a small-scale copy of the statue found in the Vatican Basilica. Nearby there is a white marble statue of St Vincenzo Pallotti, the Roman priest who founded St Peter's. The main altar and tabernacles are made of Italian marble, and the paintings in the sanctuary were executed in the baroque style by Italian painters in the 19th C. The beautiful statue of Our Lady of Mount Carmel, which stands towards the back of the church to the right of the main altar, depicts the Virgin Mary holding the infant Jesus. This statue is the focus of attention in the Procession of Our Lady of Mount Carmel (see below).

There is a strong musical tradition at St Peter's. Italian opera singers such as Enrico Caruso often sang here at mass in the 19th C and early 20th C.

THE PROCESSION OF
OUR LADY OF MOUNT CARMEL

The feast day of Our Lady of Mount Carmel (the Virgin Mary) falls on 16 July, and on the following Sunday a procession in her honour is held in the streets around St Peter's Church. The procession was first held in Clerkenwell and Holborn at some time in the mid-1880s, and excepting the war years has been an annual event since 1896.

The start of the procession outside St Peter's is marked by a peal of bells at 3.30pm. Viewed by thousands of spectators, mostly of Italian origin, the procession makes its way from Clerkenwell Road into Back Hill, up Bakers Row, down Farringdon Road, across St Cross Street, up Leather Lane and back down Clerkenwell Road to St Peter's.

Dozens of groups take part. Live tableaux from the life of Christ are carried on motor floats which blare out taped religious music. Groups of women wear Italian regional costumes, and young girls the bridal-like dresses of First Communicants. There is normally some participation from Irish Catholics in the form of an Irish pipe band.

The focus of the procession is the garlanded statue of Our Lady of Mount Carmel, which is carried shoulder high by four bearers towards the rear of the procession. The statue is accompanied by several priests, one of whom walks in front of it swinging a censer which contains burning incense.

At the tail end of the procession, three boys carrying the Italian, British and Papal flags precede a large group of parishioners who walk in ordinary dress. The procession programme advises them: 'This procession is intended to be a solemn and public act of faith. You are asked to walk in it devoutly, and take part by praying or singing with the other walkers'.

The procession usually takes about 45 minutes. A sagra (fete) then commences in Warner Street. Vendors sell Italian food and drink, and you can try your hand at the coconut shy, the hoop-la or the 'Mount Carmel Lucky Dip'.

At the turn of the 20th C Procession Sunday was the biggest celebration of the year for the inhabitants of the Italian Quarter. People would save for months beforehand to make sure there would be plenty to eat and drink on the day. Houses and streets were cleaned and decorated, and households on the route of the procession made up altars in their front windows which were judged by a priest and a prize awarded for the best.

In the anthology *Living London* (1902), the curiously named Count E Armfelt gives this description of Procession Sunday, the day when 'Italian London reveals her heart':

'It is on that occasion that Little Italy displays all its artistic genius for decoration. Imposing triumphal arches are erected at the entrances of the streets, garlands of flowers span the roadways, flags wave high and low, coloured lamps reach from house to house, gay tapestries hide the dilapidated walls, transparencies of the Virgin and the Saints appear at the windows, the street-corners are ornamented by large illuminated frames which bear the statue of the Madonna, and even the narrow courts and alleys blaze with flowers and brilliant coloured light.'

When Armfelt made his visit the procession stretched for 2 miles, and roofs, windows, balconies and pavements were crowded with onlookers. Armfelt urged his readers to 'listen to the sonorous and solemn Gregorian chant of the priests and friars, the strains of the numerous bands, the well-trained voices of the children; look at the white-robed little virgins who have devoted their young lives to the Sacred Heart or the Blessed Virgin, and

Italian Procession.

Italian Procession.

whose wreaths and floral crowns are partly hidden by the long white veils which reach nearly to the ground; hearken to the deep voices of the rosary-bearing, psalm-singing men, whose sunburnt bearded faces, long hair, slouched hats and general appearance recall the artist models one meets on the broad steps of the Roman Pincio; and you will admit that no religious procession of modern Italy can compare in grandeur and quaintness with that of Little Italy in London'.

In Armfelt's day celebrations carried on all evening after the procession, and there was music and dancing in the natural 'piazza' formed by the intersection of Eyre Street Hill, and Warner Street. People would move freely from house to house, eating and drinking into the early hours until they finally retired wearily to bed to compose themselves for a return to the normal grind of daily life.

'Inside Out'

Interviews with Anglo-Italians attending or participating in the Italian Procession . . .

"I'm playing Christ in the crown of thorns. It's a fabulous role to play. It's got everything. the soldiers have shoved this crown of thorns on his head, he's being totally humiliated, and yet the person himself, from what we know about the scriptures, had great humility. I'm a great traditionalist. I just hate things dying away. The procession has been going a hundred years and it would be awful if it was forgotten."

*

"I've walked in the procession since I was a girl. It's very emotional for me because it reminds me of my grandmother and my mother,

Eyre Street Hill looking north c 1920 on Procession Sunday.

because they walked in it. Now my daughter is in the Procession. She's just fine. She's one of the angels in the float and she's so thrilled because it's her first year."

*

"The procession's changed over the last 20, 30 years. More people come now than they used to. There are less people in the area, but I think people now consider it as a focal point for the community, so they all come. Every year there are coach loads that come down from Bedford, Peterborough, lots of places. The procession's less religious now than it used to be. It's become more of a carnival, which is bad, I suppose. Nevertheless, I think it's very good. It attracts all the community together".

*

"There's no longer any community in the area, but we all come back on procession Sunday. We meet old friends we haven't seen for a year and we catch up with all sorts of gossip . . . who got married, how many grandchildren, and what's going on. So it's a great community spirit that's involved, a great sense of coming together."

*

"The Italian church is literally the sweat and tears of the Italians. It is still the focal point, where we come to be baptised, to be married, and to be seen off in a wooden box, and it is in the heart of the procession of course."

*

"Years ago, the Italians living in the quarter, they were singing and dancing till 3 or 4 in the morning. Now after the procession and sagra people just go home - and it's finished. you've still got a few hanging about in the café or in the pub, they go and have a drink, but it's not like it was years ago."

*

'THE ITALIAN BELT'

A great number of the sites that are of Italian interest in London lie in a belt which sweeps across the centre of the city from Clerkenwell and Holborn in the east to Mayfair in the west. That trajectory is followed in the listings below.

Clerkenwell and Holborn
The premises of *The Mazzini and Garibaldi Club* (see *page 105: Mazzini*) are at 51 Red Lion Street.
Dante Gabriel Rossetti (see *page 106*) lived at 17 Red Lion Square (marked by a plaque) in 1851.
See also **The Italian Quarter,** *page 81.*

Bloomsbury
Sicilian Avenue is a short pedestrian street at the centre of an eye-catching Italian-style development that occupies the whole corner of the block. Completed in 1905, the shops and offices are clad in red brick, white terracotta and Sicilian marble, and are topped with miniature turrets. Each end of the avenue is marked off with Ionic columns. In the summer, tables

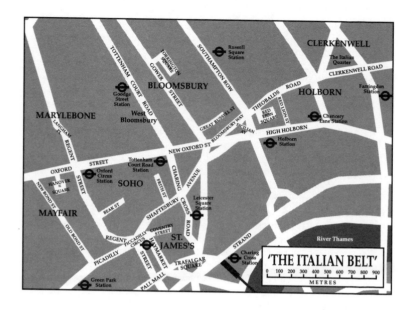

and chairs placed outside the Spaghetti House Restaurant at 20 Sicilian Avenue, WC1 (071-405 5215) make this a perfect place to sit and watch the world go by, continental-style. Espresso and cappuccino coffee and cakes can be ordered on their own from 3pm to 5pm Monday to Saturday, but at other times you must order a full meal.

The British Museum, Great Russell Street, WC1 (see *page 92),* houses a large collection of Roman antiquities. Mazzini studied here in the British Library.

Mazzini lived at 183 Gower Street, WC1 (marked by a plaque) from his arrival in London in 1837 until 1840.

Christina Rossetti (see *page 106)* lived at 30 Torrington Square, WC1 (marked by a plaque) from 1876 until her death there in 1894.

Tottenham Court Road Underground Station is situated at the intersection of New Oxford Street and Tottenham Court Road. The extensive mosaics which decorate the walls of the platforms and walkways were designed by *Eduardo Paolozzi,* a long-time resident of London who was born to Italian parents in Edinburgh in 1924. Paolozzi was one of the leading figures in the development of British pop art, and he has work exhibited in the Tate Gallery and in the Victoria and Albert Museum. The Tottenham Court Road mosaics, which were completed by Paolozzi in 1982, are intended to reflect the spirit of Tottenham Court Road, a shopping street known for its bargain-priced electrical goods. If you stand back from the walls (not too far on the platforms!), you will be able to make out the abstracted patterns of transistors, capacitors and printed circuits. Given that so many of London's mosaic floors and walls were laid by Italian workers, it is appropriate that Paolozzi should have received this commission.

See also **Shopping: Bloomsbury,** *page 94.*

Soho

Soho has attracted Continental immigrants since the late 17th C. Many Italian political exiles lived here in the 19th C, and a small Italian residential community survived through to the 1930s. Soho is noted today for its numerous Italian restaurants and delicatessens.

The Bar Italia, 22 Frith Street, W1, is a typical Italian-style stand-up snack bar which is always busy with British-Italian customers. Recordings of Italian football matches and opera are shown on a large video screen at the back of the bar.

Canaletto (see *page 102)* lived at 41 Beak Street, W1 (marked by a plaque) from 1746 to 1755.

See also **Food and Drink: Restaurants,** *page 97* & **Shopping,** *page 99.*

St James

The National Gallery, Trafalgar Square, WC2 (see *page 92),* houses an excellent collection of Italian paintings.

Casanova (see *page 103)* visited the Orange Coffee-House, Haymarket, SW1 (since demolished) on his first evening in London. The same evening he found lodgings in Pall Mall.

Piccadilly Circus

In the centre of Piccadilly Circus, W1, stands one of London's best-loved statues, created by Sir Alfred Gilbert, R.A. When it was erected in 1893 it was intended to symbolise the Angel of Christian Charity, but it has since become known as *Eros,* the Greek God of Love. Modelling for artists was an Italian speciality in late 19th C London, and it is known that it was an Italian model who posed for Eros.

Marylebone

Lord Charles Forte is the most successful catering entrepreneur to emerge from the Italian community. He came to Britain in 1913 with his father at the age of four and started off in business for himself in 1935 at the Meadow Milk Bar, 289 Regent Street, W1. Today Lord Forte is the Chairman of Trusthouse Forte, the largest hotel and catering group in Britain, and the Dome Restaurant, which now occupies 289 Regent Street, is but one tiny part of his empire.

Dante and *Christina Rossetti* were baptised at All Soul's Church, Langham Place, W1.

Mayfair

Marconi (see *page 107)* was married in 1905 at St George's Church, Hanover Square, W1.

See also **Shopping: Mayfair,** *page 94.*

OTHER PLACES TO VISIT ─────────

Victoria and Albert Museum, Cromwell Road, SW7 (071-938 8500). Open from 10am to 5.50pm Tuesday to Sunday. Admission is free, but there is very strong pressure to make a 'donation'. Extensive collection of Italian antiquities. Sculpture is particularly well represented, and a convincingly realistic plaster copy of Michelangelo's statue of David is on display in the Italian Cast Court.

British Museum, Great Russell Street, WC1 (071-636 1555). Open from 10am to 5pm Monday to Saturday, 2.30pm to 6pm Sunday. Admission free. Extensive collection of Italian antiquities, plus several rooms dedicated to Roman Britain.

The National Gallery, Trafalgar Square, WC2 (071-893 3321). Open from 10am to 6pm Monday to Saturday, 2pm to 6pm Sunday. Admission free. Contains one of the finest collections of Italian paintings in the world outside Italy itself. A number of paintings by Canaletto (see *page 102*) are on display, usually including one or two of his paintings of British scenes.

Tate Gallery, Millbank, SW1 (071-821 1313). Open from 10am to 5.50pm Monday to Saturday, 2pm to 5.50pm Sunday. Admission free. Contains British paintings up to the turn of the 20th Century and British and foreign paintings and sculptures. Rossetti (see *page 106*) and Paolozzi (see *page 90*) are two artists of Italian extraction who have made an important contribution to British art. One or two of Rossetti's works are usually on display in the Pre-Raphaelite section, and Paolozzi has sculpture and prints in the Tate collection which are sometimes on display. The Tate also has a good collection of Italian futurist paintings.

Museum of London, London Wall, EC2 (071-600 3699). Open from 10am to 6pm Tuesday to Saturday, 2pm to 6pm Sunday. Admission fee. The Museum presents the history of London from its founding by the Romans to the present day. A large gallery covers all aspects of Roman life in London using bright, imaginative displays and an impressive collection of relics. A life-sized Roman-style dining room is fully fitted out with original cutlery, glass and pottery. Artefacts originating from across Europe emphasise Roman London's importance as an international trading centre. Curiosities include a leather bikini bottom that was probably worn by an entertainer of some kind, and fire debris from the sack of London in AD 60 by rebels led by Queen Boudicca (Boadicea).

A large picture window in the Roman Gallery looks out on to remnants of the old Roman city wall, which originally stretched two miles around the city from the Tower of London in the east to Blackfriars in the west.

The *Museum Shop* sells a large selection of books on the history of London, plus miscellaneous gift items including maps of Roman London and replicas of Roman coins.

The Italian Institute at 39 Belgrave Square, SW1 (071-235 1461), compiles a fortnightly list of exhibitions, concerts, cinema, opera, drama, radio programmes and lectures in Britain that are of Italian interest. The list is published in English in the British-published Italian magazine *Londra Sera,* which is available at some foreign language newsagents in central London.

Homage to Leonardo, a statue based on a famous drawing by Leonardo De Vinci, *The Vitruvian Man, is* situated on the edge of the private park in the centre of Belgrave Square, SW1, where it faces the Italian Institute. The statue was conceived by the Italian sculptor Enzo Plazzotta (1921-1981) and completed by his assistant Mark Holloway in 1982.

Italian Academy, 24 Rutland Gate, Knightsbridge, SW7 (071-225 3474). The Italian Academy exists to make 'the finest examples of Italian Art and Design, both ancient and modern, accessible to the public of Britain'. There are exhibitions of the visual arts, lectures, drama and music. The Italian bookshop contains books in English about Italy, and Italian-language books. You can order any Italian book in print through the bookshop.

'Inside Out'

Interview with Rosa Letts, who founded and runs the Italian Academy . . .

"The Italian Academy was a dream. I left Italy, married an American man and settled in Britain, and I was missing my own traditions. The Italians have a mania for doing things in an aesthetic sense. It's just the Italian sense of beauty, they form it wherever they are.

Now with the Academy I have a stage for the genius of Italy. No, perhaps that sounds too pompous. Let us say instead that I have a stage to show this great rapport the Italians have always had with the arts.

I bring a message which I know finds a lot of echoes, certainly in most British people. Because the British have been flirting with Italian art for very many centuries. The British have gone on the grand tours to see all the monuments of the Renaissance, of the baroque period, and they have responded in their own way, with their own art, to the stimulus. I believe that art brings people together, and I would like this message to be more widely spread."

SHOPPING ─────────────────────────

Italian clothes, leather goods and furniture have a well-earned reputation for stylish design. These goods are widely available in shops in central London, though they seldom come cheap.

'Inside Out'

Interview with Willie, an Italian fashion journalist . . .

"I've been here for 43 years, I think so - yeah! Somebody told me one day, you have a job in London, you'd better get there on Monday, so on Sunday I came over.

I think Italians wear clothing differently to the English. They give much more importance to their appearance. I think Italians move in a way that shows they want to be seen. I think an Englishman doesn't really like to be seen. He's much more contained, more reserved.

In Italy there's the question of climate. Italians dine outside. In every village, in every town, at the six o'clock promenade, everybody walks with their best clothes on, and they give it an enormous amount of thought. As they live in a beautiful country, they have a tendency to make beautiful things. I think they are obsessed by the look of things.

I think Italians make better fashion than the English in the long run. The English have a lot of talent - fashion houses in Milan have lots of young English designers - but there isn't the same quality of manufacturing here in England. And the Italians have a good sense of detailing in clothes. The English tend to go for an overall look rather than being precise in the details.

Apart from fashion, I'd say what the Italians have brought to London is food, joie de vivre and children in restaurants. Italian restaurants love to have children, whereas English restaurants really don't like having children.

What Italians get to love about England is the freedom of action, of thought, of behaviour, which doesn't really exist in Italy. In Italy, where people live in the open air, you have to watch your actions, while here, nobody cares two hoots what you do, or how you dress or know if you're rich or poor. In Italy, they care much more."

Bloomsbury

La Scarpetta, 98 Southampton Row, WCI (071-831 8837). Open from 10am to 6pm Monday to Saturday. Men's and women's footwear.

Caruso and Company, 35 New Oxford Street, WC1 (071-379 5839). Open from 10am to 6pm Monday to Saturday. A classical music record shop with some imports from Italy of opera and Neapolitan folk music. Named after the celebrated Italian opera singer Enrico Caruso.

Marco, 61 Tottenham Court Road, W1 (071-631 0355). Open from 9.30am to 6pm Monday to Saturday. Men's, women's and children's footwear and other leather goods.

Mayfair

New and Old Bond Street have long been known for expensive, high-quality Italian goods. Many shops are overseas branches of Italian firms.

Rossini, 46 New Bond Street, W1 (071-499 5076). Open from 9.30am to 6.30pm Monday to Saturday (except to 7pm Thursday). Men's clothing.

Frette, 98 New Bond Street (071-629 5517). Open from 10am to 6pm Monday to Saturday (except to 7pm Thursday). Linen and lingerie.

Mina, 75 New Bond Street (071-408 1604). Open from 9.30 to 6pm Monday to Saturday (except to 7pm Thursday). Women's clothing - mostly silk dresses - from Italy and France.

Gucci, Old Bond Street, W1 (071-629 2716). Open from 9.30am to 6pm Monday to Friday, 9.30am to 5.30pm Saturday. Leather goods, jewellery, pens, gifts.

Salvatore Ferragamo, 24 Old Bond Street (071-629 5007). Open from 9am to 5.30pm Monday to Friday, 9.30am to 5pm Saturday. Women's clothing, men's and women's footwear, plus handbags, luggage and other leather goods.

Valentino, 160 New Bond Street (071-493 2698). Open from 10am to 6pm Monday to Saturday. Shuts at 7.30pm on summer Thursdays. Women's clothing.

Trussardi, 51 South Molton Street, W1(071-629 5611). Open from 10am to 6pm Monday to Saturday. Men's and women's clothing, plus perfumes, watches, pens, bags and other gifts.

Gianfranco Ferre, 20 Brook Street, W1 (071-495 2306). Open from 10am to 6pm Monday to Saturday (except 7pm Thursday). Women's clothing, plus accessories and toiletries.

Gianni Versace, 3a Old Bond Street, W1 (071-499 1862). Open from 10am to 6pm Monday to Saturday (except to 7pm Thursday). Men's and women's clothing and accessories.

Ermenegildo Zegna, 37 New Bond Street, W1 (071-493 4471). Open from 10am to 6pm Monday to Saturday (except to 7pm on Thursday). Men's clothing.

Arzani, 40 New Bond Street, W1 (071-495 3899). Open from 10.30am to 6.30pm Monday to Saturday (except to 7pm on Thursday. Men's clothing.

Rossini, 46 New Bond Street, W1 (071-499 5076). Open from 9.30am to 6pm Monday to Saturday (except to 7pm on Thursday). Men's clothing and leather accessories.

Bruno Magli, 49 New Bond Street, W1 (071-491 8562). Open from 9.30am to 6pm Monday to Saturday (except to 7pm on Thursday). Men's and women's footwear.

Carvela, 68 New Bond Street, W1 (071-629 8673). Open from 9.30am to 6.30pm Monday to Saturday (except to 7pm on Thursday). Men's clothing and toiletries.

Fratelli Rossetti, 177 New Bond Street, W1 (071-491 2066). Open from 9.30am to 6pm Monday to Friday, 10am to 5.30pm Saturday. Men's and women's clothing, footwear and accessories.

Knightsbridge

La Cicogna, 6a Sloane Street, SW1(071-235 3845/3739). Open from 9.30am to 6pm Monday to Saturday (except to 7pm Wednesday). Mostly Italian goods. Clothes, footwear and toys for children up to the age of 14. Also maternity wear, cribs and other accessories.

Ungaro, 22 Sloane Street, SW1 (071-235 1357). Open from 10am to 6pm Monday to Saturday (except from 10.30am Saturday). Women's clothing.

Giorgio Armani, 178 Sloane Street, SW1 (071-235 6232). Open from 10 am to 6pm Monday to Saturday (except to 7pm on Wednesday). Men's and women's clothing.

Valentino, 174 Sloane Street, SW1 (071-235 0719). Open from 10am to 6pm Monday to Friday (except to 7pm on Wednesday), 10.30am to 6pm Saturday. Men's and women's clothing.

Gucci, 17-18 Sloane Street, SW1 (071-235 7607). Open from 9.30am to 6pm Monday to Saturday (except from 10am to 7pm Wednesday and 10am to 6pm Saturday). Women's clothing and accessories.

Fratelli Rossetti, 196 Sloane Street, SW1 (071-259 6397). Open from 9.30am to 6pm Monday to Saturday (except to 6.30pm Wednesday, 5.30pm Saturday). Men's and women's footwear and accessories.

Bruno Magli, 207 Sloane Street, SW1 (071-235 7939). Open from 9.30am to 6pm Monday to Saturday. Men's and women's footwear.

The Italian Paper Shop, 11 Brompton Arcade, SW1 (071-850 1668). Open from 9.30am to 5.30pm (except 10am to 7pm Wednesday). Hand-made stationary imported from Florence.

Elswhere in London

Gagliardi Design, 509 King's Road, SW10 (071-352 3663).Open from 10am to 5.30pm Monday to Saturday. Italian furniture and contemporary art.

Italian Bookshop, Italian Academy, 24 Rutland Gate, SW7 (071-225 3474). Books in English about Italy, and Italian language books. You can order any Italian book in print through the bookshop.

See also **The Italian Quarter: Shopping,** *page 84.*

FOOD AND DRINK ─────────────

It is the Italians whom we must thank more than any other ethnic group for breaking down the prejudices harboured by ordinary Londoners against foreign food. Whilst Italian cuisine has long been appreciated by the wealthy, the breakthrough into a mass market did not come until the early 1950s when Italian coffee became *the* fashionable drink and espresso coffee houses the fashionable places to drink it.

Aimed at the young, the espresso coffee houses were designed to give the impression of a Continental cafe. They were typically decked out with white plaster walls, arches, false shutters and painted tiles depicting Mediterranean scenes. A central fixture was the hissing and gleaming espresso coffee machine, which produced espresso and cappuccino Italian coffee (both black, the latter with a head of frothy milk). Customers could also buy high quality continental snacks such as spaghetti bolognese, which became a standard dish.

Although few of the proprietors of the espresso coffee houses were Italian, there were many Italians who, since the 1930s, had been running snack bars serving ordinary British food. They quickly recognised that a new market had been opened up for moderately-priced Italian food and in the late 'fifties many began to turn their premises into Italian restaurants. Trade boomed in the 1960s.

The most recent major development in the Italian food scene in Britain came in the 1970s when Italian-American pizza parlours experienced spectacular growth, providing both the American-style deep-pan pizzas and the more authentic Italian thin-dough pizzas.

The authentic Italian style of eating is not much practised in London's Italian restaurants. The proper sequence of courses is a starter (antipasto), first course (pasta, risotto or soup), second course (meat or fish dishes) and fruit to finish. In Italy pasta makes up only one of two principal courses, but in Britain it has been transformed into a main course and the portions made accordingly larger and meatier. Consequently if you do try to eat two principal courses in the Italian fashion the meal can prove both heavy-going and expensive.

As any Italian will tell you, there is much more to Italian cuisine than pasta. Their veal, beef, chicken and fish dishes all deserve exploration. The pronounced regional variations of Italian cuisine were poorly represented in London until a few years ago, when several regionally-based restaurants opened. However, most restaurants still provide little more than a couple of regional specialities on an otherwise fairly standard all-Italian menu of dishes known to be popular with the British public.

RESTAURANTS

Soho

Soho boasts the greatest concentration of Italian restaurants in London. They are particularly numerous in the vicinity of Frith Street, Old Compton Street and Dean Street.

(i) Cheap and basic. Formica tables, standard menus and the emphasis on pasta. Functional places to sip coffee or fill stomachs.

Barocco, 13 Moor Street, W1(071-437 2324). Open from 12 noon to 11pm. Cheap.

Presto Restaurant, 46 Old Compton Street, W1(071-437 4006. Open from 11.30am to 11.30pm Monday to Friday, 11.30am to 12.30am Saturday. Cheap.

Pollo, 20 Old Compton Street, W1(071-734 5917). Open from 12 noon to 11.30pm Monday to Saturday. Cheap.

(ii) Modern. Bright decor and 1990's attitudes. A sophisticated approach to convenience eating.

Pasta Fino, 27 Frith Street, W1 (071-439 8900). Open from 12noon to 11.30pm Monday to Saturday, 5 to 11.30pm Sunday from June to September. A pasta restaurant with a wide and interesting range of dishes. Moderately-priced.

(iii) Trattorias. Characterised by a 'colourful' ethnic Italian atmosphere, with Chianti flasks normally dangling somewhere amidst the homely, cluttered decor. Menus are usually unadventurous.

Trattoria da Otello, 41 Dean Street, W1 (071-734 3924). Open from 12 noon to 3pm, 6 to 11.30pm Monday to Saturday. Moderately-priced.

Trattoria Cappuccetto, 17 Moor Street, Wl (071-437 2527). Open from 12 noon to 3pm, 5.30 to 11.45pm Monday to Sunday. Moderately-priced.

(iv) Upmarket. Decor more restrained than at the Trattorias.

La Tavernetta, 63 Dean Street, W1(071-437 3990). Open from 12 noon to 3pm, 5.30 to 11.30pm Monday to Thursday, 12 noon to 11.45pm Friday, Saturday and Sunday. Cosy and romantic. Expensive.

Il Siciliano, 33 Dean Street, W1(071-437 6024). Open from 12 noon to 2.30pm, 5.30 to 11.30pm. No lunch Saturday or Sunday. Romantic and sophisticated. Some Sicilian specialities. Expensive.

Leoni's Quo Vadis, 26-29 Dean Street, W1 (071-4379585/4809). Open from 12 noon to 2.30pm, 6 to 11.15pm Monday to Saturday, 7 to 10.30pm Sunday. Old-fashioned elegance. Established in 1926 by Peppino Leoni, who wrote about his rise from waiter to high-class restaurateur in *I Shall Die on the Carpet* (1966), a book whose foreword was written by the policeman who arrested Leoni on his internment in 1940. Karl Marx (see *Jewish London, page 143*) lived at number 28, which is marked by a plaque. Expensive.

Signor Zilli, 41 Dean Street, W1 (071-734 3924). Open from 12.30pm to 3pm, 6pm to 11.30pm Monday to Saturday (not for lunch Saturday). Specialities from the Abruzzi region on Italy's Adriatic coast. Moderately priced.

Elsewhere in London

Grunt's Chicago Pizza Company, 12 Maiden Lane, W2 (071-379 7722). Open from 12 noon to 11.30pm Monday to Saturday, 12 noon to 9pm Sunday. Deep-pan pizza and pasta eaten in busy, jazzy atmosphere amidst brash Chicago Americana decor. Good Fun. Cocktail bar. Moderately-priced. Also take-away.

La Trattoria Dei Pescatori, 57 Charlotte Street, W1(071-580 3289). Open from 12 noon to 3pm, 6 to 11pm Monday to Tuesday, 12 noon to 3pm, 6 to 11.30pm Wednesday to Friday, Saturday. Specialises in fish dishes. Rather overpowering nautical decor. Expensive.

Gualtiero Marchesi, Halkin Hotel, 5-6 Halkin Street, SW1 (071-333 1000). Open from 12.30pm to 2.30pm, 7.30pm to 10.30pm Monday to Saturday (except for lunch Saturday).This is the British branch of the Michelin three star-rated Milan establishment of the same name. The Italian 'cuisine nouvelle' is exquisite but very expensive.

Osteria Antica Bologna, 23 Northcote Road, SW11 (071-078 4771). Open from 12 noon to 11pm Wednesday to Saturday, 6pm to 11pm Monday and Tuesday, 12.30pm to 10.30pm Sunday. Sicilian specialities and vegetarian dishes.

La Bersagliera, 372 Kings Road, SW3 (071-352 5993). Open from 12.30pm to 3pm, 6.30pm to 11pm Monday to Saturday. They make their own bread and pasta here, and the pizza is as authentically Italian as you'll find in London.

See also **The Italian Quarter: Eating Out,** *page 84.*

FOOD AND DRINK: SHOPPING

Soho is the best place to shop for Italian food in London. Look out for the following products:

Pasta. Soft, fresh pastas made out of egg and flour are often available alongside the myriad variants of hard, factory-made pastas.

Cheese. Parmigiano reggiano (a parmesan cheese), dolcelatte (a mild gorgonzola), pecorino romano (strong and hard, made from sheep's milk), ricotta (a bland cream cheese used for sweet and savoury fillings), mozzarella (the cheese normally used on pizzas, traditionally made from buffalo's milk but cow's milk is now more usual).

Preserved meat. Milano and Felino salamis, pancetta (pork cured with salt and spices rolled up into a salami shape).

Biscuits. Amaretti almond biscuits, Savoiardi sponge fingers, Cantuccini almond cake.

Ice-cream. An Italian speciality for many centuries, it was Italian immigrants who played a large part in popularising it in Britain.

Wine. Marsala, one of the great fortified wines of the world, has long been an English favourite, and indeed is sometimes known as 'The Englishman's wine'.

Soho.

Lina Stores, 18 Brewer Street, W1(071-437 6482). Open from 8am to 5.30pm Monday to Saturday (except 1pm Thursday). Delicatessen. Wide variety of salamis and fresh pastas. Freshly-made mozzarella cheese.

Fratelli Camisa, 1a Berwick Street, W1(071-437 7120). Open from 8.30am to 6pm Monday to Saturday . Delicatessen. Specialises in Italian (and other European) cheeses, including fresh ricotta and mozzarella. Pastas and sauces are made on the premises. Fresh truffles in season and sun dried tomatoes at all times. Note the display of coloured almonds. Italians put them in nets or small ceramic pots to make gifts known as bomboniere, which are given out as mementoes to guests at special occasions. Certain coloured almonds are associated with particular occasions; white is for weddings, pink and blue for christenings, red for graduations, green for engagements, and silver and gold respectively for 25th and 50th wedding anniversaries.

Fratelli Camisa, 61 Old Compton Street, W1 (071-437 7610/4686). Open from 8.30am to 6pm Monday to Saturday. Delicatessen. Fresh pasta.

Pasta Fino, 27 Frith Street, W1 (071-439 8900). Open from 11am to 11.30pm Monday to Saturday. Fresh pasta and sauces to take away, plus a small selection of biscuits, cakes and chocolates. Managed jointly with the Pasta Fino restaurant in the basement (see *page 97*).

A Angelucci, 23b Frith Street, W1(071-437 5889). Open from 9am to 5pm Monday to Saturday (except 9am to 1.30pm Thursday). Coffee specialist. Ask for their Espresso Blend if you want to make Italian coffee.

Vinorio, 80 Compton Street, W1 (071-437 1024). Open from 9am to 7pm Monday to Saturday (except early closing Wednesday), 11am to 1.30pm Sunday. Delicatessen, specialises in wines.

Belloni Delicatessen, 53 Charlotte Street, W1(071-6360457). Open from 9am to 6pm Monday to Friday, 9am to 1pm Saturday. Delicatessen, specialises in wines.

Fratelli Camisa, 53 Charlotte Street, W1 (071-255 1240). Open from 8.30am to 6pm Monday to Saturday. An off-shoot of the Berwick Street delicatessen of the same name.

Epifani Food Store, 78 Tavistock Road, W1 (071-243 8518). Open from 10am to 6pm Monday to Saturday (except to 7pm Saturday). Delicatessen with many take-away dishes. Pasta and sauces are home made.

Elsewhere in London

Gallo Nero, 45 Newington Garden Road, N16 (071-226 2002). Open from 8.30am to 6.30pm Monday to Saturday. This delicatessen (and its sister branch at 75 Stoke Newington High Street) specialises in home-made pasta and a wide range of Italian cheeses and wines.

Marine Ices, 8 Haverstock Hill, NW3 (071-485 8898). Open from 10.30am to 11pm Monday to Sunday. Established in 1931 and still in the hands of the same family. Using natural, fresh ingredients and traditional recipes, they make their ice cream and sorbets on the premises. These are served in the ice-cream parlour and restaurant here, and are also supplied to over a thousand hotels and restaurants in Britain.

See also **The Italian Quarter: Shopping,** *page 84.*

PUNCH AND JUDY,
PANTOMIME AND OPERA

The Italian entertainers who were familiar figures in 17th and 18th C London have left two enduring legacies in British culture - the Punch and Judy puppet show and the Pantomime.

A plaque in the piazza at Covent Garden, situated to the left of the façade of St Paul's church, marks the spot where, in May 1662, an Italian puppeteer called Pietro Gimonde, performed his puppet show for the first time in Britain. It was witnessed by the diarist Samuel Pepys, who described it as "very pretty, the best that I ever saw." That performance marked the beginning of the British tradition that became Punch and Judy, and which is still sometimes performed in the piazza today.

The anarchic and violent principal character, called Pulcinella or Punchinello, rapidly became a firm favourite with British audiences and is known today simply as 'Punch'. The British 'Punch 'n' Judy' rapidly developed its own character. Judy, as Punch's wife, arrived in the mid-18th C, when she was at first called Joan.

By the 19th C the pattern had been set and the story has changed little since then. Punch mistreats the baby, argues with his wife Judy, and is then visited by a series of figures who attempt to deal with him, including a policeman. Punch beats them all off, and when he is taken to the gallows to be hung, he tricks the hangman into hanging himself. The hanging is usually felt to be a bit too strong for modern tastes and is now commonly left out.

The Italian puppet show from which Punch and Judy developed has survived in Italy, and the character of Punch and the general sweep of the plot are still recognisably similar.

By contrast, British pantomime has departed so far from its beginnings in Italian improvised comedy (commedia dell'arte) that it can be compared with nothing else in the world today. Even so, certain basic elements have survived from the performances of commedia dell'arte that were first seen in Britain in the late 16th and early 17th centuries.

The original plot of the commedia dell'arte concerned a young couple who were trying to see each other despite the opposition of the woman's father. Around that basic plot, and using a number of stock characters, the performers created a rough and ready entertainment with no literary pretensions, and they mixed together songs, acrobatics, dance, knockabout comedy, and improvised routines which often included topical allusions.

In the early 18th C these were very popular with British theatre audiences, who knew them as 'Italian Night Scenes' or 'Italian Mimic Scenes'.

These rapidly mutated into a new dramatic form, the pantomime, in which the approach of the commedia dell'arte was applied to classical, mythological or legendary stories. Since pure entertainment was the name of the game, and the form itself was so flexible, the pantomime became a dramatic form which drew on all kinds of British theatrical traditions, from the 'breeches' role, in which a woman played the lead male (frequent in 18th C comedies), to the once common animal mimics, of which the pantomime horse or cow is now the sole surviving relic. It was recognised at the time that a new theatrical form was being created, and the pantomime was widely debated, praised and attacked.

Gradually pantomime acquired its modern form. Fairy tales began to appear in the mid-18th C, the stock Italian characters of Pierrot, the clown, and

Italian Procession, Clerkenwell.

harlequin disappeared during the 19th C, and the female 'principle boy' was firmly established by the mid-19th C. The influence of the music hall brought a stronger musical element to the pantomime and made it less middle-class.

By the early 20th C, pantomime had acquired all the elements familiar today, including its performance during the Christmas season and an emphasis on family entertainment in which children form a very large part of the audience. However, despite all these changes, pantomime still continues in the same rough, knockabout vein that was the essential element of the commedia.

Joseph Grimaldi (see *page 104*) first made his reputation as a clown in the pantomime 'Mother Goose' in 1806.

Unlike Punch and Judy and the pantomime, opera has stayed close to its Italian origins. Opera originated in Italy at the close of the 16th C and soon spread to other European countries. Over the centuries Italian singers, composers and conductors have continued to play a leading role in the development of opera, and Italian remained the customary language of librettos (opera texts) up until the Second World War.

London's main opera companies are the **Royal Opera**, who perform at the Royal Opera House, Bowe Street, WC2 (240 1066/1911), and **The English National Opera**, who perform at The London Coliseum, St Martin's Lane, WC2 (836 3161, recorded information 836 7666). There are four or five performances a week at The English National Opera and three at the Royal Opera. Although most of the tickets are fairly expensive, some moderately priced seats are also available.

The Royal Opera House was purpose-built in 1858 in the style of an Italian opera house of the period. It was originally called The Royal Italian Opera House, and as a matter of policy all the operas performed there were sung in Italian. Today the Royal Opera's policy is to perform operas in their original language. By contrast, the English National Opera performs all of its operas in English only.

Both the Royal Opera and the English National Opera stage a standard repertory of popular operas alongside new and lesser-known works. Classic operas by Italian composers include *Il Barbiere di Siviglia* (1816) by Gioacchino Rossini; *Rigoletto* (1851), *Il Travatore* (1853), *La Traviata* (1853), and *Aida* (1871) by Giuseppe Verdi; and *La Boheme* (1896), *Tosca* (1900), and *Madame Butterfly* (1904) by Giacomo Puccini.

The legendary Italian opera singer Enrico Caruso (1873-1921) made his London debut in *Rigoletto* at the Royal Opera House on 14 May 1902.

PEOPLE

The Venetian Antonio Canal (1697-1768), better known as *Canaletto,* is celebrated for his paintings of the city and waterways of Venice. In the 18th C it was the custom amongst the British gentry to go on a cultural journey around Europe that was known as the Grand Tour. Most itineraries included a visit to Venice, where these early tourists would frequently call on Canaletto to provide them with a painting of the city as a souvenir of their visit.

The British became Canaletto's chief patrons, but after the War of the Austrian Succession broke out in 1740, his work fell off drastically as fewer

Britons made the trip to Venice. Eventually Canaletto made the logical commercial decision and in 1746 he came to London, where he lived until 1755 at 41 Beak Street, W1 (marked with a plaque). In a studio in the back garden of this house Canaletto continued to paint views of Venice alongside stylistically similar views of London in which the River Thames was often featured.

Although Canaletto produced several classic paintings of London before he left the city in 1755 to resume his career in Venice, the work of his British period is not highly regarded as a whole. The largest collections of his paintings on display in London can be seen in the National Gallery and in the Wallace Collection, Hertford House, Manchester Square, W1 (071-935 0687).

The libertine and adventurer *Giovanni Casanova* was born in Venice in 1725 into a family of professional actors. By the age of 21 he had already been expelled from a seminary and earned his living as a soldier, a violinist and as the secretary to a cardinal. Supporting himself through gambling and political intrigue, Casanova travelled widely in Europe. He visited London for nine months during 1763 and 1764, and recorded his activities here in his infamous autobiography *Memoirs,* which in addition to establishing his reputation as a seducer of women is also a valuable record of high and low life in 18th C Europe.

Casanova's first impression of England was that 'Nothing . . . is as it is anywhere else. The very ground is of another colour, and the water of the Thames tastes differently to that of any other river. Everything in Albion has a character of its own; the fish, the horned cattle, the men and the women are distinct types to be found nowhere else. Their mode of life, especially with regard to cookery, is totally unlike that of other people'.

In London, Casanova left his baggage with an acquaintance in Soho Square, W1, and went to the Haymarket, SW1, to call in on the now long-gone Orange Coffee-House, 'the most ill-famed coffee-house in London, and the meeting place of the scum of the Italian population'. Here he met Vincenzo Martinelli, an Italian 'man of letters', who helped him to find lodgings that same evening in Pall Mall, SW1.

Casanova came to London with the intention of setting up a lottery, a business in which he had been involved in Paris. But this project came to nothing and with 'few friends in London and nothing to do', Casanova set about finding out what amusements the city could offer. He could not speak English, so he took on a multi-lingual black servant called Jarbe to assist him in his pursuits. Casanova gambled, visited the theatres at Convent Garden and Drury Lane (for both see *Grimaldi, page 104*), 'dined in all the taverns of good and evil repute', and 'in the evening frequented the most select bagnios, where a man of quality can sup, bathe and meet well-bred women of easy virtue. There are plenty of this sort in London'. He also met King George III, Dr Samuel Johnson and other eminent figures of the age.

Although Casanova had his customary amorous successes, his infatuation and failure with one Marianne Charpillon almost drove him to suicide. Carrying large quantities of lead shot to weigh himself down, and having 'the firm intention of drowning . . . in the Thames where it flows past the Tower of London', Casanova was crossing Westminster Bridge on his way to the appointed spot when he chanced to meet a friend who recognised his distressed state and managed to pull him out of his despair. Casanova wrote: 'I must admit here, in all humility, the metamorphosis which love wrought in me here in London at the age of 38. I consider this as the end of the first act of my life'.

It was not quite the end of this particular story however, for Casanova was then arrested on a charge of trying to 'disfigure' Marianne Charpillon, who had extracted large sums of money from him. He was briefly locked up in Newgate Prison (formerly in Newgate Street, EC1), which he described as 'a veritable hell, worthy of the imagination of Dante'. Once free, Casanova bought a parrot and, apparently, taught it to say 'The Charpillon is a greater whore than her mother' in French. He then sent his servant Jarbe about town with the bird, much to the amusement of London society but to the fury of the Charpillon family. They consulted a lawyer but were advised that the law of libel could not be applied to a parrot.

Casanova had to make a hasty exit from London after he cashed a forged letter of credit given to him as payment for winning a game of dice. Although his crime had been unwitting, it was an offence for which he could hang, and so he fled to France. To add to his misfortunes, while he was travelling he became delirious from a venereal disease. During the several months he spent recuperating from this affliction in France he had much time to rue the 'fine fortune' that he had dissipated in London.

You can read a fuller account of Casanova's London adventures in *Casanova: in London* (1969), edited by M Green.

Joseph 'Joey' Grimaldi, the most famous British clown of all time, was born on 18 December 1779 in Stanhope Street (since demolished and the site now occupied by the London School of Economics, Houghton Street, WC2), and was baptised at St Clement Danes Church, Strand, WC2. Joseph's Italian father earned his living variously as a choreographer, a comedian and a dentist, and his English mother as a dancer and singer.

Joseph Grimaldi made his first stage appearance as an infant dancer at Sadler's Wells Theatre, St John Street, EC1, when he was only 14 months old. He grew up into an accomplished comedian and singer, and became famous through his performance in 1806 as a clown in the pantomime *Mother Goose* at Covent Garden Theatre, Bow Street, WC2. He retired in 1823, worn out by many years on the stage, but returned in 1828 to make his final stage appearance taking a benefit at the Drury Lane Theatre, Catherine Street, WC2.

Both Drury Lane and Sadler's Wells are still in use as theatres, though since Grimaldi's time the former has been substantially remodelled and the latter has been largely rebuilt. The Royal Opera House now stands on the site of the old Covent Garden theatre, and Grimaldi's ghost is still said to haunt it.

From 1818 to 1828 Grimaldi lived at 56 Exmouth Market and a plaque commemorates his occupancy. Grimaldi died in Southampton Street (now Calshot Street, N1), on 31 May 1837, and was buried at St James's Chapel, Pentonville Road, N1. The Chapel has since been demolished and the open space named the Joseph Grimaldi Park. Grimaldi's gravestone has been preserved and his grave is being restored.

Grimaldi is regarded as the patron saint of Britain's clowns. He is honoured by a painting and a stained-glass window in the clown's corner at the 'clown's church' of the Holy Trinity, Beechwood Road, Dalston, E8. A service attended by clowns in their 'motley' is held at the church annually on the first Sunday in February. During the service the following prayer is read:

'O God our father we remember before you,
The life of our servant known as Grimaldi the clown;
His artistry, skills and invention.
Surely he helped you to touch the hearts
Of some of your children,
And for this we give you thanks.
Amen.'

Giuseppe Mazzini was the principal political theorist behind the movement for unification that dominated Italian politics from the end of the Napoleonic Wars in 1815 until the achievement of that goal in 1870. Born in Genoa in 1805, Mazzini received a degree in law from the University of Genoa in 1827. Exiled to France because of his political activities, he founded the 'Young Italy' movement, which advocated that freedom from domination by domestic tyrants and foreign rulers could only be achieved in a united, republican Italy. Mazzini put his faith in 'Neither Pope nor King' but in 'God and the people'.

Although Mazzini's ideas spread quickly throughout Italy, the rebellions he organised to further them proved unsuccessful and as a result of these activities he was further exiled from both France and Switzerland. He arrived in London in January 1837, and took rooms at 183 Gower Street, WC1 (marked by a plaque), where he lived until 1840.

He spent his first few months in great poverty: 'I struggled on in silence. I pledged, without the possibility of redeeming them, the few dear souvenirs, either of my mother or others, which I possessed; then things of less value; until one Saturday I found myself obliged to carry an old coat and a pair of boots to one of the pawnbroker's shops, crowded on Saturday evenings by the poor and the fallen, in order to obtain food for the Sunday. After this some of my fellow-countrymen became security for me, and I dragged myself from one to another of those loan societies which drain the poor man of the last drop of his blood, and often rob him of the last remnant of shame and dignity, by exacting from him forty or fifty percent, upon a few pounds'.

Mazzini managed to scrape a living as a teacher of Italian and as a writer while he continued his political work. He kept in contact with revolutionaries inside Italy, lobbied for support amongst the British, and wrote prolifically about his political ideals. In his studies he made extensive use of the British Library at the British Museum.

Mazzini was active too in helping the Italian community in London. In 1841 he founded a school at 5 Hatton Garden, EC1 (marked by a plaque), to teach Italian to the children of Italian immigrants. In 1864 he founded the Italian Operative's Society at 10 Laystall Street, EC1 (marked by a plaque), for the welfare of Italian workers. The society survives today under the name of the Mazzini and Garibaldi Club at 51 Red Lion Street, WC1. Garibaldi was the other great political figure in the unification of Italy, and such was his popularity in Britain on his visit in 1864, that he was honoured by having a new brand of biscuits named after him. The Garibaldi biscuit is still popular today.

In 1848 Mazzini returned to Italy after revolutions broke out across the country. He became the effective head of government in Rome after a republic was declared in the city in February 1849, but was forced back into exile in London after the city was retaken by French troops who came to the aid of the Pope.

Most of Italy was reunited in 1861 under King Victor Emmanuel, but Mazzini was unable to return due to his republican views and his determination to see Italy through to complete unification. He finally left London in 1868 for Switzerland, where he settled close to the Italian border. Even after the complete unification of Italy in 1870, Mazzini still found himself politically unwelcome. He died in Pisa in 1872 living under the guise of an Englishman, a Mr Brown. Italy did not to become a republic until 1946.

The poet and painter *Dante Gabriel Rossetti* was born in 1828 at 110 Hallam Street, W1 (marked by a plaque). His sister, the poet Christina, was born at the same address in 1830. Both children were baptised into the Anglican faith at All Souls' Church, Langham Place, W1. Their father was Gabriel Rossetti, an Italian political exile and Professor of Italian at King's College, Strand, WC2. Dante and Christina grew up in a bilingual household frequented by Italian literary figures and political exiles, including Mazzini (*see above*).

Dante Rossetti was educated at King's College and studied art at the Antique School of the Royal Academy. With Holman Hunt and Millais, he founded the Pre-Raphaelite Brotherhood, an artistic group that made a great impact on Victorian art. The Pre-Raphaelites, who criticised the academic naturalism prevailing in painting at the time, aimed to return to the more spiritual approach to art that they felt existed before the time of the Italian painter Raphael (1483-1520). In the event they became associated with a romanticised vision of the medieval past.

Dante is remembered too for his troubled personal life. His wife Elizabeth Siddal was an invalid when he married her in 1860 and she died only two years later from an overdose of laudanum. It was almost certainly a case of suicide. In remorse Dante put the only complete manuscript book of his poems into her coffin, concealing it underneath her hair. Years later, he regretted the loss of the book and ordered that it be recovered from the grave in the western section of Highgate Cemetery (see *page 107*). By the light of a bonfire and torches on an evening in early October 1868, the coffin was disinterred and the book removed from beneath Elizabeth's surprisingly well-preserved hair. Dante was not present. The poems were subsequently published.

Shortly after his wife's death Dante moved to 16 Cheyne Walk, SW3 (marked by a plaque). It was here that he painted *Beata Beatrix,* one of his most famous works, from studies of his late wife. In his last years Dante led a reclusive existence in the company of a menagerie that included a Brahmin bull, an armadillo, a wombat and a wallaby. He lived at Cheyne Walk until his death in 1882, although he actually died and was buried at Birchington in Kent. In 1887 Holman Hunt unveiled a memorial fountain to Rossetti in the Embankment Gardens opposite the house in Cheyne Walk. Designed by J P Sedding, it features a small bronze sculpture of Dante by Ford Madox Brown.

The art critic John Ruskin called Rossetti: 'A great Italian lost in the inferno of London'. Be that as it may, Rossetti never set foot in Italy.

Beata Beatrix and several other paintings by Rossetti can be seen in the Tate Gallery (see *page 92*). There are also a couple of his works on display in the Victoria and Albert Museum.

Christina Rossetti was an important poet in her own right. Her verses usually have a spiritual or melancholy air. One of the best known is *Mid-Winter:*

In the bleak mid-winter
Frosty wind made moan,
Earth stood hard as iron,
Water like a stone;
Snow had fallen, snow on snow
Snow on snow,
In the bleak mid-winter
Long ago.

Christina lived at 30 Torrington Square, WC1 (marked by a plaque) from 1876 until her death there in 1894. She was buried in the family plot in the western section of Highgate Cemetery, Swains Lane, N6. Buried in the same plot are her parents, her brother William, Dante's wife Elizabeth Siddal and a number of the Rossettis' descendants.

The western section of Highgate Cemetery is a fascinating monument to Victorian tastes in death. Choked with dilapidated ivy-smothered graves and memorials, it has something of the gloomy but tacky atmosphere of a Hammer horror film set. Public access is restricted to guided walks, which are held every day except Christmas Day on the hour every hour from 10am to 3pm in the winter and from 10am to 4pm in the summer. The Rossetti family plot will not necessarily be on the itinerary of every guided walk, so you can either take a chance in turning up and hoping the guide is going to include it (or can be persuaded to do so), or you can try to make arrangements in advance by phoning 071-340 1834.

Guglielmo Marconi, the inventor of radio, was born of an Italian father and Protestant Irish mother in Bologna, Italy, in April 1874. Apart from three years living in England as a young child, he grew up in Italy, though he spent much of his time there living with the British expatriate communities at Florence and Leghorn. Marconi spoke fluent English from early childhood, but fluency in Italian was a later development, and his grasp of the language as a young boy was poor enough to attract scorn from his Italian schoolmates.

When Marconi's innovations in radio technology were turned down by the Italian Government, a move to Britain was an obvious step. Marconi came to London in February 1896, and after a brief stay with relatives moved into lodgings at 71 Hereford Road, W2 (marked by a plaque), where he lived until 1897. It was at this address that he prepared his first patent, which was drawn up with the assistance of his cousin Henry Jameson-Davis, who worked as an engineer in London.

Jameson-Davis introduced Marconi to Sir William Preece, the Chief Engineer of the Post Office, and on 27 July 1896 Marconi made the first ever formal demonstration of his radio equipment on the roof of the General Post Office, St Martin's Le Grand, EC1 (which is marked by a plaque). As a result the Post Office and the British Admiralty became Marconi's sponsors. Marconi was based in London from 1896 to 1915, though he spent much of that time travelling in Britain and abroad. These were busy years. In 1897 Jameson-Davis assisted Marconi in the foundation of Marconi's Wireless Telegraph Company. In December 1901 the first radio message was sent across the Atlantic, and it brought Marconi world fame. In 1905 Marconi married Beatrice O'Brien, an Irish woman, at St George's Church, Hanover Square, W1. In 1909 he was awarded the Nobel Prize for Physics.

Although the early years had been marred by financial difficulties and legal struggles for control of his own invention, by the outbreak of the First World War Marconi was a rich man, his company was a powerful industrial force, and his invention was of vital military importance. Indeed the British Government was first given notice of Germany's declaration of war from the Marconi company's headquarters at 335 Strand, WC2, where they had been monitoring German broadcasts.

The First World War encouraged Marconi to renew his ties with Italy. He took up a seat in the Italian senate in January 1915 and quickly became an important diplomat. He encouraged the entry of Italy into the war on the side of the Allies, and in 1919 he was sent by the Italian Government as a plenipotentiary delegate to the Paris Peace Conference.

After the war Marconi continued to work on the development of radio. He spent a lot of time in Britain in the mid-1920s, but after marriage to an Italian woman in 1927 he turned his attention more exclusively towards Italy. Even then, he always started off his day with a British-style breakfast. Marconi died in Rome in July 1937, his death marked by a two-minute radio silence across the globe.

JEWISH LONDON

HISTORY

Although it seems likely that there were Jews living in Britain in Roman times, recorded Jewish history in this country begins with the Norman invasion of 1066, when Jews from northern France came in search of economic opportunities in the newly conquered territory.

The Jews in England were soon playing a central role in financial affairs, a field in which they excelled in an age when they were barred from most other avenues of betterment. Whereas Christians were forbidden from charging interest on loans because the Church considered it to be sinful, the Jews were authorised to do so in a moneylending system that was encouraged and regulated by the Crown, which also creamed off a large share of the profits.

The senior members of the Jewish community were the financiers, who associated closely with the Royal Court. The bulk of the Jewish working population was made up of the financiers' agents, scribes and attendants, but there were also merchants, doctors and synagogue officials within the community. Amongst themselves the Jews all spoke French, the language of the ruling classes.

Until the late 12th C the Jewish settlement seems to have been both peaceful and prosperous, but over the next 100 years it came under increasing social and economic pressure. The Crusades stirred up religious prejudice against non-Christians, and in the constitutional struggles of the period between the King and his nobles, the Jews frequently fell foul of the nobles, who were often greatly in their debt. Furthermore, the Crown took to imposing punitive levies rather than regular taxation, and the Jews faced imprisonment or expulsion if they could not pay.

The Jews became subject to periodic mob violence and increasingly severe restrictions on where they could settle and what employment they could follow. They were also forced to wear distinguishing marks on their clothing in the shape of the tabula, the two stone tablets on which the Ten Commandments are said to have been inscribed.

The Jews finally lost the patronage of the Crown after Italian and French Christians moved in to take over their role as financiers. In 1290, no longer considered to be of any use to the country, they were expelled en masse. Contemporary accounts tell of the expulsion of 16,000 Jews, but modern historians believe that 3,000 to 5,000 would be a more accurate figure. Having first confiscated most of their wealth, Edward I did make genuine efforts to give the Jews safe passage, but many were nevertheless robbed and a few also murdered as they made their way out of the country. The majority of those expelled are thought to have settled in France.

The modern Jewish settlement in Britain has its origins in the expulsion of the Jews from Spain in 1492. About 50,000 Spanish Jews accepted Christian baptism in order to avoid expulsion, but there were many amongst them, known to Spaniards as Marranos, who continued to practice Judaism in secret. In the early 16th C a small community of Marrano merchants developed in London, where they were obliged to continue living under the guise of Spanish Christians. The community was broken up by deportations on several occasions over the next 150 years, but the authorities were never able to suppress it for long.

After Britain became a Republic under Oliver Cromwell in 1649, some of London's Marranos felt that the time was ripe to press for legal toleration of their faith. They had contacts with Menasseh ben Israel, a Rabbi living in Amsterdam, who in 1654 submitted a petition to Cromwell requesting that Jews be allowed to settle again in Britain. Although Cromwell supported the proposal, opposition from the Council of State prevented an agreement. However, after war broke out between Spain and England, and the property of Marranos in London came under threat, the Marranos decided to force the issue by openly declaring themselves to be 'Of the Hebrew nation and religion' and by making a plea for religious toleration. Their stratagem proved successful, and in June 1656 Cromwell agreed verbally to the toleration of Jews in Britain, an event known by British Jews as the Resettlement.

The Jewish community in London slowly expanded in the late 17th C and the early 18th C. At first most of the immigrants were Sephardic Jews, that is, Jews of Spanish and Portuguese origin, but they were soon out-numbered by Ashkenazi Jews, of Central, Eastern and Western European origin. Wide cultural and social differences existed between these two groups of immigrants. The Sephardim spoke Spanish or Portuguese, whereas the Ashkenazim spoke Yiddish, a Jewish language which is derived mainly from German and is written in Hebrew characters. The Sephardim formed a prosperous merchant community, whereas most of the Ashkenazim were poor, finding employment chiefly in the reconditioning and sale of old clothes or in peddling goods such as fruit, jewellery and knives. Social divisions between these two groups persisted well into the 19th C in Britain, and are still significant in some other parts of the world.

The number of Jews in Britain rose from about 7,000 in 1760 to about 65,000 in 1880. In 1881 the assassination of Tsar Alexander II sparked off anti-Semitic pogroms in Russia and Poland which set in train a massive westward emigration of Jews. Most were heading for the United States, but substantial numbers settled in Britain, some only because they lacked the money to continue across the Atlantic. By 1914 the Jewish population of Britain had risen to about 250,000. The vast majority of the new immigrants swelled the existing Jewish community in London's East End, where the manufacture of clothes and footwear provided the main sources of employment.

The last large wave of Jewish immigrants to Britain was in the 1930s, when about 70,000 Central European Jews fled from fascism. Today there are an estimated 350,000 Jews in Britain, of whom perhaps about 250,000 live in Greater London, most noticeably in the north and north-west of the city in districts such as Stamford Hill, Golders Green, Hendon, Finchley and Edgware.

'Inside Out'

Interview with Michael, a businessman in his late 30's and an Orthodox Jew, about his observance of the Jewish Sabbath . . .

"I'm not sure I'm deeply religious, but I deeply enjoy the Jewish way of life.

The Bible says 'you shall rest' on the Sabbath, and the Orthodox rabbis interpret that in a particular and specific way. You don't do any kind of work. You don't drive, you don't answer the telephone, you don't cook, you don't watch TV, you don't switch on the light. If you look at it theoretically, on the Shabbat (Sabbath) we're being asked to abstain from our mastery over nature. Six days of the week we bash nature, we take control of the world, and on one day, the Sabbath, we leave nature alone and we look at our spiritual selves and our family.

I welcome in the Sabbath with the Friday evening service at the synagogue. It's a very special service. It's good-bye to the working week, all the rubbish of the week's finished and there's 25 hours of peace coming on, so it's a very joyous, relaxed service.

When I come back from the synagogue, all the family are now together for the Friday night meal, which Jews have been observing for thousands of years. It's the most important meal of the week.

Before the meal my wife lights some candles. Bringing the light into the house is the Jewish mother's role, and we have a short service around that. Then, at the beginning of the meal, I sanctify the Sabbath by saying a blessing over wine in Hebrew and then drinking the wine. I cut the challa bread, which is, again, traditional, and symbolises the manna from heaven which was sent to feed the Jewish people after they'd left Egypt and were wandering in the wilderness.

It's a cliché, the centrality of the family in Jewish life, but it's a reality. Twentieth century living takes you away from the family, so the Friday night meal is the time to talk in a more relaxed fashion.

On Saturday, during the day, we have to read, to speak to our friends, to talk to each other. We have to find out who we are. In this street, I have several close relatives. In this block, I have several close friends. It's a very family-minded time, the Sabbath, and time for friends too.

Probably the Sabbath has greater meaning and greater purpose for twentieth century man than ever. Everyone involved in the mobile phone, hurry-hurry culture knows it's a nonsense. It they could only stand back from it, they would see that the extra 10% sales they've earned by taking the stress and shortening their life is a nonsense, but they can't step back from it. With the Sabbath we're forced to step back from it and consider the things which have greater value in life. That's the absolute magic of the Sabbath."

Interview with Sharon, a painter in her early 30's . . .

"If people ask me what I am I say I'm Jewish because it's important to have some roots. But you can't assume anything about what that means today, it's so dangerous to presume.

My parents aren't religious, not at all. They were in hiding from the Nazis during the war, and after what they went through it's hard to believe, to have faith. I went only once to synagogue, but I didn't see the point.

I came here from Israel in 1968 and lived in North London, but our family seemed very different to most English Jews in the area. Our experiences were very different. Other Jews in the area were much more materialistic than my parents, very geared to a certain type of success, and, at that time, quite blinded in their allegiance to Israel no matter what government was in power. I didn't join any Jewish clubs or anything and went to an ordinary comprehensive. What happened in the war is all quite close to my family, all those people who died in the camps, and it has affected me and my personality, but I respond without having to attach myself to a Jewish faith on a daily basis.

Once my grandmother died, we no longer observed the Sabbath at all. I don't observe Yom Kippur either. I feel really sorry about not observing those days and festivities. I think it's a beautiful thing as long as it doesn't impose. There's been a choice not to follow religion in our family, but tradition has gone out of the window too and that's very sad. I can always pick that up later in life though.

My current partner isn't Jewish. At one time in my life I made quite an effort to meet a Jewish man that I liked. I put aside a lot of time for it. But in the end I preferred the non-Jewish men I met.

What will I pass on to my children? That's hard to answer. In some ways I'm very detached from my Jewishness and I don't know how much difference it will make. I'll clarify how I stand with them and tell them all the family history because it's important to give your child confidence in their roots. I'd leave the choice of lifestyle up to them though. The choice is an individual choice.

But I'd like my children to read a few Jewish writers simply because they're brilliant works of art, and I'd also like to hand down some of my parents' attitudes, which are very Jewish. There's a closeness and trust in the family, supporting each other, unquestioningly. A feeling of belonging. That's lovely, and I want to pass that on."

THE CITY &
THE TOWER OF LONDON

The Medieval Settlement

The largest Jewish community in medieval Britain was in London, which at that time extended only over the area now known as the City, the financial district of modern London.

The location of the Jewish Quarter of medieval London is marked by the street called Old Jewry. The last synagogue in medieval London stood on the north-east corner of Old Jewry. In 1272 the building was confiscated by the authorities and given to the neighbouring chapel of the Friars Penitent. London's Jews were thenceforth obliged to worship in private houses.

Jews also lived in Milk Street, Wood Street and most notably in Gresham Street, where their presence is recorded in the name of The Church of St Lawrence Jewry. Founded in the 12th C, the church was rebuilt after the Great Fire of 1666 and is now the official church of the Corporation of London.

The Jewish Quarter was attacked by mobs on a number of occasions. The first time was on the day of Richard I's coronation in 1189. Jews and women were banned from attending the coronation festivities, but when a deputation of Jews arrived at the gates of Westminster Hall (now a part of the Houses of Parliament) bearing gifts for the King, a few of them were

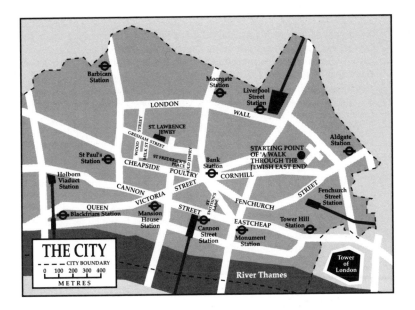

believed by the crowd to have slipped in to have a look. The whole deputation was then set upon by a mob. Some Jews managed to escape, but several were killed, and one Jew, Benedict of York, was only able to save his life by 'consenting' on the spot to becoming a Christian, whereupon he was rushed to a nearby church and baptised.

Rumours of events at Westminster quickly spread to the City of London, and the Jewry was set on fire by a mob. Many Jews found sanctuary in the Tower of London or with sympathetic Christian neighbours, but some were burnt alive in their houses or beaten to death in the streets. Thirty Jews were killed in all including a rabbi. The ringleaders of the mob were arrested and three were later hanged, though their punishment was for offences committed against Christians during the mayhem. As was often the case in medieval England, the judiciary were unwilling to come down too hard on people who had committed offences against Jews.

The Tower

Tower of London, EC3 (071-709 0765). Open from 9.30am to 5pm Monday to Saturday, 2pm to 5pm Sunday. Admission charge. The fortress of the Tower of London, which was begun in the reign of William I and was essentially complete by 1290, would have been very familiar to London's medieval Jews. Legally they came under the special protection of the Crown, and in London this responsibility was exercised by the Constable of the Tower of London, who administered justice between Christian and Jew and in certain cases between Jew and Jew.

The Tower of London loomed particularly large in the life of London's Jews in the troubled 13th C. On the one hand it was a place of sanctuary from rioting mobs and on the other hand a place of imprisonment if they were suspected of evading taxes or were unable to pay the levies that were all too frequently demanded by the Crown.

In 1210 all the wealthy Jews in England were imprisoned pending investigations into their financial affairs. Those who were found guilty of concealing transactions from the authorities were hanged or made to pay huge fines. A further fine was placed on the head of every single member of the Jewish community regardless of wealth, and as a result many of the poorer Jews were forced to leave the country.

As a precaution against mob violence, London's Jews took sanctuary in the Tower in 1220 on the occasion of Henry III's re-coronation, and again in 1236 for his wedding to Eleanor of Provence. During the rebellions against Henry between 1264 and 1267, the Jews were forced to take refuge in the Tower on several occasions, and in 1267 they took part in its defence against the rebels.

In 1272 some 600 Jews were imprisoned in the sub-crypt of St John's Chapel in the White Tower on suspicion of clipping the edges off coins and melting them down into bullion. Many of the accused were hanged and others expelled from the country, though Christians found guilty of similar offences received lighter sentences.

In 1290 a Christian judge called Henry de Bray was imprisoned in the Tower because he dared to protest against the decision to expel the Jews. He committed suicide in his cell.

London Folklore

On the expulsion of the Jews in 1290, one group of wealthy London Jews hired a ship in which to leave for France. However, when they reached Queenborough at the mouth of the Thames the ship was deliberately put aground on a sand bank and the Jews robbed and left to drown. The culprits were hanged after their return to London, convicted by their own boasts. The event has been remembered in London folklore, which tells that the water is always turbulent at the place where the Jews drowned, and that if you listen carefully over the spot their cries can still be heard.

The Modern Settlement

The Jews were prominent as merchants in the City from the earliest days of the Resettlement, but it was not until the early 19th C that they were again to play an important role in finance.

The first great Jewish financier since the Resettlement was Nathan Meyer Rothschild, who came to England from Frankfurt in 1797 and founded a bank in the City in 1804. Due to its excellent contacts on the Continent, the Rothschild bank was used by the British Government in the closing stages of the Napoleonic Wars to transfer subsidies to its allies abroad. The bank later raised money for the British Government to compensate slave owners on the abolition of slavery, to finance the Crimean war, and to buy up a large block of shares in the Suez Canal in 1875.

The Rothschilds used their influence to help the cause of Jewish emancipation, in which they had many willing allies in the City of London. In 1847 Baron Lionel de Rothschild, then head of the Rothschild Bank, became Britain's first Jewish MP when he was elected as the Liberal candidate for the City of London. At the time entry to parliament was dependent on taking a Christian oath, which Lionel refused to do. After being re-elected to his constituency five more times, the law was changed, and in 1858 Lionel was finally able to take his seat in the Commons on his own terms. In 1885 Lionel's son Nathaniel became the first Jew to sit in the

House of Lords. In 1890 the Jews finally achieved equality under the law in all respects.

Jewish bankers were a considerable force in the City in the latter half of the 19th C, but they declined in importance in the early 20th C when their private partnership banks were eclipsed by the development of larger central banks. Nevertheless, N M Rothschild and Sons Ltd is still an important financial concern in the City, and the Rothschild name itself continues to evoke 'wealth and glamour' even to those members of the public who have no idea of who the Rothschilds are or what they have done.

The headquarters of the Rothschild bank is at New Court, St Swithin's Lane, EC4, where a modern office building now occupies the site on which the bank was founded in 1804. Two busts in the foyer of the building are visible from the street through the large plate-glass windows. One is of Nathan Meyer Rothschild and the other of Lionel de Rothschild. Behind them hangs an 18th C tapestry which depicts Moses striking the rock to bring water for the Israelites.

Disraeli (see *page 142*) worked as an articled clerk at 6 Fredrick's Place (marked by a plaque), off Old Jewry.

THE JEWISH EAST END

In the late 17th C Jewish merchants established a Jewish Quarter on the eastern fringe of the City of London. From that small core the Jewish East End expanded eastwards over the centuries to take in Whitechapel, Spitalfields and Mile End.

The heyday of the Jewish East End was between 1880 and 1914, when tens of thousands of Yiddish-speaking Russian and Polish Jews settled in London. The Jewish population of the East End peaked at about 130,000 just before the First World War and then slowly declined between the wars as many Jews moved out to north and north-west London. Bombing and evacuation during the Second World War hastened movement from the area and there were few Jews left by the 1950s.

Even so, there is still much of interest to be seen in the old Jewish Quarter. Some Jewish businesses and institutions remain, and the Jewish presence has left a firm imprint on local history and custom. Walking through these streets today, the past does not seem so very distant:

'Though he had known them perfunctorily for years, the streets of the old Jewish quarter now fascinated him and day after day he returned, usually at early evening, to walk and walk through the dirty little alleys where the first great waves of Jewish immigrants had clustered towards the end of the last century. As he walked a curious strength of feeling, a kind of passionate affection went out from him to the mean, decrepit little houses . . . the very refuse in the gutters . . . Then he would catch sight of one of the old, Jewish, black garbed men, venerable and bearded, now so few in the quarter but occasionally to be seen, and his heart would lift with a kind of passionate nostalgia as if through such men he could still touch the certainty, the vitality, the rough, innocent, ambitious, swarming life of those early immigrants with so much before them of promise. He felt also a great pride.' - G Charles *The Crossing Point* (see **Literature,** *page 147*).

A Walk Through The Jewish East End

This walk is divided into two parts. Part One covers points (1) to (21),
Part Two covers points (22) to (26). The numbers in the text match with the
map provided and mark places where you should stop and read the text until
it advises you to move on. Part One of the walk is complete in itself, but if
you have a lot of energy to spare you may wish to continue onto Part Two,
which covers a much wider area but includes relatively few points of
interest.

How Long Will It Take? Part One should take about one-and-a-half hours
to complete, excluding any additional time you may spend looking around
Bevis Marks Synagogue, browsing in the market or eating in Bloom's
Restaurant. Part Two should take about 45 minutes at a brisk walk - and
there is a lot of walking to do.

When To Go. For Jews, Sunday is traditionally the main shopping day of
the week, as Jewish shops close all day Saturday (and early on Friday) in
observance of the Jewish Sabbath. Such has been the impact of Jewish
custom on the business life of Whitechapel and Spitalfields that even today
most non-Jewish shops in the area follow Jewish opening hours. The best
time therefore to go on this walk is on a Sunday, and particularly so in the
morning, when the Petticoat Lane Market is being held in Middlesex Street.
Conversely, Friday afternoons and Saturdays are to be avoided.

Prior Reading. In anticipation of your visit, you may be interested in trying
to catch some of the spirit of the old Jewish Quarter by reading Israel
Zangwill's *Children of the Ghetto* (1892), a brilliant documentary-style
novel which is quoted extensively in the following text. Wolf Mankowitz's
short story *A Kid for Two Farthings* (1953) and Arnold Wesker's play
Chicken Soup with Barley (1959) are also of interest. For autobiographical
tales try Emmanuel Litvinoff's *Journey Through A Small Planet* (1972) and
Harry Blacker's *Just Like it Was: Memoirs of the Middle East* (1974).

Part One

The walk begins at the intersection of Creechurch Lane and Bury Street,
where a plaque on the corner of the Cunard building marks the ***site of the
Creechurch Lane Synagogue (1),*** the first post-Resettlement synagogue in
Britain. In June 1656 Cromwell gave permission to Britain's clandestine
Jews to worship openly, and shortly afterwards the London community
hired a house on this spot for use as a synagogue. In so doing, they laid the
cornerstone for the Jewish East End.

Heading north up Creechurch Lane, take the first left down Bevis Marks.
Crossing over Heneage Lane, on the left there is an iron gate which leads
into the courtyard of the ***Bevis Marks Synagogue (2),*** now almost invisibly
sandwiched between towering office blocks. Purpose-built in 1701 after the
Creechurch Lane Synagogue became too small to cope with the growing
Jewish population, Bevis marks is the oldest surviving synagogue in Britain.
Now, as then, it is a Sephardic synagogue.

If you want to look around inside the synagogue, telephone 071-289 2573 to
arrange a convenient time for a visit, or alternatively go on a tour with
Historical Tours (081-668 4019), who include Bevis Marks in their walk
around the Jewish East End. In the interior, the elaborate branched candle-
holders which hang from the ceiling of the main hall strike a bold contrast
with an otherwise austere scene. Above the ground floor is the Ladies'
Gallery; following orthodox custom, the women worship separately from
the men.

At the eastern end of the hall is the ark, the focus of attention in every synagogue. It contains scrolls of the five books of Moses, which are taken out and read during Sabbath and festival services. The Bevis Marks' ark is made of wood in mock-classical style, and bears a Hebrew inscription which translates: 'Know before whom thou standest' . In front of the ark hangs a sanctuary lamp, which burns perpetually.

Sir Moses Montefiore (1784-1885), an eminent Jewish leader and philanthropist, was a member of the congregation at Bevis Marks. He sat in the front row next to the ark in seat number 354, which is now separated off from the rest of the row by an arm rest. Only Montefiore's descendants and the Lord Mayor of London are allowed to use this seat. The birth of Benjamin Disraeli (see *page 142*) was registered at Bevis Marks, where his father Isaac was a member of the congregation.

Before you leave it would be polite to make a donation to the synagogue funds.

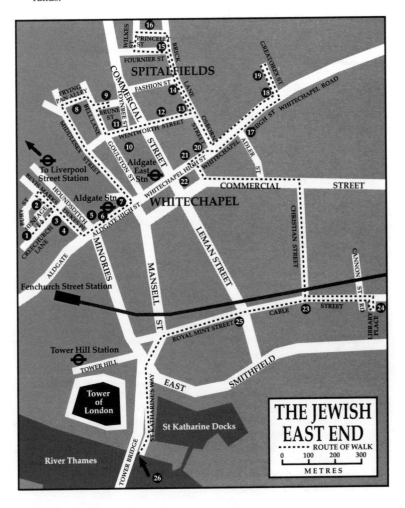

THE JEWISH
EAST END
• • • • ROUTE OF WALK
0   100   200   300
METRES

'Inside Out'

Interview with Reverend Bennaroch, the 'hazan' at Bevis Marks Synagogue . . .

"Originally, I am from Tangier in North Africa, and when I first came here, I was very much impressed with the decorum of this synagogue and its beautiful services.
We are the oldest synagogue in Britain and follow many old traditions. For example, during the services on the Sabbath and at festivals, many people in the congregation wear top hats. We are very British and we follow the tradition of England in that way. But also the first Jews to come to Britain were Spanish and Portuguese, and in our services we still do some prayers in these languages. Most of the congregation are descendants of Spanish and Portuguese Jews, although most don't understand the languages now.
In the past the Sephardim here did look down a bit on the Ashkenazim, the people who came from Poland and Russia. But we are all united now and some of my best friends are Ashkenazim.
I love my job. To be on the reading desk or to lead the congregation in prayer, to pray to the Almighty, is such a beautiful thing."

Retracing your steps back along Bevis Marks and over Creechurch Lane you enter **Dukes Place (3),** the centre of the early Jewish quarter, and now occupied by anonymous modern office buildings. Just past Creechurch Lane on the right is the **site of the Great Synagogue (4),** the first post-Resettlement Ashkenazi Synagogue in Britain. Opened in 1690, it was destroyed in 1941 by German bombs after centuries of service as Britain's best known synagogue. The site is marked by an inconspicuous plaque about 10 feet up on the wall of International House.
Leaving Dukes Place, and crossing over Houndsditch, on the corner is **St Botolph's Church, Aldgate (5),** which has made a positive response to the local Jewish presence of several centuries. The church is the headquarters of The Council for Christian-Jewish Understanding, an organisation which is concerned with bringing about mutual understanding between Christians and Jews – outside of any consideration of the issue of conversion. Inside the church you can buy pamphlets and booklets on such themes as *The Jewishness of Jesus* and *Our Debt to the Jews.*
Walking eastwards along **Aldgate High Street (6),** you are now leaving behind the early Jewish Quarter and entering Whitechapel, the centre of the 19th C and early 20th C Jewish Quarter. Standing in the shadow of the prosperous City of London, this poor, dilapidated district is in many respects little changed from when it was occupied by the Jews. Here there is much to spur the imagination in trying to bring to life the image of the Jewish East End that Zangwill presented so eloquently to his readers:
'Not here in our London Ghetto the gates and gabardines of the olden Ghetto of the Eternal City; yet no lack of signs external by which one may know it, and those who dwell therein. Its narrow streets have no speciality of architecture; its dirt is not picturesque. It is no longer the stage for the high-buskined tragedy of massacre and martyrdom; only for the obscurer, deeper tragedy that evolves from the pressure of its own inward forces, and

Petticoat Lane Market, Middlesex Street, at the turn of the century.

the long-drawn-out tragicomedy of sordid and shifty poverty. [Yet it is] a world which hides beneath its stony and unlovely surface an inner world of dreams, fantastic and poetic as the mirage of the Orient where they were woven, of superstitions grotesque as the cathedral gargoyles of the Dark Ages in which they had birth. And over all lie tenderly some streaks of celestial light from the face of the great Lawgiver.' – *Children of the Ghetto* (1892).

Continuing along Aldgate High Street, on the left you come to **Middlesex Street (7)** . This is the main shopping street of the Petticoat Lane Market, which is held here every Sunday morning, and, to a lesser extent, during the week in adjoining streets. Middlesex Street was in fact originally called Petticoat Lane, but was given its present name in 1830 as a result of prudish objections about having a street named after an item of underwear. In spite of the dictates of officialdom, the street has remained known locally as 'The Lane' up to the present day, and the market itself is still known universally by its original title.

Middlesex Street has been associated with the garment trade since the 16th C. Its original name of Petticoat Lane perhaps arose because of the production of petticoats here by Huguenot (French Protestant) silk weavers in the 17th C. Petticoat Lane Market, which has been in existence for at least 150 years, has probably always dealt in cheap clothing. The Jews, who dominated the London trade in second-hand clothes in the late 18th and early 19th C, played an important role in the development of the market, which was the first official Sunday-opening market in London. This influence is still evident today even though Jewish participation has waned considerably, in that the market is still closed on Saturdays and open on Sundays. It also closes for the holiest day of the Jewish year, Yom Kippur.

'Old clo' was the cry of many stallholders in Petticoat Lane Market until the turn of the 20th C, when the local tailoring trade pioneered the mass-production of cheap new clothes. Today the market is known primarily for its cheap new clothes, as well as clothes fabrics, footwear, leather ware, jewellery and toys. Few Jews now run stalls in the market, but a Jewish presence is still evident in some of the shops on Middlesex Street, which sport names such as Levy, Kossof, Cohen and Moscovitch.

In the late 19th C Middlesex Street was notable not only for its Sunday market, but also, as Zangwill observed, as 'the stronghold of hard-shell Judaism...into which no missionary dared set foot'. Indeed it was not unknown, he wrote, for the 'new fangled' rabbis of the middle class suburbs to be mistaken for Jewish converts to Christianity on missionary work, and to be met with a hail of vegetables and eggs.

Zangwill describes the ultra-orthodox Jews of the East End as 'Strange exotics in a land of prose, carrying with them through the paven highways of London the odour of Continental ghettos, and bearing in their eyes, through all the shrewdness of their glances, the eternal mysticism of the Orient, where God was born. Hawkers and pedlars, tailors and cigar-makers, cobblers and furriers, glaziers and cap-makers – this was in sum their life: to pray much and to work long . . . to eat not over-much and to 'drink' scarce at all; to beget annual children by chaste wives (disallowed them half the year), and to rear them not over-well; to study the Law and the prophets, and to reverence the Rabbinical tradition and the chaos of commentaries expounding it . . . to wear phylacteries and fringes, to keep the beard unshaven and the corner of the hair uncut; to know no work on the

Wentworth Street, Whitechapel, by Gustave Doré (London, 1872).

Sabbath and no rest on week-day.' – *Children of the Ghetto* (1892).

Walking up Middlesex Street and turning into Frying Pan Alley, the site of the *Jews' Free School (8)*, which operated here between 1821 and 1939, is marked by a large office building called Rodwell House. At the turn of the century the school was the largest in the British Empire, boasting 4300 pupils and 100 teachers. Israel Zangwill (see *page 146*) was a pupil, and later a teacher, here. It was while he was teaching here that he published his first novel, *Children of the Ghetto*, most of whose action takes place locally. Another pupil was the millionaire Barney Barnato, whose life could not have been more perfectly tailored to fit the phrase 'rags to riches'. Born the son of an old clothes dealer in Middlesex Street in 1852, Barnato went on to become one of the founders in South Africa of De Beers Consolidated Mines, a company which still dominates the diamond markets of the world today.

The school colours of blue and gold were adopted from the Rothschilds, who had a long charitable association with the school. The Rothschilds, as Zangwill wrote, were 'a magic name' to the poor of the Jewish East End.

Passing through Frying Pan Alley and turning right down Bell Lane, on your left is Brune Street. Half way down this street is a building which proudly announced its business in lettering engraved prominently on its frontage: *'Soup Kitchen for the Jewish Poor' (9).* The building is dated 1902 and also 5662, the equivalent year by the Jewish calendar. One of the many attempts by Jewish philanthropists to improve the lot of the Jewish poor, it closed down only in 1992.

Walking back into Bell Lane and continuing southwards, you come to the *junction (10) of Wentworth Street and Goulston Street,* the main subsidiary branches of Sunday's Petticoat Lane Market. Unlike Middlesex Street, a market is also held in these streets from Monday to Friday. You are now standing at what was the heart of the Jewish Quarter at the turn of the century. At that time the population of these and neighbouring streets would have been almost exclusively Jewish, and the walls and hoardings would have been covered in Yiddish posters advertising local events. On Jewish festivals and holidays Goulston Street was the location of a poultry market, which Zangwill described as 'a pandemonium of caged poultry, clucking and quacking, and cackling and screaming'. The birds would be bought alive and then killed in accordance with Jewish religious law by an official slaughterer for a small fee.

'Inside Out'

Interview with Anna, an elderly Jewish woman who used to act in the Yiddish Theatre in the East End, and still lives in the area . . .

"I was born in Rumania, and our family spoke Yiddish. Yiddish is a German dialect, plus a lot of Hebrew plus the language where the Jews happened to be settled. The Rumanian Jews used a lot of Rumanian in their Yiddish, and when I first arrived in England I found that the Jews who spoke Yiddish here used a lot of English in their Yiddish.

At one time there were four Yiddish theatres in the East End of London. Between the two world wars we're talking about, when the East End was a Jewish district and many of the immigrants could hardly speak any English or understand it. There was no television in those days, so for the working class people of the area the Yiddish theatre was their place of entertainment, where they used to go after a hard week's work to be entertained and to forget all their troubles for a few hours.

What was it like? The Yiddish theatre had a flavour of gefilte fish, a flavour of strudel, a flavour of roast chicken, a flavour of cholent. It was frequented by the same people every week, they sat in the same seat in the same row. Because we were a rep company, we changed the repertoire each week.

A Yiddish play had to have everything in it, three for the price of one. My father, God rest his soul, said to me when I was still a very little girl, 'remember my child', he said, 'if you will have to make a living working in the Yiddish theatre, you will have to give your audience what they love, that is, a song, a laugh and a tear, and you have to have all three ingredients in the one play'.

Of course, there's no Yiddish theatre now, and I am the last of the Mohicans. The way of life then was different. The striving to keep up with the Joneses was low key in those days, you were pleased with the little you had, whereas nowadays you've never got enough. Am I right? In those days everyone helped one another, and if there was a dispute you could go to the rabbi for his counsel. It's a selfish society today, but young people can't see that."

Walking east along Wentworth Street, on the corner of the junction with Toynbee Street is the Jewish delicatessen *Mark's of the Lane (11),* at 57-59 Wentworth Street (071-247 1400/4294). It is open from 6.30am to 4pm Monday to Saturday, 6.30am to 3pm Sunday.

The street cries of Jewish women who sold beigels were once a notable feature of Petticoat Lane Market. Today you can hear only the occasional cry of 'beigels'' on a Sunday morning, and that comes from Mark's delicatessen. You can also buy hot salt beef sandwiches and latkes here, and all are recommended. Mark's is a well-stocked shop, and on Sunday morning it is always crowded with expatriate Jewish East Enders.

Zangwill described Wentworth Street of the 1880s as: 'The noisy market street, where serried barrows flanked the reeking roadway exactly as of old, and where Esther trod on mud and refuse and babies. Babies! they were everywhere; at the breasts of unwashed women, on the knees of grandfathers smoking pipes; playing under the barrow, sprawling in the gutters and the alleys. All the babies' faces were sickly and dirty'.

The bad housing and unhealthy conditions in which poor Jews lived in the East End were a matter of concern to many of London's wealthy Jews. If you cross over Commercial Street and continue along Wentworth Street, on the left you will see a relic of their concern in a large free-standing *arch (12)* , which now serves as an entrance to a modern housing estate. It is marked with the words *'Erected by the Four Per Cent Industrial Dwellings Company 1886'.* This company was set up by wealthy Jews to finance the construction of such buildings as the Charlotte de Rothschild Model Dwellings (opened in 1887), which stood beyond this arch until the early 1980s. The arch now leads on to a small estate of modern model dwellings erected by the Toynbee Housing Association. The new estate stands on the site of Flower and Dean Street, the birthplace in 1908 of Abraham

Sapperstein, who emigrated to the States in the 1920s, where he founded the famous Harlem Globetrotters basketball team of New York.

Turning left out of Wentworth Street, you enter **Brick Lane (13)**, the heartland of the East End Bengali community. The district of Spitalfields, which lies to the north of Whitechapel, has been noted for its immigrant population for over 300 years, having been occupied in turn by Huguenots, Irish Catholics, Jews, and since the early 1960s, Bengalis.

Walking north along Brick Lane, on your left is **Fashion Street (14)**. Israel Zangwill grew up in Fashion Street, as did Arnold Wesker and Wolf Mankowitz. At its eastern end Fashion Street contains a number of wholesale outlets for local clothing manufacturers. Spitalfields has been a manufacturing centre for the garment trade since the 18th C, and every major immigrant group to settle in the area has played a prominent role in the business. Yesterday it was the Jews, today it is the Bengalis.

There are numerous workshops in the vicinity of Brick Lane in which clothing is manufactured. The working conditions today are often little changed from the turn of the century, when tailoring was the most important source of employment for local Jews. Hours were long (frequently 12 to 14 hours a day), pay was low, and the premises dirty and unhealthy.

Rudolph Rocker, a leading figure in the local Jewish anarchist movement at the turn of the century, was deeply involved in the struggles of the Jewish tailors to improve their conditions of work. This was his view of their basic problems:

'The clothing industry in the East End was run by hundreds of small master tailors who were sub-contractors for the big firms in the City and the West End. In order to get the contract they underbid each other mercilessly, thus creating their own hell. They passed that hell on of course to their workers . . . The new immigrants, who had just arrived from Poland or Russia or Rumania and had to earn their bread, went to these small sweat shops to learn to be pressers or machinists. . .This lower grade of worker was employed and paid not by the master tailor but by the presser or machinist. It suited the master tailor because it placed responsibility of driving the workers on the upper grade of the workers themselves.'

Continuing along Brick Lane, on the corner of Fournier Street stands a mosque, the **London Jamme Masjid (15)**. This was erected as a Huguenot Church in 1744, was the headquarters of a Christian evangelical society to the Jews between 1801 and 1892, and housed Spitalfields Great Synagogue from 1898 to 1965. During the heyday of anarchism in the East End between 1880 and 1914, Jewish anarchists organised atheistic celebrations of their own to coincide with Yom Kippur, the holiest day on the Jewish calendar. The anarchists further demonstrated their contempt for religion by marching up Brick Lane to the Great Synagogue ostentatiously smoking (reckoned a great sin on a holy day) and eating ham sandwiches (considered offensive in the extreme because of the Orthodox ban on eating pork). Such provocation would often lead to trouble, and in 1904 there was a riot outside the Great Synagogue in which several anarchists were badly beaten up by their religious brethren.

There are many decaying old houses in the vicinity which give some flavour of the old Jewish Quarter. It was close by to this spot that a Government survey in 1885 found a house with nine rooms that had an average of seven people in each room, and only one bed per room. The inhabitants, the report said, were 'all respectable people.' Even today you may be surprised to find residents going in and out of buildings that look completely derelict. Since the mid 1980's some of the period houses have been restored and Fournier Street, in particular, is once more a fashionable address.

Turning down Fournier Street, right into Wilkes Street, and right again down Princelet Street, at number 19 is the *Heritage Centre, Spitalfields (16)*, which was once the United Friends Synagogue. The building is being generally restored for use as a multi-cultural resource centre, and there are plans for public displays relating to the various ethnic groups who have lived in the locality. There isn't that much to see yet, but if you do want to look around inside the centre, telephone 071-377 6901 to arrange a convenient time for a visit.

Walking all the way back down Brick Lane, and past Wentworth Street, you enter Osborn Street. Turning left at the end of Osborn Street, and walking along Whitechapel High Street, on your right is *Adler Street (17)*, named after Chief Rabbi Hermann Adler (1839-1911). Approaching the East London Mosque on your right, and reaching Greatorex Street on your left, you are entering the *Whitechapel Road (18)*. In the late 19th C this street was the location for the open-air hiring of labour for the clothing workshops, an event known contemptuously as the 'hazer mark' (the pig market). Whitechapel Road itself was known amongst Jews as 'monkeys' parade' because of the Jewish teenagers who promenaded here in the evenings and on the Sabbath. Dressed in their best clothes, they often strolled along four or six abreast, sometimes singing the latest popular songs.

Turning left down Greatorex Street, 50 yards down the road on the left is *The Kosher Luncheon Club (19)* at Morris Kasler Hall, 13 Greatorex Street. Open from 12 noon to 3pm Monday to Friday, it is the last relic of the cheap eating houses set up to cater for poor Jews in the East End, and although it has the look of a club, it is open and friendly to all comers. Here one can still get a sense of the old spirit of the Jewish East End. Fish is the speciality.

Retracing your steps down Whitechapel High Street, continue past Osborn Street to the *Whitechapel Library (20)*. Over the stairway on the first floor hangs a portrait of Rudolph Rocker, 'libertarian philosopher, trade union organiser, and leader of the Jewish immigrant poor'. Of German origin, Rudolph Rocker was not in fact Jewish himself, though he was able to speak Yiddish. The reference reading room was once a meeting place for Jewish intellectuals. Isaac Rosenberg, the First World War poet, and Israel Zangwill the novelist were among visitors here. The Library functioned as a first aid post on 4 October 1936 (see below), when many a cracked head was nursed on the premises.

Another 50 yards down the road is *Bloom's Restaurant (21)* at 90 Whitechapel High Street. This is indeed 'The most famous kosher restaurant in Britain', as is proclaimed with all due modesty on the restaurant front, but that does not mean it is the best. You may wish to eat a meal here, or just buy a salt beef sandwich at their take-away counter.

Incidentally, it was in the East End that the word 'nosh' was adopted from the Jews and brought into the English language as a slang word for food. In its original use, in Yiddish, it means a tasty titbit of food and is derived from the German 'naschen' - a snack between meals. Non-Jewish East Enders were also so struck by Jewish religious dietary laws that by the mid-19th C, the phrase 'is it kosher' had become part of cockney slang, though with the meaning: 'Is it fair/genuine/proper?'

Mural depicting 'The Battle of Cable Street', St George's Town Hall, Cable Street.

Part Two

Leaving Bloom's, you look out onto a traffic intersection that was once known, before its redevelopment, as *Gardiners Corner (22)*. This was a key rallying point on Sunday 4 October 1936, when a large number of local inhabitants (estimates range from 10,000 to 100,000!), both Jews and gentiles, went on to the streets to prevent a march through the area by uniformed members of the British Union of Fascists.

Over the previous days there had been many preparations to oppose the march. Pavements and walls were chalked and whitewashed with the Spanish Republican slogan 'They shall not pass', and loudspeaker vans toured the streets appealing to local people to rally against the fascists. By the Sunday morning first aid posts were ready with doctors and nurses in attendance, legal aid was prepared for people who might be arrested, and a network of runners and telephones was poised for action.

By late Sunday morning Gardiners Corner had been blocked by a huge crowd. They were confronted by many of the thousands of policemen who had been mobilised to keep the roads clear for the fascist march. In his autobiography *Out of the Ghetto*, Joe Jacobs describes the scene: 'Around midday, the police were beginning to show their hand. There were skirmishes all over the place . . . Young people were perched on all the lampposts and other vantage points, displaying posters and directing the crowds towards the weak spots in the front with the police. The crowds were roaring 'They shall not pass'. The police were making periodic baton charges, both mounted and on foot, in an effort to keep the crowds back . . . As anyone was grabbed by the police there were determined efforts made by others to secure their release'.

The police proved unsuccessful in their efforts to clear a route for the march. By the early afternoon, as the Morning Post described, '2500 fascists had formed themselves going into a procession along Royal Mint Street, isolated and closely guarded by police. In every surrounding street dense crowds were being held back by cordons of mounted and foot police'.

It was clear that the fascists were not going to be able to march past Gardiners Corner, so an alternative route was chosen further to the south, passing along Cable Street. When the news filtered through to the protesters of this change of plan, thousands of demonstrators streamed down from Gardiners Corner towards Cable Street.

Following the path taken by the protesters, cross over into Commercial Road, turn right into Christian Street, and walk down to the junction with *Cable Street (23)*. As the police advanced up Cable Street to clear away through for the fascists, they were met with barricades manned by missile-throwing crowds. One barricade was erected close to where you now stand, and it was defended by people gathered on the railway bridge at the end of Christian Street, who showered the police with milk bottles. The police were also put under fire from the upper windows of the terraced houses which then lined both sides of the street, and found kitchen rubbish and even furniture being thrown down on top of them. The barrage was so fierce that a handful of policemen actually surrendered to the protesters, who confiscated their truncheons.

Turning left down Cable Street, and continuing across Cannon Street, off Library Place on the side of St George's Town Hall, 236 Cable Street, is a *large mural depicting the 'Battle of Cable Street' (24)*. Designed and painted mainly by David Binnington, the mural was started in 1978 and finally completed in 1983 following a long delay after it was vandalised by latter-day fascists. It is without doubt one of London's best public murals, capturing the drama of the original events with a stirring, dynamic design.

Retracing your steps down Cable Street and past Christian Street, you come to the *junction (25) with Royal Mint Street and Dock Street*. This was the point at which the fascists 'did not pass'. Although the police fought their way some distance up Cable Street, the fascists never set foot in it. The Police Commissioner decided it would be foolish to allow the march to continue through the East End and the leader of the fascists, Sir Oswald Mosley, was obliged to lead the march west through the empty streets of the City to the Embankment, where the marchers dispersed.

In his autobiography, Joe Jacobs describes the protesters' reaction when they heard that the march had been cancelled: 'As the news spread, cheers could be heard all over the area and into the surrounding streets some distance from the battleground itself. The air was full of sound. People shouting slogans: "They did not pass"; "They shall not pass". As the police withdrew their forces from the major points of conflict, all the cafes and other public places were full of laughing people swapping stories . . . There were many people bandaged and bloody. The debris left by the fight was everywhere'.

That October Sunday is of some significance historically in that it was the only occasion in pre-war Europe in which large numbers of ordinary Jews and gentiles (as opposed to political activists) joined together to stage mass physical resistance to fascism. The events of that day also brought about changes in British law, for the Government reacted by bringing in the Public Order Act of 1937, which banned political groups from wearing uniforms in public.

Crossing Leman Street into Royal Mint Street, and down into St Katherine's Way, from the jetty at the end of the street you can see *Irongate Stairs (26),* a flight of stone steps which rises out of the Thames directly beneath Tower Bridge. Many Jewish immigrants docked here in the late 19th and early 20th C and first set foot in Britain on these steps.

In the anthology *Living London* (1902), the writer describes the arrival of Jewish immigrants at these steps . . . 'Let us meet a ship from Hamburg, laden with men and women who will presently be working in the dens of the sweaters. It is a pouring wet day. The rain is coming down in torrents, and one has to wade through small lakes and rivulets of mud to reach the narrow pathway leading to Irongate Stairs, where the immigrant passengers of the vessel lying at anchor in the Thames are to land. This is a river steamer, and so the wretched immigrants are taken off in small boats and rowed to the steps. Look at them, the men thin and hungry-eyed, the women with their heads bare and only a thin shawl over their shoulders, the children terrified by the swaying of the boat that lies off waiting to land when the other boats have discharged their load! What must these people feel as they get their first glimpse of London? All they can see is a blurred and blotted line of wharves and grim buildings, and when at last they land it is in a dark archway crowded with loafers and touts all busily trying to confuse them, to seize their luggage, almost fighting to get possession of it. Fortunately Mr. Somper, the Superintendent of the Poor Jews' Temporary Shelter, is here also. As the scared and shivering foreigners step ashore he speaks to them either in Yiddish or Lettish, and finds out if they have an address to go to. Most of them have something written on a piece of paper which they

Gerrard Street, Chinatown.

Waiters in Chinatown.

Cake shop in Chinatown.

Notting Hill Carnival.

Turkish Cypriot Café/Chinatown.

Cypriot Shop, Harringay.

Notting Hill Carnival.

Italian Procession, Clerkenwell.

Italian Procession, Clerkenwell.

produce creased and soiled from a pocket. It is the address of a friend or relative, of a boarding house. Others have no idea where they are going. Many, asked what money they have, confess to twenty or thirty shillings as their entire fortune. Others at once begin to unfold a tale of robbery at the frontier, and moan that they have scarcely anything. These are at once taken charge of and housed in the shelter until their friends can be found for them. For most of them have friends "somewhere". It may be a brother, it may be only a fellow townsman or fellow villager, who came to London years ago. In the shelter they are taken care of with their money and their "baggage"

Jewish immigrants landing at Irongate Stairs at the beginning of this century.

until their friends can be communicated or employment obtained.'

Our walk ends here, though if you still have any surplus energy, you may wish to make a visit to The Tower of London on the other side of the bridge. Regular walks around the Jewish East End are organised by Historical Tours (081-668 4019), City Walks (071-700 6931) and All About London (071-607 5026). The London Museum of Jewish Life (see *page 136)* also occasionally organises guided walks.

GOLDERS GREEN

Golders Green was one of the last Jewish districts to be established in London, acquiring a permanent synagogue only in 1922. Today it is the area of London most closely identified with the Jewish middle classes. It is also notable for its large Orthodox community, whose men folk are readily identifiable by the skull-caps ('yarmulkes') or dark trilby-style hats with which they keep their heads covered in observance of their faith.

There are many things of Jewish interest in Golders Green, but bear in mind that they are scattered over a wide area which is not particularly well served by public transport. The Jewish presence is most evident in the shopping parade on the stretch of Finchley Road between Portsdown Avenue in the south and Alberon Gardens in the north.

Local newsagents stock the British-published weekly newspaper *The Jewish Chronicle.* On the front page of its first edition in 1841 it made the appeal: 'Readers, will you be the gardener, and make us the fruit tree?' The Jewish Chronicle has been cultivated with some care, and it is now the oldest Jewish newspaper in the world.

'Inside Out'

Interview with Fiona, aged 17, about Jewish teenage life in North London . . .

"The main social scene in North London now is round Golders Green. It used to be Edgware but a lot of non-Jews came down and picked on us and there was a lot of fights and police down there. I think it's more secure here in Golders Green, because there's lots of Jewish restaurants and Jewish places and lots of Orthodox people round here.

Me and my friends go down to Golders Green every Thursday and Saturday. Because we're Jewish, we're not allowed out on Friday night, it's Shabbat (the Sabbath), so instead of Friday nights, we go out on Thursday nights. So it's like extending the weekend a bit longer, but minus the Friday. The scene here is more reform Jews, not Orthodox.

We hang out in Golders Green road, and lots of people there know each other because they went to the Jewish Free School and grew up together. You get some girls hanging out who we call *becs.* How can I put it? I personally think a bec is a Jewish princess, someone who's spoilt by their parents and drives fast cars in the middle of Golders Green and Edgware. I think the word comes from the name Rebecca, but I'm not sure. But it's a word that everyone uses. It's

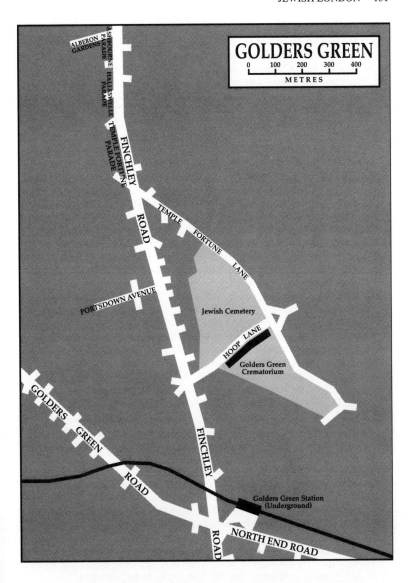

GOLDERS GREEN

0   100   200   300   400
METRES

ALBERON GARDENS
ASHBOURNE PARADE
HALLSWELLE PARADE
TEMPLE PARADE
TEMPLE FORTUNE PARADE
FINCHLEY ROAD
TEMPLE FORTUNE LANE
PORTSDOWN AVENUE
Jewish Cemetery
HOOP LANE
Golders Green Crematorium
FINCHLEY ROAD
GOLDERS GREEN ROAD
Golders Green Station (Underground)
NORTH END ROAD

like an expression, oh she's a bec, oh look at her with all the
flaunting jewellery and the mini skirts and designer clothes. They
have like a three hour conversation about boys on the phone and
then come out and talk about it again!"

*Interview with Pippa, a nurse in her early thirties, who belongs to
an Israeli folk dance troupe in North London . . .*

"The dances and the costumes we use are taken from the early East
European pioneers who went to Israel in the 1920s. It's more than

exercise. It's a way of identifying with the Jewish culture and the Jewish Israeli culture as opposed to the Jewish religious culture.

Quite a few Jewish kids go to youth clubs when they're young and get the fun of summer camps and weekends away. When I left my youth club I was looking for something to take over and someone suggested Israeli dancing. I'm still coming ten years later.

As the years have progressed, the other things I used to do within the Jewish community have lessened and this is virtually the only thing that I now do on a regular basis. It's where I meet Jewish friends. As well as dancing together, we do other things together. We often celebrate Jewish festivals together or go to Israel together and spend Friday nights together. It's more than just dancing. Dancing breaks down the stereotypes, because people I don't think normally associate Jewish people with such active and striking activity. When we go out to perform in the non-Jewish community it really makes people think in a different way about Israel and Jewish people.

It's quite difficult for minorities to exist in a wider culture. I've always had double pulls, double ties, double commitments, double responsibilities. At school I wasn't mixing with Jews all the time and there were lots of pulls to go out on the Sabbath, to go to parties on holidays, to eat non-kosher food. All the time you've got to weigh up where you stand on these issues.

It's an ongoing battle for many of us about whether to settle in Israel. I mean you've got the sunshine, which is lovely, you've got a lot of very energetic people in a very alive country, and you've got the Jewish identity all the time. You don't have to think about observing the holy days, or not eating kosher food, because it's just not there and everything happens fairly automatically."

SOUTHERN GOLDERS GREEN

Shopping

Jerusalem the Golden, 146a Golders Green Road, NW11 (081-455 4960, 458 7011). Open from 9.30am to 6pm Sunday to Thursday, 9.30am to 5pm Friday. Israeli arts and crafts, Israeli folk music, Jewish religious music, books and prints on Jewish themes, religious requisites and silver Kiddush cups.

Merrorah Print and Gift Shop, 227 Golders Green Road, NW11 (081-458 8289). Open from 9.30am to 6pm Monday to Friday (except early Sabbath closing Friday), 9.45am to 1pm Sunday. Books, music cassettes.

Shopping (Food and Drink)

Cousin's Bagel Bakery, 109 Golders Green Road, NW11 (081-201 9694). Open 8am to midnight Monday to Thursday, 9am to 3pm Friday and Saturday. Beigels, pretzels and other Jewish speciality breads.

Sussers, 113a Golders Green Road, NW11 (081-455 4336). Open from 9am to 6pm Monday to Wednesday, 11.30am to 3pm Sunday, 9am to 8pm Thursday, 8am to Sabbath early closing on Friday. Kosher wines and liqueurs from Israel, U.S.A. and Europe. Polish Vodka.

The Jewish penicillin (see page 139): notice in the window of a Golders Green kosher butcher.

COLDS or COUGHS?

PRESCRIPTION....

A HOT PLATE OF
CHICKEN SOUP!

Carmelli's Bakery, 128 Golders Green Road, NW 11 (081-455 2074). Open from 12 noon to 12 midnight Sunday to Friday, (except early closing Friday afternoon). Most popular Jewish bakery in the area. Beigels etc.

Europa Country Market, 136-140 Golders Green Road, NW11 (081-455 3595/3289). Open from 9am to 10pm Monday to Sunday. Now a member of the Europa chain, most customers are Jewish and the supermarket specialises in Kosher food and drink. There is a good fresh fish section.

Grodzinski, 223 Golders Green Road, NW11 (081-458 3654). Open from 7am to 8pm Sunday to Friday (except early closing Friday afternoon). Also open after the Sabbath on Saturday evening.

Kosher King Supermarket, 235 Golders Green Road, NW11 (081-455 1429). Open from 8am to 11pm Sunday to Friday (except early closing Friday afternoon). All produce is strictly Kosher.

Kay's Delicatessen, 2 Princes Parade, Golders Green Road, NW11 (081-458 3756). Open from 9am to 10pm Sunday to Friday (except early Sabbath closing Friday). A general delicatessen but specialising in Jewish food.

Eating Out

For further information on the restaurants and snack bars listed below, see *page 141*.

Bloom's, 130 Golders Green Road.

Amor's Take-away, 8a Russell Parade, Golders Green Road, NW11.

GOLDERS GREEN CREMATORIUM AND THE JEWISH CEMETERY

Golders Green Crematorium, Hoop Lane, NW11 (081-455 2374). Open from 9am to 5pm Monday to Sunday. Sigmund Freud (see *page 141*) was cremated here, as was Israel Sieff, the Marks and Spencer magnate and prominent Zionist. Their ashes are housed in the Ernest George Mausoleum. Call into reception on your arrival at the Crematorium, as you may need a key to enter the Mausoleum and you will certainly save a lot of time in locating Freud's ashes if you seek guidance here first. The Mausoleum was cold, sombre and rather eerie on the winter's afternoon on which I made my visit. Each room contains dozens of cinerary urns and caskets, but once you have found the correct room the location of Freud's ashes is obvious, surrounded as it is by many well-kept flowers and plants. Freud's ashes, together with those of his wife, are contained in his favourite Greek urn, which stands on a small column. On the shelves behind the vase stand caskets containing the ashes of his daughter Anna and his son Oliver. In the adjacent area, close to the connecting doorway, a plaque marks the casket containing the ashes of Sieff.

Jewish Cemetery, Hoop Lane, NW11 (situated directly across the road from the Crematorium). Open from 9am to 6pm (summer), 9am to dusk (winter) Sunday to Friday. Closed Jewish holidays.

The cemetery was founded in 1895. In its eastern section are the tombstones of Sephardic Jews, which are inscribed with names such as Sassoon, Mercado and Henriques. These tombstones are flat, and from a distance look much like a huge collection of stone coffins laid end to end. Sephardic Jews are traditionally buried with their feet pointing towards Jerusalem, but there is a distinct difference in the orientation taken by the older and newer tombstones in this cemetery. If we assume that the newer tombstones have been correctly orientated, then the older ones are pointing rather more towards the direction of Mecca!

In the western section of the cemetery are the tombstones of Reform Jews, which are upright, as in Christian cemeteries. Both Ashkenazi and Sephardic Jews are buried in this section, but Ashkenazi names, such as Stein, Strasberg and Mendilov, are predominant. Lord Leslie Hore-Belisha (see *page 146*) of Belisha-beacon fame is buried here. Ask at the gatehouse if you want to find his grave.

NORTHERN GOLDERS GREEN

Shopping

Aisenthal, 11 Ashbourne Parade, Finchley Road, NW11 (081-455 0501). Open from 9am to 6pm Monday to Friday (except Friday early closing), Sunday 9.30am to 1.15pm. Jewish bookshop, mainly English-language, some Hebrew. Also stocks music from Israel and Jewish religious music.

Shopping (Food and Drink)

Northern Stores, 722 Finchley Road, NW 11 (081-455 3590). Open from 8.45am to 6.30pm Sunday to Thursday, 8.45am to 2pm Friday. Kosher grocers and delicatessen.

Froheims's, 1095-7 Finchley Road, NW11 (081-455 9848). Open from 8am to 5pm Monday, 8am to 6pm Tuesday to Thursday, 8am to 12.30pm Friday and Sunday. Kosher butchers. Excellent sausage counter.

Moshe Israeli Food and Delicatessen, 1099 Finchley Road, NW11 (081-455 3611). Open from 8am to 7pm Monday to Friday (except early closing Friday), 8am to 7pm Sunday. Jewish groceries, including many Israeli products. Good for snacks and wines.

Sam Stoller, 28 Temple Fortune Parade, Finchley Road, NW11(081-458 1429). Open from 8am to 1pm Monday, 7am to 5pm Tuesday to Thursday, 7am to 4pm Friday. A kosher fishmongers, so they don't stock shellfish, or fish without scales such as eels or skate. They do stock Israeli carp and schmaltz (pickled) herrings.

Platters, 10 Halleswelle Parade, Temple Fortune, Finchley Road, NW11

(081-455 7345). Open from 8.30am to 5pm Monday to Friday, 8.30am to 5pm Saturday, 8.30am to 2pm Sunday. Delicatessen.

Daniels Bagel Bakery, 13 Halleswelle Parade, Temple Fortune, Finchley Road, NW11 (081-455 5826). Open from 7am to 9pm Sunday to Friday (except early Sabbath closing Friday). Kosher bakers.

Eating Out

See *page 141* for further details on ***Marcus's,*** 4 Halleswelle Parade, Temple Fortune, Finchley Road, NW11.

STAMFORD HILL ⸺⸺⸺⸺⸺⸺⸺⸺⸺⸺⸺⸺⸺

Stamford Hill is notable for its large population of ultra-orthodox Jews known as 'Hasidim'. The men are very conspicuous in their black eighteenth century frock coats topped by black hats. The women are less conspicuous. They dress modestly, and though you probably wouldn't guess it, they all wear wigs, as they believe that only their husbands should see their real hair.

The Hasidim have their origins in 18th C Poland when a charismatic religious leader, Ba'al Shem Tov, led a mystical and ecstatic movement which emphasised closeness to God. It attracted rich and poor devotees with its emphasis on a non-intellectual relationship with God and adherence to strictly defined rules for life.

Various sects grew up in Poland, Russia and Hungary, each taking the name of their birthplace - Belz, Sadigor, Satmar, Lubavitch. The kind of clothing worn by the nobility in 18th C Poland became their traditional dress, and their headwear distinguishes one sect from another.

The first language of the Hasidim is Yiddish, and they are the only community of Jews in Britain who have retained this ancestral tongue. All of the community are also fluent in Hebrew and English.

The Hasidim lead a very conservative, very traditional life. Families are very large, divorce is extremely rare, and men and women are not allowed to mix together unless they are married or are related. Theirs is a close-knit world in which family life has changed little down the centuries. Very few Hasidim ever leave the community, and their life is one in which they purposely have very little contact with non-Jews, and even with other less orthodox Jews.

The Hasidim manage their own community, and the appointed authorities give legal judgements on all inter-community matters. These are regarding as binding on all members. It is considered unforgivable to bring the established law of England into inter-community affairs, such as a dispute between two different parties.

The commercial centre of Stamford Hill is at the cross-roads of Stamford Hill and Amhurst Park.

The Hebrew Book and Gift Centre, 18 Cazenove Road, N16 (081-254 3963, 081-802 4567). Open from 10am to 6pm Monday to Thursday, 10am to 1pm Friday and Sunday. Religious literature in Hebrew, English and Yiddish, plus religious music on LP and cassette, and religious requisites. Most of the customers are Hassidic Jewish men.

Ross Bakeries, 84 Stamford Hill, N6 (081-806 4002). Open 8am to 6.30pm Monday to Thursday, 8am to 4pm Friday and Sunday. Closed Saturdays.

Moses Supermarket, 182 Stamford Hill, N16 (081-800 1883). Open from 8am to 7pm Sunday to Thursday (except to 2pm Friday), 7am to 4pm Sunday. Large Jewish supermarket.

OTHER PLACES TO VISIT ————————

The Jewish Museum, Woburn House, Tavistock Square, WC1 (071-388 4525). Open from 10am to 4pm Tuesday to Thursday, 10am to 1pm Friday and Sunday (except to 4pm Friday in summer). Closed Jewish and public holidays. Admission charge.

Elaborately-fashioned Jewish ritual art and antiques make up the bulk of the items on display in this small museum. The significance and use of such items as the Chanukah lamp, circumcision bench and illustrated marriage contracts are explained in two ten-minute audio-visual presentations that can be run at your request by the attendant. One presentation takes the viewer through the festivals of the Jewish year, and the other through Jewish life 'From the cradle to the grave'.

Some exhibits illustrate Jewish history in Britain. These include 13th C wooden tallies given to Jews as receipts by the Royal Exchequer, a portrait of Rabbi Menassah ben Israel, early 19th C porcelain figures of a Jewish peddler and an old-clothes man.

Museum Shop. Prints, postcards and books (see also *page 137* for details of the *Jewish Memorial Council Bookshop,* which is in the same building). Also stocks replicas of a limited selection of objects from the Museum, including a Chanukah lamp and a Passover plate.

The London Museum of Jewish Life, The Sternberg Centre for Judaism, The Manor House, 80 East End Road, N3 (071-346 2288). Open from 10.30am to 5pm Monday to Thursday, 10.30am to 4. 30pm Sunday (except August). Admission free. A museum that traces the history of Jewish settlement in London, it features reconstructions of a tailor's workshop, a bakery and a typical Jewish domestic scene. See also *page 137* for details of *Manor House Books,* which is on the same site.

The Freud Museum, 20 Maresfield Gardens, NW3 (071-435 2002). Open from noon to 5pm Wednesday to Sunday. Admission charge. When Sigmund Freud (see *page 141*) left Austria in 1938 after its annexation by the Nazis, he was able to ship over all his possessions to his new home at 20 Maresfield Gardens, where he recreated his Viennese consulting room (complete with consulting couch), study and library. After his death in 1939, these rooms were left undisturbed, and following their restoration were finally opened to the public in 1986.

Ben Uri Art Gallery, 21 Dean Street, W1(071-437 2852). Open from 10am to 5pm Sunday to Friday (closed Friday in winter). Changing exhibitions by Jewish artists or by non-Jewish artists on Jewish themes.

Holocaust Memorial Garden, Hyde Park, W2. A small garden, south-east of the Bell Restaurants at the east end of the Serpentine Lake, commemorates the Holocaust.

SHOPPING

If you intend to go shopping, bear in mind that most of the premises listed in *Jewish London* close all day Saturday and early on Friday in observance of the Jewish Sabbath.

Jewish Memorial Council Bookshop, 2nd Floor, Woburn House, Upper Woburn Place, WC1 (071-387 3081). Open from 10.30am to 12.45pm Sunday, 10am to 5.30pm Monday to Thursday, 10am to 2pm (October to April) and 10am to 4pm (May to September) Friday. Situated in the same building as the *Jewish Museum* (see *page 136*). Stocks a variety of books in English and Hebrew, both religious and secular. Specialises in Biblical and Talmudic studies, old Judaic books and children's literature. Wedding, birthday and New Year cards are also available.

Faculty Books, 98 Ballards Lane, Finchley, N3 (081-346 7632). Open from 9.30am to 5.30pm Monday to Saturday. A wide selection of books includes many of Jewish interest.

Carmel Gifts, 62 Edgware Road, Edgware (081-958 7632). Open from 9am to 5.30pm Monday to Thursday, 9am to 1.30pm Friday. Religious requisites.

Marlborough Shop, 159 Clapton Common, N16 (081-809 2566). Open from 6.30am to 7.30pm Monday to Saturday, 9am to 6.30pm Sunday. This newsagent sells Kosher confectionery and Jewish festive cards.

Jewish Chronicle Bookshop, 25 Furnival St., EC4 (071-405 9252). Open from 9.30am to 5.30pm Monday to Thursday, 9.30am to 5pm Friday, closed Saturday. Books of Jewish interest.

Manor House Books, 80 East End Road, N3 (081-349 9484). Open from 10am to 4pm Monday to Thursday, 10am to 1pm Sunday, closed Friday and Saturday. Large selection of music of Jewish interest, including kletzmer, the East European Jewish folk music that is currently enjoying a revival.

See also **Golders Green: Shopping,** *pages 132, 134,* **Stamford Hill,** *pages 135, 136.*

FOOD AND DRINK

Jewish cuisine has developed under the dual influence of Jewish travels and Jewish religious law.

When Jews settled in a new country they took the cuisine of their previous homeland with them and in so doing transformed it into 'Jewish cuisine', which therefore varies enormously around the world depending on the origins of any particular community. In Britain, like British Jews, it is largely of East and Central European origin.

Orthodox Jews are required to follow a strict dietary code. Eating the meat of certain animals, such as pigs and shellfish, is forbidden. Animals whose meat may be eaten must be killed in a prescribed manner and the blood drained off from the meat before it can be consumed . Meat and dairy dishes cannot be eaten at the same meal. Cooking, as with all work, is not permitted on the Sabbath. Food which is eaten in accordance with Jewish religious law is called kosher.

Religious constraints have concentrated the attention of Jewish cooks on particular aspects of cookery. The main meal of the week is traditionally on

Saturday, yet it has to be prepared on Friday if the Sabbath is to be properly observed. This situation has encouraged the use of cold foods such as fried fish, pastries, and cakes, and dishes such as casseroles that can be left to cook overnight. Jewish cooks have also developed a wide range of *pareve* foods, which contain neither meat nor milk, in order to ease problems in drawing up menus. Pareve ice-cream, for example, is made from vegetable oils.

The most ancient types of Jewish food are associated with religious festivals. Passover, which normally falls around Easter, commemorates the escape of the Jews from slavery in Egypt. They were in such haste that the dough they took with them was unleavened, and they were forced to eat unleavened bread. In memory of this event, Orthodox Jews are forbidden to eat any food which contains leaven during the eight days of Passover, when all baking is done with leaven-free matza meal. A piece of commercially-made unleavened 'bread', known as a matzo, looks and tastes much like a cream cracker.

Although the standard of food in Jewish snack bars in London is generally good, the Jewish restaurants have a poor culinary reputation. As a Jewish American acquaintance said to me after we ate at one of the best-known Jewish restaurants in London: 'They wouldn't stand for this in New York'. Nevertheless, if you're unfamiliar with Jewish food the novelty value alone should make it a worthwhile enough experience.

'Inside Out'

Interview with David, who works in a Jewish restaurant as a 'Shomer'...

"A Shomer is someone who is knowledgeable about all Jewish laws appertaining to food, and he supervises the kitchen so that everything that goes on conforms with those laws, so that it is kosher. For example, I prepare the vegetables, and when I cut lettuce I must examine it to check to see that there are no eggs or small insects inside the leaves because we cannot eat any insects, worms or things like that. Then before we cook eggs, I examine them to make sure that there is no blood in them. According to Jewish law we must not eat blood from an animal, so if we find a blood spot we throw the egg away.

I learnt all this mainly from living at home, seeing how my mother did things and asking questions and just being brought up in that way of life with Judaism. I always wanted to be involved with Jewish things, and there's other things I have done as well. Like last year I went to Russia for two months to Takzikistan and taught Jewish children Hebrew and Judaism. It was beautiful, doing that."

Whether shopping or eating out in Jewish London, look out for the following:

Bread and Sandwiches.
Challa: A plaited loaf made from white flour and egg.
Beigel (or bagel): A bread ring.
Sandwiches: Usually made with rye bread. Typical fillings include salt beef,

pastrami (spicy salt beef), chopped liver and chopped herring.

Soups. Clear chicken broth forms the basis of most soups. Amongst East European Jews, chicken was once the only type of meat that they were likely to eat regularly because they were able to raise the chickens themselves. Chicken soups are named according to the principal additional ingredient, whether that be kneidlach (dumplings), kreplach (ravioli) or lockshen (noodle). Chicken soup has acquired the nickname of the 'Jewish penicillin' because of its reputation amongst Jews as a cure-all.

Fish. The subject of fried fish sent the author Israel Zangwill (see *page 146*) into ecstasies in the 19th C:

'Fish was, indeed, the staple diet of the meal. Fried fish, and such fried fish! Only a great poet could sing the praises of the national dish, and the golden age of Hebrew poetry is over . . . With the audacity of true culinary genius, Jewish fried fish is always served cold. The skin is a succulent brown, the substance firm and succulent. The very bones thereof are full of marrow; yea, and charged with memories of a happy past. Fried fish binds Anglo-Judea more than lip-professions of unity. Its savour is early known of youth, and the divine flavour, endeared by a thousand childish recollections, entwined with the most sacred associations, draws back the hoary sinner into the paths of piety.' - *Children of the Ghetto.*

Although fried fish may no longer bind Anglo-Judea, it is still much in evidence in Jewish delicatessens and restaurants. Herring, the staple fried fish, is served in everything from sour cream to red wine. Other Jewish specialities include round balls of minced fish called gefilte fish, and fish fried in batter made out of egg and ground down matzos. Fried potato cakes called latkes go well with most fish dishes.

Preserved meats. Salt beef (pickled beef), viennas (pure beef sausages), wurst (a German salami often served with eggs), smoked turkey.

Pastries and puddings. Many originate from France, Austria and Hungary. Thin strudel pastry is used to make cherry, apple and cheese pastries. Patisseries sell Continental-style biscuits.

Wine. There is an ancient tradition of Jewish wine making. When Moses sent men out to reconnoitre the promised land after the Jews had been wandering in the wilderness for 40 years, they brought him back a cluster of grapes. Sweet Kosher wines have long been used in Jewish religious ceremonies, but are now gaining in popularity in secular use. Their growth and fermentation is strictly controlled by Jewish law, and although they are expensive, buyers can be assured of their outstanding natural content and purity. Kosher wines are available in some restaurants and delicatessens and specialist off licences.

FOOD AND DRINK: SHOPPING

East London

Marks of the Lane, 57-59 Wentworth Street, E1 (071-247 1400/247 4294). Open from 6.30am to 4pm Monday to Sunday (except closes Sunday at 3pm). A long-established Jewish delicatessen whose smoked salmon is justifiably famous.

Beigel Bake, 159 Brick Lane, E1 (071-729 0616). Open 24 hours Monday to Sunday. Famous for its beigels, Beigel Bake is as much a 'stand up' café as a bakers. Very lively late night Saturday/early Sunday morning.

A. Baum, 6 Toynbee Street, E1 (071-347 3168). Open from 10am to 5pm

Monday to Saturday, 12 noon to 2pm Sunday. Kosher vodka and Israeli kosher wines.

Grodzinski, 235 Whitechapel Road, E1 (071-247 8516). Open from 7am to 4.30pm Monday to Friday, 8am to 12 noon Sunday. An outlet of the chain of Jewish bakers which has been on this site for about a century.

Elsewhere in London

Keene's Patisserie, 120a Ballards Lane, N3 (081-346 5348). Open from 8am to 5pm Monday to Friday (except closed 4pm Friday), Sunday 8am to 1pm. Jewish pastries and breads - Beigels only on Sunday.

Ridley Bagel Bakery, 13-15 Ridley Road, E8 (081-241 1047). Open 24 hours Monday to Sunday. Jewish bakery and delicatessen. Beigels, breads and pastries are all made on the premises. Kosher.

Ross Bakery, 84 Stamford Hill, N16 (081-806 4002). Open from 8am to 6.30pm Sunday to Friday (except early Sabbath closing Friday). Jewish bakery with a wide range of traditional cakes. Kosher.

Sharon's Bakery, 154 Stamford Hill N16 (081-800 9769). Open 24 hours Sunday to Friday (except early Sabbath closing Friday). Jewish bakery. Kosher.

Carmel, 145 Clapton Common, N16 (081-800 9033). Open from 8.30 am. to 6pm Monday to Friday (except early Sabbath closing Friday). 8.30am to 2pm Sunday. Jewish delicatessen.

Grodzinski, 170 Clapton Common, N16 (081-802 4166). Open from 6.30am to 6pm Sunday to Friday. Jewish bakery.

See also **Golders Green: Shopping,** *page 132, 134*, **Stamford Hill:** *page 137.*

EATING OUT: RESTAURANTS AND SNACK BARS

Central London

Grahame's Sea Fare Restaurant, 38 Poland Street, W1 (071-437 3788/0975). Open from 12 noon to 2.45pm, 5.30 to 9pm Monday to Saturday (but closes at 8pm Friday and Saturday). Bright and bustling, specialises in traditional Jewish fish recipes. Take-away service. Moderately-priced. Kosher.

Reubens Snack Bar and Take-Away, 20a Baker Street, W1 (071-486 7079). Open from 11am to 9pm Monday to Thursday, 11am to 3pm Friday, 11am to 10pm Sunday. Snack bar. Moderately-priced. Kosher.

Reubens Restaurant, 20a Baker Street, Wl (071-935 5945). Open from 12 noon to 3pm, 5 to 10pm Monday to Thursday, 12 noon to 3pm Friday, 12 noon to 10pm Sunday. Situated above the snack bar. A stylish restaurant which offers Jewish and 'international' cuisine. Moderately-priced. Kosher.

Phil Rabin's Restaurant, 39 Great Windmill Street, Wl (071-434 9913). Open from 11am to 11pm Monday to Saturday. Small stand-up snack bar. Hot meals and take-away.

Nosherie Restaurant, 12-13 Grenville Street, ECI (071-242 I591). Open from 8am to 4pm Monday to Friday. Spacious but homely snack bar. Hot meals and take-away. The sandwiches aren't cheap, but you get your money's worth. Moderately-priced.

Gatby's Continental Bar, 30 Charing Cross Road, WC2 (071-836 4233). Open from 8am to midnight Monday to Saturday, 11am to 9.15pm Sunday. Snack bar. Beigels, salt beef sandwiches, falafel.

Kosher Meat Restaurant, 1-2 Endsleigh Street, WC1 (071-388 0801). Open from 12.30pm to 2pm Monday to Thursday (closed during students holiday periods). The restaurant aims to provide modestly priced kosher food to Jewish students, but everyone is welcome. Food and surroundings are basic.

The East End

Bloom's Restaurant, 90 Whitechapel High Street, El (071-247 6001/6835). Open from 11am to 9.30pm Sunday to Friday (except closes at 9pm in winter and early closing Friday). Take-away open from 9am to 10pm Sunday to Friday (except early closing Friday). Bloom's was founded in 1920 in Brick Lane by Morris Bloom, whose face still looks down sternly on diners from an oil painting which hangs on the back wall of the present premises. The restaurant is bright and functional, and at its best when crowded, as it invariably is on Sunday lunchtimes. In the entrance a take-away counter displays Bloom's own-brand kosher food products - the kneidlach and kreplach soups are recommended. Moderately-priced. Kosher.

The Kosher Luncheon Club, Morris Kasler Hall, 13 Greatorex Street, E1. For further details see *page 125*.

Golders Green

Bloom's, 130 Golders Green Road, NW11 (081-455 1338/3033). Open from 12 noon to 9.30pm Sunday to Thursday, sunset to 3am Saturday. Bright, canteen-like restaurant similar to the East End branch, but much smaller. Good take-away counter. Moderately priced. Kosher.

Amor's Take away, 8a Russell Parade, Golders Green Road, NW11 (081-458 4221 daytime, 081-802 5569 evening). Open from 8.30am to 6.30pm Monday to Friday (except to 3pm Friday), 8.30am to 2pm Sunday. Kosher take-away food.

Marcus's, 4 Halleswelle Parade, Finchley Road, NW11 (081-458 6690 restaurant), (081-458 4610, 458 1041 take away). This is an unusual restaurant that offers a choice of Chinese or Jewish food, all kosher. Take-away dishes are served next door at number 5.

PEOPLE ───────────────────────

Sigmund Freud was born in 1856 in Moravia (now part of Czechoslovakia), and spent most of his life in Vienna, Austria. One of the most influential thinkers of the modern age, Freud's pioneering work in psychiatry provoked a fundamental reassessment of human nature through its emphasis on the power of the unconscious and the importance of sexuality and aggression as basic instincts.

Freud rejected Judaism along with all religion, but he 'gladly and proudly' acknowledged his Jewishness, to which he gave credit for his intellectual daring: 'Because I was a Jew . . . I found myself free of many prejudices which restrict others in the use of their intellect: as a Jew I was prepared to be in opposition and renounce agreement with the compact majority'.

Freud always had a special regard for Britain, which he first visited at the age of 19 on a trip to see his half-brother in Manchester. Freud considered emigrating to Britain on several occasions. In a letter to his wife-to-be in 1882, he wrote:

'I am aching for independence so as to follow my own wishes. The thought of England surges up before me, with its sober industriousness, its generous devotion to the public weal, the stubbornness and sensitive feeling for justice of its inhabitants; . . . all the ineffaceable impressions of my journey of seven years ago, one that had a decisive influence on my whole life . . . I am taking up again the history of the island, the works of the men who were my real teachers - all of them English or Scotch; and I am recalling what is for me the most interesting historical period, the reign of the Puritans and Oliver Cromwell . . . Must we stay here, Martha? If we possibly can let us seek a home where human worth is more represented'.

Freud named his son Oliver after Oliver Cromwell, whom Freud admired for a number of reasons, not least for his role in the readmission of the Jews to Britain in 1656.

Freud eventually moved to Britain only after the annexation of Austria by Germany in 1938. He was a prime target for the Nazis, and his daughter Anna had already suffered interrogation at the hands of the Gestapo before diplomatic pressure enabled them to leave for Britain. Shortly after his arrival in London, Freud wrote:

'Here there is enough to write about, most of it pleasant, some very pleasant. The reception in Victoria Station and then in the newspapers of these first two days was most kind, indeed enthusiastic. We are buried in flowers . . . Finally, and this is something special for England, numerous letters from strangers who only wish to say how happy they are that we have come to England and that we are in safety and peace'.

At his home at 20 Maresfield Gardens, NW3 (marked by a plaque), Freud received visits from Salvador Dali, H G Wells and Chaim Weizmann (see *page 144*). Even though he was suffering badly from cancer, Freud was able to complete his book *Moses and Monotheism,* in which, controversial to the last, he argued that Moses had not been a Jew but an Egyptian. Freud believed that the story of Moses being abandoned by his Jewish mother and reared by an Egyptian princess was an invention designed to conceal the embarrassing fact that Moses actually *was* the son of the princess.

Freud died at Maresfield Gardens shortly after the outbreak of war in 1939. He had been confident that the war would see the end of Hitler, but this was to happen too late for his four sisters, who died in the holocaust. Freud was cremated at Golders Green Crematorium (see *page 133),* where his ashes are contained in a mausoleum. His home at Maresfield Gardens has now been turned into The Freud Museum (see *page 136).*

The Freuds have continued to make an impact on British society. Freud's daughter Anna helped to establish London as a centre for psychoanalysis, and his grandsons Lucien and Clement are respectively a notable painter and a well known MP, gourmet and humorist.

Benjamin Disraeli, the great Victorian statesmen, was born in 1804 at 22 Theobalds Road, WC I (marked by a plaque). The son of the eminent writer Isaac d'lsraeli, Benjamin was raised in the Jewish faith. His birth was registered at Bevis Marks Synagogue (see *page 116),* and at school he was exempted from Christian prayers and received tuition from a rabbi once a week. However, Benjamin's father Isaac broke with Judaism after the death of his own devout father, and though Isaac never became a Christian himself, he had Benjamin baptised into Christianity at the age of 13 at the Anglican Church of St Andrew's, Holborn Circus, EC1.

Benjamin Disraeli worked as an articled clerk at 6 Frederick's Place, EC2 (marked with a plaque), between 1821 and 1824, and subsequently dabbled unsuccessfully in share speculation and journalism. In 1826 he launched into a successful career as an author with his first novel *Vivian Grey*. After standing unsuccessfully for Parliament several times as an independent candidate, he joined the Tory Party and was eventually elected as an MP in 1837.

Although all the evidence demonstrates that Disraeli's Anglican faith was sincere, he was at the same time exceedingly proud of his Jewish origins. He spoke vociferously in favour of the entry of Jews into the House of Commons even though he knew his views damaged his political standing. He declared: 'Has not the Church . . . made the history of the Jews the most celebrated history in the world? On every sacred day you read to the people the exploits of Jewish heroes, the proofs of Jewish devotion, the brilliant annals of past Jewish magnificence'. In 1876 the *Jewish Chronicle* claimed: 'Benjamin Disraeli belongs to the Jewish people, despite his baptismal certificate'. Today he is considered Jewish enough to merit a bust in the Jewish Museum.

Despite opponents within his own party who ostentatiously referred to him as 'The Jew', Disraeli rose to become the leader of the party and to serve as Prime Minister in 1868 and between 1874 and 1880. He was a key figure in the transformation of the Tory Party from a narrowly-based party which represented the landed gentry into a national party which drew support from all classes. A political theorist in a party which has produced very few until the 1980s, Disraeli laid the foundation for modern populist Conservatism through overseeing a combination of policies that wedded social reform and the extension of the vote with support for the Empire and the establishment. The most famous quotation from Disraeli's novels is found in *Sybil* (1845):

'"Two nations; between whom there is no intercourse and no sympathy, who are as ignorant of each other's habits, thoughts and feelings, as if they were dwellers in different zones, or inhabitants of different planets; who are formed by a different breeding, are fed by a different food, are ordered by different manners, and are not governed by the same laws." "You speak of . . ." said Egremont, hesitatingly. "THE RICH AND THE POOR".'

Disraeli lived at 93 Park Lane, WI (marked by a plaque) from 1839 to 1873. He died in 1881 at 19 Curzon Street, Wl (marked by a plaque). A statue of him stands at the north side of the central traffic island in Parliament Square, SW1.

Karl Marx, the prophet of world revolution, was born in 1818 in Trier, Germany. The grandson of a rabbi, he was baptised into Christianity at the age of six following the conversion of his father, a successful lawyer.

Marx became involved in radical politics while studying law and philosophy at university. He became an atheist who believed that revolution would lead to an irreversible decline in religion, and that the Jews would consequently merge into the rest of the population. While Marx had no time for any religion, he seems to have reserved a particular venom for his denunciations of Judaism.

Many commentators have interpreted Marx's hostility to the Jews as a measure of his own anxiety to distance himself from his own origins. Be that as it may, the Jewish author Chaim Bermant argues that Marx's Jewish origins were an important influence in the development of his politics:

'The Hebrew for the code of Jewish laws is Shulchan Aruch, which means, literally, the prepared table, and it lays down a system of laws covering one's existence from the time one rises in the morning till one goes to bed, from the torment of birth till the moment of death . It does not deprive the observant Jew of initiative or the need for decisions, but it assures him that he is operating within a divine order . . . Marx, too, introduced a system, which was not, of course, divine, but which laid down iron laws, operating irrespective of human will and human effort but which, on the contrary, determined the direction of effort. It suggested an inevitability to the course of human history, it promised certainties. It did not give a ready answer to every question, but it offered sufficient guidance from which an answer might eventually be obtained. It was a Shulchan Aruch . . .' - *The Jews* (1977).

Marx settled in London in 1849 after his expulsion from Prussia following the failure of the 1848 revolution. In 1850 he moved with his wife and children to 28 Dean Street, W1 (marked by a plaque), where he earned a precarious living as a freelance journalist. The Marx family lived in great poverty for several years, and three of Marx's six children died at this address.

The Marx's financial position gradually improved through the generosity of Engels and their receipt of family inheritances, and in 1856 they moved on to better housing at 9 Grafton Terrace, NW5 (now number 46).

For the last 20 years of his life Marx spent much of his time in the British Library at the British Museum, where he worked on *Das Kapital,* the critical analysis of the capitalist economic system that forms the intellectual cornerstone of Communism.

For Marx, London was not just a place of refuge; as the capital of the most industrially developed country in the world it was also a social and economic laboratory in which he could observe 'developed on the greatest scale the despotism of capital and the slavery of Labour'. The squalor and destitution that he saw around him served only to confirm his belief that 'the workers have nothing to lose but their chains. They have a world to gain'. As George Bernard Shaw later observed, the Russian revolution was 'built on English history, written in London by Karl Marx'.

Only one of the three volumes of *Das Kapital* was published within Marx's lifetime and he died in relative obscurity 14th March, 1883 in a house (since demolished) in Maitland Park Road, NW3. His ideas spread rapidly after his death.

Marx's grave is in the eastern section of Highgate Cemetery, Swain's Lane, N6. A large granite plinth is topped by a powerful bust of Marx, looking like nothing so much as an Old Testament prophet. Two of Marx's most famous phrases are engraved on the plinth: 'Workers of all lands unite', and 'Philosophers have only interpreted the world in various ways. The point however is to change it'. The grave still attracts visitors from across the world, ranging from the idly curious to the relics of the Communist world bearing wreaths of red flowers.

Chaim Weizmann, a prominent Zionist, was born in Russia in 1874 and came to settle in Britain in 1904. He was soon on the staff of Manchester University, where he became a Professor of Chemistry. It was here that he was approached in 1915 by David Lloyd George, then the Minister of Munitions, to see if he could help solve a worrying military problem. There was a shortage of chemical acetone, which was needed for the manufacture of high explosive, and was then made from natural fermentation.

Building on the work of Louis Pasteur, Weizmann isolated a bacteria that was capable of synthesising acetone, and the problem was quickly solved. Weizmann's work was not only an important step in the development of what we know today as biotechnology, but almost certainly had an impact on the creation of Israel. Grateful to Weizmann, Lloyd George offered to recommend him for an honour. Weizmann refused, but instead raised the question of a homeland for the Jews.

Shortly afterwards, Lloyd George became Prime Minister and in that capacity discussed the issue with his Foreign secretary, Arthur Balfour. Weizmann was not the first nor the last Zionist who lobbied the government, but his personal contribution was undoubtedly an important one.

Britain was then at war with the Ottoman Empire, which controlled Palestine. Further lobbying by Weizmann and other British Zionists finally led to the British Government issuing 'The Balfour Declaration' to Lionel Rothschild (see *page 114*) on 2 November 1917. It stated: 'His Majesty's Government view with favour the establishment in Palestine of a national home for the Jewish people, and will use their best endeavours to facilitate the achievement of this object, it being clearly understood that nothing shall be done which may prejudice the civil and religious rights of existing non-Jewish communities in Palestine'.

The original Balfour Declaration is held by the Manuscripts Department of the British Library at the British Museum. It is not on public display, but photocopies can be provided on request.

Britain took full control of Palestine in 1918 and ruled the country until 1948. Weizmann played a key role in negotiations for the British withdrawal from Palestine and became the first President of the state of Israel on its foundation later in 1948.

Weizmann lived at 67 Addison Road, W14 (marked by a plaque) from 1917 to 1920.

'Inside Out'

Interview with Leon, a retired Jewish man, on his feelings about Israel...

"I would say that the founding of the State of Israel is the single most important thing that ever happened to every single Jew, however little observant he is. It gives the individual Jew a dignity that he never had before.

When I was a young man there was no state of Israel. When I was at school, some of the boys were very nasty to me because I was Jewish. One boy said to me, "you Jews are cowards, you're no good at fighting". Well, no-one could say that to a Jew today, could he? But in those days it seemed it might be true, that the Jews wouldn't stand up for themselves, that we were used to being persecuted and accepted it as a fact of daily life.

Now, for every young person, the State of Israel has existed all their lives - they know of nothing else. They can look at a country which has fought valiantly and which has done pretty well, and which matters in the conferences of the world. They will be able to walk the streets in a different way to the way I did when I was young."

Numerous other Jewish figures of note have lived in or visited London over the centuries. The following is a brief selection:

Heinrich Heine (1797-1856), the celebrated German poet, was a convert to Christianity. On a visit to London he stayed at 32 Craven Street, WC2 (marked by a plaque), between April and July in 1827. Heine wrote: 'Send a philosopher to London, but by no means a poet. This bare earnestness of everything, this colossal sameness, this machine-like movement, this moroseness of joy itself, this exaggerated London, oppresses the imagination and rends the heart in twain'.

Rufus Isaacs (1860-1935) was Viceroy of India between 1921 and 1926. He lived and died at 32 Curzon Street, W1 (marked by a plaque).

The writer *Israel Zangwill* (1864-1926) is remembered chiefly for his novel *Children of the Ghetto* (see *Literature below*). He lived at 288 Old Ford Road, E2 (marked by a plaque), between 1884 and 1887, and taught at the Jews' Free School in Middlesex Street.

Sir Jacob Epstein (1880-1959) was born in New York and settled in Britain in 1905. A pioneering sculptor of the modern school, many of his pieces are on display in public places around London. He lived at 18 Hyde Park Gate, SW7 (marked by a plaque), from 1929 until his death there in 1959.

Harold Laski (1893-1950) was an influential figure in the Labour Party, of which he was made Chairman in 1945. He lived at 5 Addison Bridge Place, W14 (marked by a plaque), from 1926 until his death.

Lord Leslie Hore-Belisha (1893-1957) was Transport Minister in the National Government of the 1930s. He gave his name to 'Belisha beacons', the yellow globes which mark zebra crossings. He is buried in the Jewish Cemetery at Golders Green (see *page 134*).

Bud Flanagan, (1896-1968). A famous music-hall star who wrote 'Underneath the Arches', amongst other songs.

Sir John Cohen (1878-1979). Founder of the Tesco Supermarket chain. Born in the East End, he started his working career on a market stall.

Isaac Rosenberg (1890-1918). Famous world War One poet, killed in action. Born in East London.

Sir Carol Reed (1906-1976). Film director whose most famous film was 'The Third Man'. Born in London, a plaque at 311 Kings Road, SW3, commemorates his occupancy.

LITERATURE

Children of the Ghetto by Israel Zangwill (1892). A vivid, panoramic novel that brings to life the joys and tragedies of everyday life in the Jewish East End of the 1870s and 1880s. Zangwill's large cast includes humble and proud, rich and poor, and represents many facets of Jewish life from religious zealotry to militant trade unionism. The single most important theme is that of religious conflict between the Orthodox immigrant and the British-born generation, an issue which Zangwill treats with a refreshing frankness. *Children of the Ghetto is* not only essential reading for anyone interested in the Jewish East End, but an excellent piece of literature to be enjoyed in its own right. *Recommended.

The King of Schnorrers by Israel Zangwill (1894). A brilliantly comic tale set on the eastern fringes of the City of London at the end on the 18th Century. Manasseh da Costa is a Sephardic Jew, and a schnorrer (beggar).

But he is no ordinary beggar. He is a proud and imposing man who is a master of manipulation and Rabbinical reasoning, and uses his talents to the full to extract the maximum of donations from wealthier Jews. When an Ashkenazi Jew, and a fellow beggar, wants to win his daughter's hand, de Costa gives him a task to truly try his wits - to be invited to dinner by the most notorious miser in town. *Recommended.

A Kid for Two Farthings by Wolf Mankowitz (1953). A short, light and charming story about a young boy growing up in the East End of the 1930s. He watches the tailors at work, wrestles in the local gym, and gets lost in his own fantasies. It was made into a British film of the same name in 1955.

The Crossing Point by Gerda Charles (1960). A novel centered around the relationship between a woman who lives with her fanatically religious father and a rabbi who is desperately in search of a wife. An engaging and compassionate look at 'Jewish guilt . . . and melancholy' in post-war suburbia. *Recommended.

Madame Sousatzka by Bernice Rubens (1962). Marcus is eleven years old, a talented pianist and the only son of an adoring but pushy mother. When Marcus is taken up by the eccentric piano teacher, Madame Sousatzka, he is introduced to an exciting new world in her West End house far away from his home in Stamford Hill. 'Madame Souatzka' was made into a film recently by John Schlesinger, but with the Jewish theme eliminated - Marcus and his mother are cast as Asians and Madame Sousatzska is not noticeably Jewish. *Recommended.

Mate In Three by Bernice Rubens (1966). Jack's parents are wealthy, non-observant Jews who left Germany in the early 1930s for London and who still blame their poorer Jewish brethren for their exile. Ruth's family are poor, but Jewish through and through and proud of it. When Jack and Ruth get married, no-one else is very pleased and their marriage is soon on the rocks. However, when Ruth arranges a trip to South Africa, it seems as if Jack's emotional response to apartheid may enable them to heal the rift.

The Elected Member by Bernice Rubens (1969). Norman Sweck is a successful young barrister with a brilliant career ahead of him when he has a mental breakdown. The book slowly reveals the family pressures and tragedies that have driven him to madness. An intense examination of how the best of parental intentions can lead to tragic consequences. *Recommended.

Spring Sonata by Bernice Rubens (1979). An unusual baby is conceived by a Jewish woman. Its past life has not been erased and, while still in the womb, it is conscious of everything that goes on around it in the troubled family into which it is to be born. When the time comes for its birth, it not only refuses to come out but also takes up an interest in music, eventually being able to strike up a duet with its mother, a failed classical musician. The tone of the story is given in the following quote - "The parents sin, and the children atone; the fathers eat sour grapes, and the children's teeth are set on edge".

By The Waters of Whitechapel by Bernard Kops (1969). In the late 1960's, Aubrey and his mother are still living in the East End, having not joined 'the second most famous exodus in history - from Whitechapel to Golders Green'. Aubrey's mother owns a sweetshop, and totally controls Aubrey's life, and he despairs of ever escaping. But when he meets Zena, an attractive young woman from Stamford Hill, he pretends to be a successful barrister, and with the aid of money he steals from his mother's account, he embarks on a wild life in the guise of this alter ego. A comic treatment of the traditional Jewish mother and son theme. *Recommended.

Blood Libels by Clive Sinclair (1985). A darkly comic story about how events at a boy's Bar Mitzvah in Hendon in 1961 lead, through a bizarre sequence of events, to an antisemitic pogrom in 1980s London by latter-day fascists. A surrealistic vision of an England gripped by antisemitism that is set against the backdrop of real events of the period.

So Long As They're Cheering by Sue Dinsman (1986). The upbeat story of a Jewish theatrical family in the years before the First World War, following their exploits from underground theatre in Poland to theatrical success in the Yiddish theatre of London's East End.

Drama

The post-war East End has generated a wealth of talented Jewish playwriters.

Harold Pinter is undoubtedly the most famous, although it is difficult to identify anything specifically Jewish in work such as *The Homecoming, The Birthday Party* and *The Dumb Waiter*. The same could be said for **Steven Berkoff**, who has written the plays *East, West, Greek* and *Decadence*.

Arnold Wesker and **Bernard Kopfs** have both written about Jewish life in the East End. Wesker's best-known play, *Chicken Soup with Barley* (1959) is a stage drama about a Jewish family and their involvement with the Communist Party. The play begins with the triumph of the Battle of Cable Street in the East End in the 1930s and ends with political disillusionment in Hackney in the 1950s.

IRISH LONDON

HISTORY

Irish immigration to London began in the late 12th C in the wake of the Anglo-Norman invasion of Ireland. A steady trickle of merchants, scholars and vagrants made their way to London over the following centuries, but it was not until after the re-conquest of Ireland in the 16th and early 17th C that Irish immigration made any significant impact on the city. By the late 17th C there were sufficient Irish people in London for the district of St Giles (which surrounds St Giles in the Fields Church, St Giles High Street, WC2) to be known as an area of Irish settlement.

In the 17th and 18th C London's Irish community had to cope with fierce anti-Catholic prejudice. In the Gordon riots of 1780, huge mobs went on the rampage in London after Parliament lifted some of the restrictions under which Catholics were forced to live. Irish people were attacked on the streets, Irish shops looted, and Irish chapels burnt down in Spitalfields and Moorfields. The rioting, which soon escalated into an indiscriminate assault on authority, was eventually suppressed by the military at the cost of several hundred lives.

The number of Irish people in Britain remained fairly low until the early 19th C, when economic turmoil in Ireland led to a huge exodus of rural labourers and small farmers. There were substantial numbers of Protestants amongst those who came to Britain, but the Irish immigrants who settled in London were overwhelmingly Catholic, many of whom spoke only Gaelic.

The 19th C wave of immigration peaked in 1847 and 1848 during the Great Famine in Ireland, in which it is thought that about 800,000 people died after the potato crop was decimated by blight. By 1851 there were some half a million Irish people in England and Wales, of whom over 100,000 lived in London, where they made up about one in 20 of the population.

Unlike Jewish immigrants of the 19th C, the Irish did not congregate in one particular quarter of London, but settled in enclaves of a few streets or alleys dotted about the working-class districts of the city. There were particularly large Irish populations in the districts of St Giles, Whitechapel and Southwark.

The poverty of many Irish immigrants forced them into the worst parts of working-class districts, known as rookeries. Here they faced appalling overcrowding, with whole families living in single rooms, and insanitary conditions that bred cholera, typhus and scarlet fever. Vivid descriptions of such localities have been left to us by 19th C social observers such as Blanchard Jerrold:

'On our way to the City on the tide of Labour, we light upon places in which the day is never aired: only the high points of which the sun ever hits. Rents spread with rags, swarming with children of mothers forever greasing the walls with their shoulders; where there is an angry hopelessness and carelessness painted upon the face of every man and woman; and the oaths are loud, and the crime is continuous; and the few who do work with something like system, are the ne'r-do-weels of the great army.'

'And yet in the midst of such a scene as this we cannot miss touches of human goodness, and of honourable instinct making a tooth-and-nail fight

The Rookery, St Giles: Irish London in the mid-19th C.

against adverse circumstances. Some country wenches, who have been cast
into London - Irish girls mostly - hasten out of the horrors of the common
lodging-house to market, where they buy their flowers, for the day's
huckstering in the City. They are to be seen selling roses and camellias,
along the kerb by the Bank, to dapper clerks. There is an affecting
expression in the faces of some of these rough bouqetieres, that speaks of
honourable effort to make headway out of the lodging-house and the rents.'
- *London* (1872).

The 19th C Irish immigrants worked mainly in unskilled and semi-skilled
manual jobs. Men worked as labourers in the building trade, and on the
docks, roads, railways, underground and canals. Women worked in the
clothing trade and in domestic service. Both men and women worked as
street vendors, dealing in fruit, flowers and trinkets. Children worked from
an early age at anything that would pay, from selling wood to sweeping
road crossings.

Irish immigration fell off sharply in the late 19th C, and it was not until a
massive surge in the 1950s that the number of Irish-born residents of
London passed the peak of the mid-19th C. This 20th C wave of
immigrants contained a larger urban and middle-class element than in the
19th C, but for the men labouring was still an important occupation (though
many of the construction companies they worked for were now Irish-
owned), and for the women nursing formed the modern equivalent of
domestic service. Factory work, transport and catering were other major
sources of employment.

Immigration eased off during the 1960s, when Ireland was experiencing an
economic boom, but rising unemployment in the 1980s sent many young
Irish people back along the well-trodden path to London. The census of
1991 recorded 256,470 Irish-born people living in London. Districts in
London with large Irish populations include Paddington, Kensington,
Hammersmith, Islington, Camden Town and Willesden.

PLACES TO VISIT

Westminster Cathedral, Morpeth Terrace, SW1 (071-834 7452). If there is
one enduring testament to Irish immigration to this country then it is in the
revival of the English Catholic Church. The Catholic population of England
in the wake of the Reformation was very small - at the end of the 17th C it
was estimated that there were only about 30,000 Catholics in the whole of
England and Wales, whose total population was then some six million. It
was not until the mass Irish immigration of the 19th C that Catholicism
became a significant religious force in England once more. The
achievements of that century culminated in the construction between 1895
and 1903 of Westminster Cathedral, the first Catholic cathedral to be built
in England since The Reformation. Constructed in brick in a striking early
Christian Byzantine style, it now stands in bold contrast to the adjacent
modern office blocks of Victoria Street.

The Chapel of St Patrick and the Saints of Ireland is situated off the west
aisle of the Cathedral. It is handsomely decorated in Irish style, with much
use made of interlacing Celtic patters, and of Cork red marble and
Connemara green marble . Prominent features include a bronze statue of St
Patrick, and a frieze of shamrocks inlaid with mother of pearl. The badges

of Irish regiments displayed around the chapel commemorate Ireland's contribution to the First World War. A book listing the names of the 50,000 Irish soldiers who died in the conflict rests in a casket to the left of the altar. Situated on the aisle wall adjacent to the Chapel of St Patrick is a mosaic depicting Oliver Plunket (born County Meath 1629), Archbishop of Armagh. Falsely accused of conspiracy against the British Crown, Plunket was hung, drawn and quartered in 1681 at Tyburn Gallows situated close to the junction of Edgware Road and Bayswater Road, W2. His was the last Catholic martyrdom in England. In 1975 he was made Saint Oliver Plunket, the first Irish person to be canonised since Laurence O'Toole in 1226.

See also *page 156 St Paul's Bookshop,* and *Gift Shop, Westminster Cathedral.*

St Patrick's Church, 21a Soho Square, W1 (071-437 2010). This is the oldest Roman Catholic mission in England that is dedicated to St Patrick. A chapel was founded on the site in 1792 by Father O'Leary (born County Cork 1729) when the parish housed a large number of Irish Catholics. The present church, which was built in 1893, holds services in Spanish and Cantonese as well as English, but it is still a traditional venue for Irish baptisms, weddings and funerals.

In the entrance to the church there is a memorial dedicated to Father O'Leary, 'whose useful Labours in the Vineyard of the Lord, in France, England and Ireland his native country . . . bear testimony to his fervent Piety, discreet Zeal, and steady Loyalty'. Although there is no mention of it here, his holy reputation was somewhat tarnished following his death in London in 1802 when it was discovered that he had been an informer in the pay of the British Government.

FESTIVALS

St Patrick's Day

St Patrick (c AD 385-461), the patron saint of Ireland, was kidnapped from his home in Britain by Irish raiders at the age of 16. Taken to Ireland as a slave, he was forced to work as a herdsman in Antrim, but managed to escape back to Britain after six years. Patrick eventually returned as a missionary to Ireland, where he played an important role in establishing Christianity.

Tradition has it that St Patrick died on 17 March, which is observed as St Patrick's Day. In Ireland it is a national holiday. For the Irish in London it is a day to remember the old country and to celebrate being Irish.

In the book *An Irish Navvy* (1964), an autobiographical account of life as a labourer in England in the 1950s, Donall MacAmhlaigh describes St Patrick's Day festivities in London. His account could be equally applicable today.

'St Patrick's Day. I put on a bit of shamrock in the lapel of my coat and went down to Mass in Camden Town at nine o'clock. The church was full and everyone had their bit of shamrock . . . I feel as light-hearted as a lark every St Patrick's Day and when the congregation started to sing *Hail Glorious Saint Patrick* my heart swelled out with pride for my race. Hundreds of thousands of people all around the world will be wearing the shamrock today in the Saint's honour and in honour of the country that gave them birth and who can say that the empire that we, the Irish people, have built is not greater and nobler in the four corners of the world than one that John Bull built with the help of his guns? . . . You could hardly walk in the street outside the church after Mass, there were so many Irish meeting there and having a bit of sport. Hundreds come up from the country for the Feast-day and most of them don't go back until they have spent all they have.'

Wearing a sprig of shamrock on St Patrick's Day is an ancient tradition. St Patrick is said to have used the shamrock to illustrate the doctrine of the Holy Trinity to the pagan Irish. Like the three leaves of the shamrock, he taught, The Father, The Son and The Holy Ghost form three distinct parts of an integral whole.

Shamrock for St Patrick's Day is frequently posted to the Irish in Britain by obliging relatives in Ireland who have picked it from the wild. Commercially grown shamrock is flown in from Ireland to London, where it is sold in Irish shops and distributed free at church services and in pubs and clubs.

On St Patrick's Day it is customary to attend mass, phone relatives in Ireland, and to end the day either in the pub or at one of the St Patrick's Night dances which are held in church halls and clubs across London. Music for the dance is usually provided by an Irish group, and at many venues children give a formal performance of Irish dancing, earning admiring applause from proud parents.

'Inside Out'

Interview with Robert, a teacher of Irish dancing . . .

"I've been teaching Irish dancing since 1982 and my main base is here in London. I was born here, and my mother was Irish. She didn't push me to do Irish dancing, and she got quite a shock when I asked to do it. I'm second generation Irish and almost all my students are in the same situation - English children of Irish parents. The children come to the classes because of a combination of reasons - they've been pushed into it by their parents or seen it on TV or their friends do it. We've got pupils here from four up to eighteen, nineteen, and most of them enjoy it, whatever level they get to. The majority of my students will attend at least three lessons a week. They compete all the time, and travel all over England. They go over to Ireland three times a year and enter all the major championships. Some even go to the American Nationals. So I mean they are very dedicated and get a lot out of it. They make a lot of friends.

If you compare Irish dancing to any other national dance, theirs is so basic compared to ours! I certainly believe that it's on a par with ballet and it could become even more popular in future.

I think it is important for children of Irish parents to do Irish dancing, to be educated in their own culture. It helps when they visit Ireland. Myself, I really like Ireland and I'm engaged to an Irish woman. In fact, I don't know anybody who isn't Irish or of Irish descent."

London Irish Festival

The London Irish Festival or Fleadh is held on the first Sunday in July at Roundwood Park, Willesden. Access is from Harlesden Road and Longstone Avenue, NW10. There is an admission charge.

Tens of thousands of Irish people attend between mid-morning and the early evening. Tents representing each of Ireland's 32 counties provide information and sell caps and rosettes decked out in the colours of their county. Other stallholders include Irish companies and cultural and political organisations. Several stages feature live music and Irish dancing, and Gaelic football can be viewed on the playing fields. Further details can be obtained near to the date in the British-published weekly newspaper the *Irish Post,* or by writing to The Irish Festival c/o The Irish Centre, 52 Camden Square, NWI (071-485 0051).

SHOPPING (incl. Food and Drink) ─────────

Jewellery. The Claddagh ring, which depicts two hands holding a crowned heart, is an Irish love symbol dating back hundreds of years. The ring gets its name from a small fishing village called Claddagh (now part of Galway City), where it is said that married women were once legally obliged to wear such a ring.

There are traditional rules about how the ring should be worn: if it is worn on the right hand with the crown pointing inwards then the wearer is single and uncommitted; if it is worn on the right hand with the crown outwards then the wearer is romantically attached; and if it is worn on the left hand with the crown inwards then the wearer is married.

The Tara brooch was the name given to an 8th C Celtic ring brooch that was unearthed in County Louth in 1850. Copies of the brooch have become popular items of jewellery, and are often used to fasten the shawls worn by costumed Irish dancers.

A great number of the pieces of jewellery on sale in the shops listed below feature the Irish emblems of the shamrock, harp or Celtic cross.

Clothing and Fabrics. Aran knitwear is identified by its distinctive chunky patterns woven in creamy-white wool. It is best known in the form of jumpers and cardigans, but hats, scarves, gloves and socks are also made to match.

Although Aran knitwear is promoted as a traditional Irish craft, it was in fact created in the 1930s by a German-born textile journalist, Heinz Edgar Kiewe. On a visit to Dublin he came across a single white jumper with an interesting design that he thought was worth developing. Coincidentally, he saw Robert Flaherty's documentary film *Man of Aran* about the fisherfolk of Aran, an island off the west coast of Ireland . Although no-one in the film wears anything remotely like an 'Aran' jumper, Kiewe decided to use the name of the island to market his new range of jumpers. He could not even find the right sort of wool for his jumpers anywhere in Ireland, and ended up commissioning them from the Outer Hebridies off the west coast of Scotland. Nevertheless, many fruitful years have passed since Aran knitwear's birth of dubious parentage, and in that time it has developed by adoption into a genuine Irish tradition.

Ireland is also noted for its high quality clothing made from tweed (especially Donegal tweed) and other woollen fabrics.

The Irish linen industry, which had been established by French Protestant refugees in the 17th C, was by the early 20th C the largest in the world. Linen production has drastically declined since then due to the advent of cheaper and more convenient to use mass-produced fabrics, but there is still a call for Ireland's high quality product. Irish specialities include the decorative damask tablecloth (which is woven in Celtic, shamrock and chrysanthemum designs), and embroidered handkerchiefs (though today the embroidering itself is likely to have been done in China).

Glassware and China. Quality and tradition are the hallmarks of Waterford crystal glassware, which was first produced in Waterford in 1783. The glasses, decanters and jugs are blown by mouth and cut by hand to traditional designs.

Belleek porcelain china has been produced in County Fermanagh since 1857. It has a distinctive creamy white colour and an appealing 'folksy' look.

Drink. Guinness originated in Dublin, where it has been brewed since 1778. The original proprietor, Arthur Guinness, was first encouraged to export his drink to Britain when his opposition to the nationalist United Irishmen (see *Tone, page 159)* led to threats of a boycott of what was dubbed 'Guinness's black Protestant porter'. The drink has long since ceased to be politically controversial.

Amongst the Irish it is widely held that Guinness brewed in Dublin tastes better than that which is brewed in England. It's the water, they claim, that makes the difference. The Guinness brewing company stoutly denies that there is any difference in the quality of their product.

Shops

The Irish Shop, 11 Duke Street, W1 (071-935 1366). Open from 9.30am to 5.30pm Monday to Saturday closes 7pm Thursday. *The Irish Shop,* 14 King Street, WC2 (071-379 3625). Open from 9am to 5pm Monday to Friday, 9.30am to 3pm Saturday, 9.30am to 4.30pm Sunday. Both of these shops are managed by the same company and stock a similar range of goods, including Waterford crystal, Belleek china, embroidered linen handkerchiefs, jewellery, woollen travel rugs and Aran knitwear, alongside an entertaining array of touristy knick-knacks such as shamrock-shaped cufflinks, 'lucky leprechaun' dolls.

Irish Linen Company, 35-6 Burlington Arcade, W1 (071-493 8949). Open from 9am to 5.30pm Monday to Friday, 9am to 4.30pm Saturday. 'Specialists in fine linens since 1875' boasts the Irish Linen Company, and framed on the wall are letters from some of its more illustrious customers - Charlie Chaplin strikes an odd contrast with the British, Japanese and Greek royal families. A Royal Warrant to supply Irish linen to Queen Elizabeth II has been awarded. The shop stocks a good line in fancy embroidered linen alongside its wide range of functional items such as sheets and huckaback towels.

Givan's Irish Linen, 207 King's Road, SW3 (071-352 6352). Open from 9.30am to 1pm, 2 to 5pm Monday to Friday. About a third of the stock is Irish linen. Sheets, huckaback towels, damask tablecloths.

Gaelic Goodies, 706b Holloway Road, N19 (071-272 7885). Open from 10am to 5pm Monday Saturday, 11am to 1pm Sunday. Limited stock of

Irish music on video, record, CD, and cassette. Also gifts and Catholic religious objects, and Catholic identity cards - 'I am a Catholic. In case of accident or sickness please call a priest'.

St. Paul's Bookshop, Morpeth Terrace, SW1 (071-828 5582). Open from 9.30am to 5.15pm Monday to Friday. Religious literature, some religious music.

Gift Shop, Westminster Cathedral, Morpeth Terrace, SW1 (071-828 4962). Open from 9.30am to 5.15pm Monday to Friday, 10am to 4.45pm Saturday and Sunday. Various items of interest to Catholics, from statuettes of the Virgin Mary to jigsaws of the Pope and videos. There is little of specific Irish interest except for a few models of Celtic crosses.

Four Provinces Bookshop, 244-246 Gray's Inn Road, WC1 (071-833 3022). Open from 11am to 5.30pm Tuesday to Saturday (except to 4.30 Saturday). Small Irish book shop which specialises in Gaelic literature, socialist writing and language-learning material. Also stocks Irish newspapers and journals.

The Kilburn Bookshop, 8 Kilburn Bridge, NW6 (071-328 7071). Open from 9.30am to 5.30pm Monday to Saturday. General book shop with a good selection of books of Irish interest. Gaelic dictionaries.

Acushla Flowers, 95 Lever Street, EC1 (071-253 3301) and 57 Baylis Road, SE1 (071-633 0911). Flower shops which stock shamrock for St Patrick's Day. Home delivery is available.

The Willard Book shop, Willesden Green Library Centre, High Road, NW10 (081-451 7000). Open from 10am to 6pm Monday to Saturday. Books of Irish interest.

Greek Ink Books, 8 Archway Mall, N19 (071-263 4748). Open from 10am to 6pm Monday to Saturday (except to 5.30pm in winter. Books either by Irish writers or about Irish subjects.

Mandy's, 161 High Road, NW10 (081-459 2842). Open from 8.30am to 7pm Monday to Sunday. This shop is of interest chiefly for its stock of Irish foods: Nash's red lemonade, Erin soups, Boland's biscuits, Ballygowan spring water, Barry's tea, Emerald chocolate caramels, Irish jams, traditional Irish soda bread, Irish varieties of potatoes and Galtee brand sausages, black and white puddings, Irish smoked salmon and cheeses. They also stock Irish music on record and cassette, Catholic religious objects and a large selection of Irish newspapers.

The Irish Shop, 1 Leytonstone Road, E15 (081-519 4205). Open from 9am to 7pm Monday, Tuesday and Thursday, 9am to 9pm Friday and Saturday, 9am to 5pm Sunday. Irish foods, gifts, jewellery, videos, newspapers, magazines.

The Irish Kiosk, 419 High Road, Leytonstone, E15 (in the forecourt of the Plough and Harrow public house). Open from 2pm to 6pm Monday to Friday, 10am to 6pm Saturday and Sunday. This small kiosk stocks Irish foods plus Irish newspapers and magazines.

MUSIC

Live music plays an important role in the social life of the Irish in London, as might be guessed from the numerous music events advertised in the *Irish Post.* 'Irish' music as played in the pubs, clubs and dance halls of London is usually an eclectic mix of folk, pop, rock, ballads and country and western.

A typical live group is like a jukebox, playing a bit of everything to please everybody - though the influence of country and western is strong and its rhythms tend to sneak into everything else the group plays. This style of live music emerged in Ireland in the 1960s, and the groups who play it are known as 'showbands'. In recent years, however, the success of the rock group U2 has spawned a number of imitators, and to a certain degree rock music has eclipsed the showband style on the Irish music circuit in London.

However it is Irish folk music in its traditional acoustic form that will probably be of the greatest interest to non-Irish readers of this book. Irish folk music has a vigour and a popular following that has long since departed from its English cousin. Although Irish folk is primarily a dance music, it also incorporates non-dance forms such as sean nós, a style of unaccompanied individual singing that is associated with the Gaelic language. Distinctive Irish musical instruments include the bodhrán (a hand-held side drum) and the union or uilleann pipes (bagpipes that are held flat across the lap). Other characteristic instruments used in Irish folk include the tin whistle, wooden concert flute, fiddle, accordion and guitar. Details of many Irish folk events can be found in the folk listings of the weekly magazine *Time Out*.

A large number of pubs which feature live Irish music can be found in and around the Holloway Road, N7/N19. Some, like the *Archway Tavern* and the *Half Moon*, have groups playing every night, while for others live music is confined to weekends or just one evening during the week.

If you fancy an evening out, a walk around some of these pubs on a Friday or Saturday is recommended. The best starting point is the *Archway Tavern,* Archway Close, N19 (071-272 2840), directly opposite the Archway Underground Station. There is a large music lounge at the back of the pub. The traditional Irish dish of bacon and cabbage is available along with other meals between 5.30 and 8pm in the front bar which is open every night until 12.30am (last admission 11pm). Videos of Gaelic football matches are also shown here.

Going south down the Holloway Road, within ten minutes' walk of the Archway Tavern are *The Norfolk Arms,* 557 Holloway Road, N19 (071-272 0518), *The Cock,* 596 Holloway Road, N7 (071-263 7723), *The Half Moon,* 471 Holloway Road, N7 (071-272 3634) and *The Good Intent,* 52 Wedmore Street, N19 (071-263 5267). Other pubs in the vicinity which feature Irish music include: *The Whittington Cat,* 89 Highgate Hill, N19 (071-272 3274) and *The Victoria,* 203 Holloway Road, N7 (071-607 1952), music Thursday to Sunday.

Other Irish music venues in London include:
Molly Malone's, 75 Harrow Road, N16 (071-284 1943) Live music most evenings.
Edinburgh, 125 Newington Green Road, N1 (071-226 6604). Live music Saturday 9pm to 11pm.
Weavers Arms, 98 Newington Green Road, N1 (071-226 9611). Music at weekends.
Finsbury Park Tavern, 263 Seven Sisters Road, N4 (081-809 0192). Music at weekends plus Gaelic football videos.
Plough and Harrow, 419 High Road, Leytonstone, E15 (081-539 1683). Music 10pm to 1am weekdays, 8pm to midnight Sunday.

'Inside Out'

Interview with Yvonne, 19, a nurse . . .

"I came over here because for me it was the only way of getting a decent job. I didn't really want to fill in lots of forms to go to college. I'd done a secretarial course in Ireland but I didn't really want to be a secretary. I suppose coming to England is one way of getting a job and there are a lot of nurses in the same boat as me. Loads of people who came nursing with me when I started were Irish. Out of the 45 in my set, half are Irish and we have our own little Irish ways. Being an Irish nurse means something over here. Definitely on the wards it's like if you're Irish you should be that bit more kind and caring and extra nice to your patients.

I love it over here, the freedom is great. When I came over here first of all I thought it would be terrible, but it's not, it's brilliant. There are great night clubs like the Swan in Stockwell, The Shannon, The Plough and Harrow and all the Irish pubs. I feel really a part of the Irish community and I think that we have made our mark here with everything. We have everything we want, we stand out and I don't feel a bit English. No, I don't feel that the English have touched me one bit. I feel I'm Irish over here, but I don't miss Ireland at all, only my family over there."

SPORT

On every Sunday afternoon during the summer teams with names like Acton Gaels and Father Murphy's are out on sports fields across London playing the Irish sports of Gaelic football and hurling. To the uninitiated, Gaelic football looks rather like a cross between rugby and soccer, and hurling bears some resemblance to hockey. Gaelic football and hurling are both 15-a-side games played on a pitch with rugby-style posts. Gaelic football is played with a soccer ball, which is struck by hand or foot, and hurling with a small leather ball, which is struck by wooden sticks similar to those used in hockey.

Both games use the same scoring system: a single point if the ball passes over the crossbar, and a goal, worth three points, if the ball goes under the crossbar. On a scoreboard the single points and goals are listed separately, with the goals first. Therefore if a team's score is listed as 3-10, they have a total of 19 points and this would beat a score of 4-5, which totals only 17 points.

Hurling is fairly easy for an uninitiated observer to follow. Not so Gaelic football, where knowledge of the following rules is advantageous:

- Throwing the ball is not allowed. When it is passed it must be struck with the fist or the palm of the hand.

- The ball cannot be picked up directly off the ground. It must be intercepted in the air, or chipped up off the ground by foot.

- Players may run with the ball for as long as they are able to do so, provided only that they bounce the ball from foot to hand every four paces.

- Players are not allowed to push, trip, elbow or rugby tackle (though you may find this hard to believe when watching some matches!).

London fixtures of Gaelic sports are listed on the sports page of the *Irish Post*. The best place to see Gaelic football and hurling in the London area is at the **Ruislip Gaelic Athletics Ground**, West End Road, Ruislip (081-841 2468), where several matches are played on every Sunday afternoon between March and September.

PEOPLE

Politics

Modern Irish republicanism began with the United Irishmen, an organisation founded in 1791 under the inspiration of the American and French revolutions. **Theobald Wolfe Tone** (born Dublin 1763) was the most prominent of its leaders. Tone came to London in January 1787 to study law at the Middle Temple, EC4, and lived nearby in Hare Court, EC4. He returned to Dublin in December 1788 to complete his legal studies and to take up radical politics.

Tone's declared purpose was: 'To subvert the tyranny of our execrable government, to break the connection with England, the never ending source of our political evils . . . and to substitute the common name of Irishman in place of the denominations of Protestant, Catholic and Dissenter'. He himself was a Protestant.

In 1798 the United Irishmen staged an unsuccessful insurrection, and Tone was captured while he was accompanying French troops who had been sent to assist the rebels. Sentenced to death, Tone killed himself in his prison cell after being refused a military execution. Many United Irishmen were held in London's prisons. The best known was **Arthur O'Connor,** who was held in the Tower of London, EC3. After his release he went into exile in France, where he became a general in the French Army.

As a result of the uprisings of 1798 the British Government decided that the Irish Parliament was not fit to handle its own affairs, and coerced this exclusively Protestant body of men into assenting to the Union of Britain with Ireland in 1801. Irish MPs were thenceforth elected to the British Parliament, and the House of Commons in London thus became the stage for the great Parliamentary debates of the 19th C on 'The Irish Question'.

Daniel O'Connell (born County Kerry 1775) was the dominant Irish political figure of the early 19th C. Educated in London at a private school from 1793 to 1794, and at Lincoln's Inn college of law, WC2, between 1794 and 1796, he then returned to Ireland where he led the fight for the admission of Catholics into Parliament. O'Connell's campaign roused such mass support amongst the Irish people that by 1829 the British Government felt it prudent to concede to this demand. The Prime Minister at the time was the Duke of Wellington (see *page 162*), who was himself of Irish birth. O'Connell, elected as an MP, attended the House of Commons regularly until his death in 1847.

Feargus O'Connor (born County Cork, 1796?), was elected MP for Cork in 1833 and for Nottingham in England in 1847. O'Connor was a leading national figure in the Chartist movement, which proposed a six-point programme of democratic reform: the vote for all men, vote by ballot, equal electoral districts, the abolition of property qualifications for MPs, payment for MPs and annual parliaments. Mass petitions in support of these demands were presented to Parliament in 1839, 1842 and 1848.

On the last of these occasions the Chartists planned to rally on Kennington Common (now Kennington Park, SE11) and then to march on the Houses of Parliament to present the petition. Fearing a revolutionary uprising, the Government banned the march and appointed the Duke of Wellington to oversee the enforcement of the law. The Queen was sent to the Isle of Wight to ensure her safety, Government buildings were prepared for defence against assault, and 7000 soldiers were lined up along the Thames Embankment to prevent the marchers from crossing the river.

London's Commissioner of Police met with O'Connor just before the rally on Kennington Common and persuaded him to call off the march. Speaking at the rally, O'Connor asked the crowd to disperse peacefully afterwards, and they did so, though not without some angry opposition to this change in plan from the likes of William Cuffay (see *page 208*), who was the chairman of the committee organising the march but had not been consulted. O'Connor later presented the petition to Parliament himself.

Chartism diminished rapidly as a political force after 1848. O'Connor continued in his work as an MP until 1852, when he was certified insane. Committed to a lunatic asylum in Chiswick until 1854, he died in Notting Hill in 1855. O'Connor's funeral was attended by tens of thousands of mourners, and a monument was erected by subscription 'chiefly from the working classes' over his grave in Kensal Green Cemetery, Harrow Road, NW10 (071-969 0152). The monument bears the inscription: 'While philanthropy is a virtue and patriotism not a crime will the name of O'Connor be admired and this monument respected'.

The Irish Republican Brotherhood, founded in 1858, aimed to bring about Irish independence by the use of force. Many of its members, who were known as Fenians, ended up in London's prisons. On 12 December 1867 a disastrous attempt was made to rescue two Fenians from Clerkenwell Prison (formerly in Clerkenwell Close, ECl). The detonation of a barrel of gunpowder next to a prison wall not only failed to free the prisoners but also demolished a number of nearby houses, causing the deaths of at least half a dozen civilians. *Michael Barrett* (born County Fermanagh 1842) was found guilty of causing the explosion and was executed outside the walls of Newgate Prison (formerly in Newgate Street, ECl). It was the last public execution carried out in England.

In the early 1880s the constitutional movement for Irish Home Rule gathered pace under the Parliamentary leadership of *Charles Stewart Parnell* (born County Wicklow 1846). In 1885 the Irish Home Rulers won 85 out of the 103 Irish Parliamentary seats, and as a result the Liberal Party decided to support Home Rule, the first time a major British political party had done so. Even so, not all Liberal MPs supported their party leadership on this issue and the Home Rule bill of 1886 was defeated.

Parnell remained a powerful political figure until 1890, when he was named in a divorce case as the lover of Katharine O'Shea, the wife of a former member of his own Home Rule Party. The scandal created divisions within the Home Rule Party, and in Irish opinion at large, that persisted even after Parnell's death in 1891.

The Irish Home Rule Party remained split until 1900, when *John Redmond* (born County Wexford 1856) became its leader. He led the party through to the Home Rule bill of 1912, which was opposed by Irish Unionists under the Parliamentary leadership of *Edward Carson* (born Dublin 1854), a successful London barrister (see *Wilde, page 165*). Carson played a leading role in the formation in the north of Ireland of the Ulster Volunteers, an illegally-armed 100,000-strong Protestant paramilitary army, which threatened to set up a Protestant-led Government by force in the north if the Home Rule Bill was passed.

The Home Rule bill was indeed passed in 1914 but its operation was immediately suspended until the end of the war. On Easter Monday 24 April 1916 over 1,000 Irish nationalists took matters into their own hands when they occupied the centre of Dublin and declared Irish independence. The rebels were defeated by British Government troops after a week of street fighting, but although they had received little support from Irish Catholics during the rising itself, public opinion swung rapidly behind them upon the execution of 14 of the rebel leaders.

Sir Roger Casement (born Dublin 1864) was one of those martyrs to the cause. He had worked for many years in the British Consular Service, in which he had attracted much public attention through his exposure of colonial cruelty and exploitation in Africa and South America. Following his retirement from the service in 1912 he worked full-time in support of the Irish nationalist cause, and when war broke out in 1914 he went to Germany to muster support for a rebellion in Ireland. Casement was captured by the British when he returned to Ireland accompanying a cargo of weapons that were intended for use in the Easter Rising.

They took Sir Roger prisoner and sailed for London Tower,
And in the Tower they laid him as a traitor to the Crown.
Said he, 'I am no traitor', but his trial he had to stand.
For bringing German rifles to the lonely Banna Strand.

'Twas in an English prison that they led him to his death.
'I'm dying for my country', he said with his last breath.
He's buried in a prison yard far from his native land
The wild waves sing his Requiem on lonely Banna Strand.
- Lonely Banna Strand (traditional Irish ballad).

Casement was imprisoned in St Thomas' Tower at the Tower of London, and was hanged on 3 August 1916 at Pentonville Prison, Caledonian Road, N7. His body, which had been unceremoniously dumped into a prison lime pit, was disinterred in 1965 and reburied in Ireland after a state funeral.

Michael Collins (born County Cork 1890) emigrated to London in 1906 where he lived for nine years in Netherwood Road, W14. He worked for most of that time as a clerk in a Post Office Savings Bank. In 1909 he joined the Irish Republican Brotherhood, and when the call came in 1916 he returned to Ireland to take part in the Easter Rising. In the following years he emerged as a leading figure in the Irish Republican Army, which fought the British authorities in the Anglo-Irish War between 1919 and 1921. Collins' military tactics and theories have inspired guerilla and terrorist movements throughout the world, from Chairman Mao to anti-Nazi resistance groups, and of course, the modern I.R.A.

Terence MacSwiney (born Cork 1879), was elected as the Mayor of Cork in 1920. Arrested by the British at an IRA conference, he was sentenced to two years in prison. MacSwiney died in Brixton Prison, Jebb Avenue, SW2, on 24 October 1920 after serving 73 days of a hunger strike that attracted international attention. An annual commemorative Mass is held at 11.30am in Westminster Cathedral on the Sunday nearest to 24 October.

The Anglo-Irish War was brought to an end through negotiations in London in 1921 between the British Government and an Irish delegation that was jointly led by Collins. It was agreed by treaty that the Irish Free State, a self-governing dominion of the British Commonwealth, would be established in 26 counties of Ireland. The remaining six counties in the north-east of Ireland, where the Protestants were in the majority, would remain part of the United Kingdom.

However, there were many militant Irish nationalists who disagreed with the terms of the treaty and were determined to go on fighting the British until they obtained a united, independent Ireland. In 1922 civil war broke out in Ireland between the pro- and anti-treaty factions, and later in that year Collins, the Commander-In-Chief of the Free State Forces, was killed in an ambush. The anti-treaty faction called off its military campaign in 1923 and many of its members eventually entered constitutional politics.

One such was *Countess Constance Markievicz* (nee Gore-Booth). Born in London in 1868 into an Irish aristocratic family, she grew up in Ireland, returning to London in 1887 where she was presented to the Royal Court as a 'society beauty'. After studying art at the Slade School, University College, WC1, and marrying a Ukranian Count, she settled in Dublin in 1903§ . An active participant in the Easter Rising, Markievicz was interned at Holloway Prison, Parkhurst Road, N7, between May 1918 and March 1919. During her imprisonment there she was elected as a Sinn Fein MP for Dublin, the first woman ever to be elected to the British Parliament.

The start of 'The Troubles' in Northern Ireland in the late 1960s brought Irish affairs back to the centre stage of British politics. According to Tim Pat Coogan's authoritative book *The IRA* an abortive attempt to resolve the conflict in the province was made at a secret meeting in July 1972 at 96 Cheyne Walk, SW10, between an IRA delegation and the British Government. On the Irish side was *Sean MacStiofain,* the Chief of Staff of the Provisional IRA in the early 1970s, and one of its founders in 1969. Born John Stephenson in Leytonstone, London in 1928 to Irish parents, MacStofain left England for Ireland in 1959.

Over the last 20 years London has experienced numerous bombings by Irish republicans, as well as other incidents such as hunger strikes in Brixton Prison and the siege of IRA men in Balcombe Street, NW1. These events have left many dead or injured, and there is still no end in sight.

Soldiers and Adventurers

Service in the British Army formed an important source of employment for the Irish for several centuries. The Irish contribution reached its peak in the early 19th C when it was estimated that they made up about half the entire army.

Christine Kavanagh (born Dublin 1667) joined the army by pretending to be a man. Although some of the details of her life that have been passed down to us are probably fictional, it is known for certain that her sex was only revealed when she was wounded in battle. Kavanagh then became a minor celebrity, and was awarded a pension. She died in London in 1739 while on a visit to her husband at the Chelsea Hospital, Royal Hospital Road, SW3, and was buried in the Hospital churchyard with full military honours.

Arthur Wellesley, later the Duke of Wellington, was born in Dublin in 1769 into the Irish Protestant aristocracy. Educated at Eton and a French military academy, he achieved national fame in a military career that climaxed with his command of British forces in the defeat of Napoleon at Waterloo in 1815. Wellington subsequently entered politics as a Tory, and served as Prime Minister from 1828 to 1830 (see *pages 159, 160*). He lived in London at Apsley House, 149 Piccadilly, W1, from 1817 until his death in 1852. It is now the *Wellington Museum* .

Wellington was buried in the crypt at St Paul's Cathedral following a funeral procession that was attended by an estimated 1,500,000 people. A life-size reclining statue of the Duke rests on top of a separate memorial situated in the Cathedral's north aisle. Wellington's Irish origins were so little known even during his own time that when Tennyson wrote an *Ode on the death of the Duke of Wellington* in 1854, he called Wellington 'England's greatest son'.

Horatio Herbert Kitchener (born County Kerry 1850) was educated in Switzerland and at the Royal Military Academy, Woolwich, SE18. After a notable military career in Africa and India, he was appointed Minister for War in 1914. One of the few men in power who did not believe that the troops would be 'home by Christmas', his was the face, finger and moustache that appealed to the British public in the famous recruiting poster that declared 'Your country needs YOU!'.

A plaque at 2 Carlton Gardens, SW1, marks the house in which Kitchener lived from 1914 to 1915. He was killed in 1916 when a ship in which he was travelling to Russia was sunk by a mine. Kitchener was honoured with a memorial chapel at St Paul's Cathedral, the Chapel of All Souls, where the dominant theme is 'the spirit of sacrifice'. The chapel is not normally open to the public, but it is on the itinerary of most guided tours.

Thomas Blood (born 1618?, very probably in Ireland) fought for Parliament in the Civil War and was given lands in Ireland as a reward. After the Restoration of the monarchy in 1660, his estates were confiscated and he became an outlaw, mixing in all kinds of intrigue. In 1671, posing as a clergyman, he stole the Crown Jewels from the Tower of London, but was caught red-handed as he tried to escape from the scene. Blood was locked up in the Tower itself for two months, but in an extraordinary turn of events he was then pardoned, had his Irish lands restored, and was awarded a pension. Quite what determined this change in fortunes we shall probably never know.

James MacLean, the son of an Irish clergyman, was a notorious highwayman who terrorised Londoners in the mid-18th C. His hunting ground was Hyde Park, W2, then on the edge of London. After many 'daring exploits', in 1750 he was hanged at Tyburn Gallows (situated at the junction of Edgware Road and Bayswater Road, W2) apparently to the distress of a good many society ladies, with whom he had acquired a reputation for gallantry.

Writers

The group of famous Irish writers dealt with in this section is a remarkable one, not least in that few of their number are remembered for anything they wrote about Ireland or the Irish and many are indeed often wrongly assumed to have been English. That all were Protestants who left Ireland while still young has undoubtedly been an important factor in obscuring their Irish origins.

If there is any unifying factor in the work of Swift, Sterne, Goldsmith, Sheridan, Wilde and Shaw, it is in their witty and incisive observation of English social manners. Whereas their Irishness gave them an outsider's perspective on the English, their Protestant upbringing also gave them an insider's feeling of allegiance. Evidently this is a productive combination when it comes to making the English laugh at themselves.

Jonathan Swift (born Dublin *1667) is* best known for *Gulliver's Travels (1726),* a satire on contemporary life and politics that has survived in the public mind largely because of its fantasy appeal to children. Swift lived in London for long periods from his early 20s through to his mid-40s, residing at addresses in Leicester Square, WC2, New Bond Street, W1, and Bury Street, SW1. Ordained as an Anglican clergyman in 1694, he returned to settle in Ireland for good in 1714 following his appointment as Dean of St Patrick's Cathedral in Dublin.

A brilliant social critic, Swift condemned the complacency of the authorities in the face of the suffering of Ireland's poor. In the macabre satire *A Modest Proposal for Preventing the Children of Poor People in Ireland from being a Burden to their Parents or Country* (1729), he suggests that these children be used as food for the rich: 'I have been assured by a very knowing American of my acquaintance in London, that a young healthy child well nursed is at a year old a most delicious, nourishing and wholesome food, whether stewed, roasted, baked, or boiled, and I make no doubt it will equally well serve in a fricassee, or a ragout'.

Laurence Sterne (born County Tipperary 1713) is the author of *The Life and Opinions of Tristram Shandy,* a humorous and inventive novel that was denounced for lewdness at the time of the publication. The son of an army ensign, Sterne was raised in various Irish garrison towns before being sent to school in Yorkshire at the age of ten. Ordained as an Anglican clergyman, in 1738 he became vicar of Sutton-on-the-Forest in Yorkshire. Following the instant success of the first volume of *Tristram Shandy* in 1760, Sterne was feted in London literary society. He died of pleurisy in Old Bond Street, W1, in 1768 .

Oliver Goldsmith (born County Longford 1728) *is* best known today for the poem *The Deserted Village* (1770), the novel *The Vicar of Wakefield* (1766) and the play *She Stoops to Conquer* (1773). The son of an Irish clergyman, he left Ireland for Scotland in his early 20s after failing in his efforts to enter the Church himself. Following travels on the Continent, Goldsmith arrived penniless in London in 1756, where he struggled to make a living as a writer. He was under imminent threat of arrest for debt when his friend Doctor Samuel Johnson managed to sell the manuscript of *The Vicar of Wakefield.* Goldsmith died in 1774 in Brick Court, WC2. He was buried in the churchyard of the Temple Church, off Inner Temple Lane, EC4, and a monument was erected to him in Westminster Abbey, SW1.

Richard Brinsley Sheridan (born Dublin 1751) left Ireland at the age of eight to attend Harrow School, High Street, Harrow. He settled in London where he made his name as the author of the witty stage comedies *The Rivals* (1775), *The School for Scandal* (1777) and *The Critic* (1779). As an MP between 1780 and 1812, Sheridan was a noted speaker in the House of Commons. Here he delivered one of the neatest ripostes in Parliamentary history: 'The Right Honourable Gentleman is indebted to his memory for his jests, and to his imagination for his facts'.

Sheridan was in serious financial difficulties towards the end of his life, and in 1816, as he lay on his death bed, his house at 14 Saville Row, W1 (marked by a plaque), was repossessed by bailiffs. Ironically, he was then given a lavish public funeral and an honoured, and expensive, burial in Westminster Abbey.

Abraham 'Bram' Stoker (born Dublin 1847), began his working life as an Irish civil servant. He moved to London in 1878 to join the management of the Lyceum Theatre, Wellington Street, WC2. Of his many novels only *Dracula* (1897) is still widely read. Notwithstanding its treatment in film and comic book, this is a surprisingly good novel, a powerful and genuinely chilling piece of writing. Stoker died in 1912 and his body was cremated at Golders Green Crematorium (see *page 133*). A plaque at 18 St Leonard's Terrace, SW3, marks the house in which he lived from 1896 to 1906.

Oscar Fingal O'Flahertie Wills Wilde was born in Dublin in 1854. After education at Trinity College, Dublin, and Magdalen College, Oxford, Wilde settled in London where he established a reputation as an aesthete and wit. A master of the witty one-liner, many of his epigrams still bear repetition in modern conversation, as for example: 'There is only one thing in the world worse than being talked about, and that is not being talked about'. In his literary output Wilde is best known for the novel *The Picture of Dorian Gray* (1891), the play *The Importance of Being Earnest* (1895) and the poem *The Ballad of Reading Gaol* (1898).

A plaque at 34 Tite Street, SW3, marks the house in which Wilde lived between 1884 and 1895. It was while he was at this address that he became embroiled in one of the most celebrated scandals of Victorian times. The Marquees of Queensberry threatened to expose Wilde as a homosexual because he disapproved of Wilde's relationship with his son, Lord Alfred Douglas. Although Wilde was a homosexual, he decided to sue Queensbury for libel. Wilde's case fell apart under cross-examination by Edward Carson (see *page 160*) and Wilde was then put on trial himself at the Central Criminal Court, Old Bailey, EC4, for his homosexual activities.

Sentenced to two year's hard labour, Wilde served six months at Wandsworth Prison, Heathfield Road, SW18, and the rest of his sentence at Reading Gaol in Berkshire. After his release he lived in Italy and France. He died in Paris in 1900, converting to Catholicism on his death bed.

George Bernard Shaw (born Dublin 1856) started working life as a clerk in an estate office in Dublin. He came to London in 1876 where he spent many years struggling as a writer before he made his name as a playwright with *The Devil's Disciple* in 1897. Other plays by Shaw that are still frequently performed include *Arms and the Man* (1894), *Man and Superman* (1903), *Pygmalion* (1913), *Heartbreak House* (1919) and *Saint Joan* (1923). His plays on Irish themes - *John Bull's Other Island* (1904) and *O'Flaherty, VC* (1915) - are seldom revived. *Pygmalion,* which was set in London, was made into a British film of the same name in 1938, and into the very successful American musical *My Fair Lady,* filmed in 1964.

In his plays Shaw was very fond of commenting on 'the English', as for example: 'There is nothing so bad or so good you will not find an Englishman doing it; but you will never find an Englishman in the wrong. He does everything on principle. He fights you on patriotic principles; he robs you on business principles; he enslaves you on imperial principles.' - *The Man of Destiny* (1895).

A plaque at 29 Fitzroy Square marks the house in which Shaw lived from 1887 to 1898. Shaw left London in 1906 and moved out to Hertfordshire, where he died in 1950. He was awarded the Nobel Prize for Literature in 1925.

William Butler Yeats was a central figure in the Irish literary revival at the turn of the century, and co-founded the famous Abbey Theatre in Dublin. Although he wrote a number of plays, such as *The Countess Cathleen* (1892), he is best known for his poetry. He was awarded the Nobel prize for Literature in 1923.

Yeats' family moved to London shortly after his birth in Dublin in 1865. He lived at 23 Fitzroy Road, NWI (marked by a plaque), from 1867 until 1873. After attending the Godolphin School, Hammersmith, W6, he returned with his family to Ireland in 1880 where he went to art school in Dublin. Yeats came back to London in 1887, and in 1895 took up residence at 5 Woburn Walk, WC1 (marked by a plaque). He kept these rooms until 1919, though he spent much of the intervening period in Ireland. Yeats then settled permanently in Ireland, where he served as a senator in the Irish Parliament between 1922 and 1928. He died in the south of France in 1939.

Sean O'Casey (born Dublin 1880) wrote his best known plays - *The Shadow of a Gunman* (1923), *Juno and the Paycock* (1924) and *The Plough and the Stars* (1926) - while he was working as a manual labourer in Dublin. *Juno and the Paycock,* which dealt controversially with the Irish civil war, met with riotous protests at its premiere at the Abbey Theatre in 1926. Hurt by attacks on his work, O'Casey left for London and a career as a full-time writer. O'Casey lived in London until 1938 when he moved to Devon where he died in 1964. He was cremated at Golders Green Crematorium (see *page 133),* where his ashes were scattered in the Garden of Remembrance between the Shelley and Tennyson rose beds.

In some of his later plays O'Casey casts a critical eye on intolerance and superstition in Irish society. In *Cock-a-Doodle Dandy* (1949) a young woman returns from London to a narrow-minded Irish rural community, attracting suspicion even from her own father: 'Since that one come back from England, where evil things abound, there's sinister signs appearin' everywhere, evil evocations floatin' through every room'. At the conclusion of the play, the woman decides to return to England, 'A place where life resembles life more than it does here'.

LITERATURE

Girls in their Married Bliss by Edna O' Brien (1964). A bleak tale with an ironic title about two Irish girls who emigrate to London and get married to expatriate Irishmen. *Recommended.

London Irish by John Broderick (1979). When an elderly, rich Irish building contractor living in London decides to marry his young American secretary, alarm bells ring for his erstwhile heirs, his niece and nephew in Dublin. They travel to London to investigate and slowly start to uncover an unsavoury tale of deception. *Recommended.

Duffy Is Dead by J.M. O'Neill (1987). A slice of Irish low life in North-East London. Calnan runs a pub in Dalston, and when a regular called Duffy dies, Calnan ends up arranging his funeral. The rather rambling storyline takes in a raid by the anti-terrorist squad, dodgy goings-on by his fellow Irish drinkers, and Calnan eventually losing his job because of an undeclared criminal conviction coming to light.

Builders, Chancers and Crack by Brendan Ward (1985). A collection of good-humoured anecdotal tales about Irish building workers in England. The 'crack' in the title of the book is a much-used Irish term for 'fun'.

'Inside Out'

Interview with Ian, late 20's, a building worker . . .

"I've been over here seven years. I didn't have a job when I came over, I just walked around looking into building sites. A friend of mine helped get me a job and now the vast majority of people I work with are Irish. It all depends if you're qualified or not, most of the people I work with they're not very well qualified. So they've got trades.

I came from a rural background, a little village with a population of ninety people to London where the population is nearly ten million. That was very strange. All the people, everybody rushing, no one would talk to you, everything was just a mad rush. I don't know if I'm going to settle here but I do like it. You get more freedom of choice, more facilities here. All you have to do is walk around the corner to bars, shops, cinemas, swimming pools, sports complexes, whatever, you get a lot wider range of things you can do socially and you don't have to travel whereas back home you do. Ireland's a very expensive country to live in and I'd get bored there probably because I've got used to a different lifestyle.

After seven years here I still haven't lost my accent. I don't go to mass anymore but I still pray. I usually work six days a week and Sunday is a day to rest and get over a hangover, and to buy an Irish paper to keep up with what's happening back home. I think many people in London treat the Irish as being backward, which is totally wrong. Some of the most educated people here are Irish. A lot of qualified Irish people come over here and get top jobs. People see an Irishman as an ignorant builder which most of them aren't anyway. I don't think the Irish stand up for themselves very well. We're a bit easy going. If something bothers us we more or less put up with it, rather than complain. We learn to cope even though we mightn't like it, but we take it as part of life."

Turkish Cypriot café, Green Lanes.

GREEK &
TURKISH LONDON

HISTORY

It may strike some readers as odd to join Greeks and Turks together in one section of this book, but until very recently, almost all Greeks and Turks in London were from Cyprus, and Cypriots, whether Greek or Turkish, share a common culture and history - if not religion.

Cyprus, the third largest island in the Mediterranean, is peopled by a Greek-speaking majority (Greek Orthodox Christians) and a Turkish-speaking (Muslim) minority. The island came under British control in 1878, and in the 1920s Cypriots began to settle in Britain, attracted chiefly by work in the catering trade. By 1941 there were some 10,000 Cypriots in Britain, but it was not until the mid-50's that immigration really gathered pace, with most arrivals coming from the villages of Cyprus.

Greek Cypriot immigrants of the 1950s settled around Camden Town, where a small community had been established in the 1930s, whilst the Turkish Cypriots settled over a wider area across Islington and Hackney. Most Cypriots found work in catering, the garment industry or in the manufacture of leather goods - trades that remain important sources of employment today.

Emigration from Cyprus was encouraged not only by economic opportunities in Britain, but by the violence that broke out in 1955 when the National Organisation of Cypriot Fighters (EOKA) took up arms against the British authorities. EOKA's aim of uniting Cyprus with Greece was opposed by Turkish Cypriots, and the consequent inter-communal violence further complicated the situation. A compromise was eventually reached, and on 19 February 1959 an agreement to establish Cyprus as an independent republic was signed in London by the British, Turkish and Greek Governments, with the approval of the Greek Cypriot and Turkish Cypriot representatives. However, it was not independence but the Commonwealth Immigrants Act of 1962 that checked Cypriot immigration to Britain, which peaked at 25,000 arrivals in 1961.

In 1974 troops from the Turkish mainland invaded Cyprus in response to the overthrow of the Cypriot Government in a coup d'etat backed by the mainland Greek junta. The Turkish occupation of the northern half of the island led to the displacement of about 180,000 Greek Cypriots from the Turkish sector, and 20,000 Turks from the Greek sector. Over 10,000 of these people left for Britain, where many had friends and relatives. However, with no legal right of residence here, and the British Government unwilling to grant them refugee status, most have now been forced to return to Cyprus.

Today Cyprus remains partitioned, but the rancour of events in Cyprus has mercifully been kept out of community relations between Greek and Turkish Cypriots in London. However, linguistic and religious differences remain, and a greater degree of social mixing is limited not so much by hostility as by the social inertia of two communities who are no longer forced to come to terms with each other through sheer necessity.

Cypriots moved out of Camden Town in the late 1960s and the 1970s, and today Cypriot Greeks and Turks live chiefly in Hackney, Palmers Green, Islington and, in particular, Harringay.

The census of 1991 recorded 50,684 Cypriot-born people living in London, and the Cypriot community can probably be numbered at around 100,000 (there are only about 650,000 people in Cyprus itself). In Cyprus the Turks make up about 20 percent of the population, and it is thought that they account for roughly the same proportion of Cypriots in Britain. In comparison with the Cypriot community, the number of mainland Greeks and Turks in Britain is relatively small, but there has been a significant increase in mainland Turkish immigration since the mid-1980s.

'Inside Out'

Interview with 'Cleopatra', a 'BBC' (British-born Cypriot) dress designer . . .

"I studied at St Martin's school of art. I've always had lots of English friends and my whole influence there is of British Culture and British fashion eccentricity. My other design influence is mainly the Greek wedding, in which everyone goes completely over the top, and there is complete happiness. My designs are expressing the extravagant side of my Greek nature, I suppose.

My parents came over here in the late 50's and they actually met over here. I've got to admit there's a real identity crisis going on. You have people who came over in the late 50's and early 60's and they can get stuck in a time warp, stuck in their own communities and in a certain way of thinking. Of course like in Cyprus things have progressed, the modern world has taken over and they've changed with the times.

It's hard when I was growing up. I'd have to be a nice Greek girl at home, with the family and doing the chores that are expected. Then you go to school and mix with the British, with all different other communities. So it's like almost leading a double life. It's hard when you get involved in relationships outside because it's hard to mix the two, because it's a real difference in cultures. What we have to do is find a happy medium, really.

I think we need to get out of ourselves a bit more. Because in our community, everyone is quite passionate and everyone loves everyone else. Outside of the community we tend to be more reserved and not ourselves really. I don't know if it's like the British way or whatever, but I think we need to be more ourselves."

GREEN LANES, HARRINGAY ——————

The Green Lanes area of Harringay is the most important Cypriot residential and shopping district in London. In some of the streets that lead off Green Lanes over half the houses are occupied by Cypriots, and on Green Lanes itself, between Hermitage Road in the south and Falkland Road in the north, there are many Cypriot shops, take-aways, travel agents and banks.

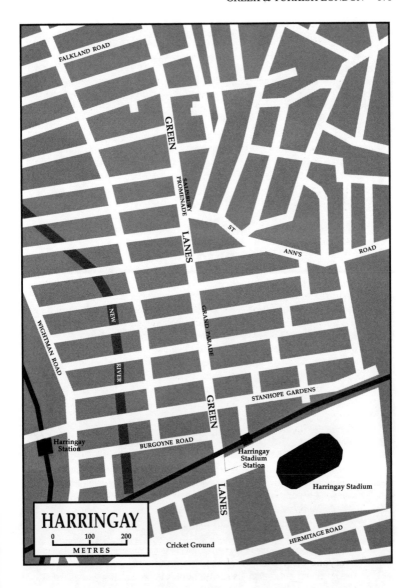

HARRINGAY

0   100   200
METRES

Cypriot cafes are a distinctive feature of the area, though as is made clear by the net curtains or boards that screen their interiors, they are not intended for use by the general public. Cypriot men (no women) meet here to chat, drink coffee and brandy, play tavli (a kind of backgammon) and read the newspapers (Greeks are most likely to read the British-published Greek-language weekly *Parikiaki Haravghi,* and Turks the European edition of *Hurriyet,* a Turkish mainland daily). The cafes are usually associated with particular towns or villages in Cyprus, some of whose populations have been transplanted almost in their entirety to London.

From top to bottom: 1. Kneading dough; 2. Baking bread; 3. The shop.

On your visit to Green Lanes keep an eye out for 'eyestones', the Cypriot good luck charms that resemble small glass eyes. They can be spotted hanging up in shops, dangling from car mirrors and as amulets worn around children's necks. Eyestones are supposed to have the power to ward off bad luck brought by the evil eye - an envious look from someone who is attracted by a show of wealth, achievement or beauty.

HARRINGAY: SHOPPING

Trehantiri, 367 Green Lanes, N4 (081-802 6530). Open from 10am to 7pm Monday to Saturday, 11am to 6pm Sunday. Large stock of Greek (mainland and Cypriot) music on record and cassette. Also Greek books, newspapers, magazines and a limited range of gifts (eyestones, worry beads, model bouzoukis, dolls in national costume). Musical instruments include bouzoukis.

Greek City, 50 Grand Parade, Green Lanes, N4 (081-800 9685). Open from noon to 10pm Monday to Saturday, 12 noon to 10pm Sunday, (closed Wednesday). Video rentals of Greek films.

Bahar Video, 343 Green Lanes, N4 (081-802 1391). Open from 10am to 8pm Monday to Sunday. Video rentals of Turkish films (some English-subtitled), small selection of Turkish music cassettes.

SHOPPING (FOOD AND DRINK)

Most Cypriot shops stock a fairly similar range of goods from Cyprus, Greece and Turkey - though shops run by the Muslim Turks will not stock any pork on religious grounds.

Popular Cypriot vegetables such as artichokes and aubergines are conspicuous in the greengrocers. In the grocers look out for yoghurts, halva sweets (hard, flat blocks made from crushed sesame seeds), olives and vine leaves (sold both packaged and loose), and white cheeses such as feta (which tastes like a cross between cottage and cheddar cheese) and halloumi (which is pungent, salty and rubbery).

In both grocers and butchers you can find lountza (smoked loin of pork), zalatina (jellied pork), sheftalia (minced pork, beef or lamb wrapped up in a skin of fat), and sausages such as loukanika (minced beef or pork with wine) and bastourma (beef and garlic). Grocers and off-licences stock Cyprus sherry, ouzo (a clear aniseed drink that tastes rather like Pernod), plus Cypriot brands of beer (Keo), wines (Othello, Aphrodite, Arsinoe) and brandies (Brandy '31, Anglias).

Nobody should neglect to visit the Cypriot patisseries on a trip to Green Lanes. Try the cheesecakes, which have been made in the Greek world for over 2,000 years, and the rich, sweet pastries such as baklava, kataifi, trigona and galatopoureko. Sweetbreads called flaounes are particularly associated with Easter celebrations, but are also available the rest of the year round. Made out of cheese, raisins, sesame seeds and eggs, they look like huge Cornish pasties. The patisseries also sell large, disc-shaped white loaves, and some savoury snacks.

Both of the patisseries listed below specialise in elaborate made-to-order wedding cakes, which can often be seen on display in their shop windows. These cakes can vary in construction from a modest three-tier structure to an astonishing eight-tier extravaganza incorporating a revolving upper tier, a water tank with live fish and a middle compartment from which doves are released!

Halepi Patisserie, 24 Grand Parade, Green Lanes, N4 (081-802 5585, 800 9272). Open from 9am to 9pm Monday to Thursday, 9am to 10pm Friday to Sunday. Greek Cypriot. Also stocks the huge white candles which are carried in church during Greek christening services.

Yasar Halim Patisserie, 495 Green Lanes, N4 (081-340 0811). Open from 8am to 10pm Monday to Sunday. Closes 9.30pm Monday. Turkish Cypriot. Try their Cypriot pizza - the Italian idea, but using Cypriot sausage, yoghourt and white cheese.

Andreus Michlis Grocers, 33 Salisbury Road, N4 (081-802 0188). Open from 9.30am to 7pm Monday to Saturday. Specialises in watermelons, a Cypriot favourite.

Kimon and Venus, 75/76 Grand Parade, Green Lanes, N4 (081-800 5268). Open from 9.30am to 9pm Monday to Saturday, 12 noon to 2pm Sunday. Off-licence, specialises in Greek drinks.

HARRINGAY: EATING OUT

Green Lanes is not a centre for Cypriot restaurants, and those in the area are nothing special. There are however many take-aways serving doner and shish kebabs, sheftalia, etc, that are worth visiting.

Helicon Restaurant, 395 Green Lanes, N4 (081-348 8858). Open from 6pm to midnight Monday to Thursday, 6pm to 2.30am Friday and Saturday. Cypriot restaurant. Live music and belly dancing Friday and Saturday.

Faros, 52 Grand Parade, Green Lanes, N4 (081-802 5498). Open from 12 noon to 3pm, 5.30pm to midnight Monday to Sunday. Cypriot restaurant.

'Inside Out'

Interview with Elias, owner of a factory in the Green Lanes area which makes wedding dresses . . .

"In the early fifties, one of my brothers, who was a tailor, and one of my sisters, who was a seamstress, they came over to England looking for work. They were offered some dresses to make and they turned out to be wedding dresses. And that's how this whole business started.

To me there is no Turkish or Greek Cypriot. We are all Cypriot. They are Muslims, the others are Christians. I happen to be baptised Christian, that's all, but I am a Cypriot. We have Muslims here working with us. They don't mind us and we don't mind them. We get on very well. Where wedding dresses are concerned, there are no differences in style between the two communities. By tradition, both prefer white. In the old days, with Muslims, they preferred higher necklines and closer sleeves but that's a thing of the past. We are modernised, we are anglicised.

Pinning money to the wedding dress at the wedding is a Cypriot tradition, both Muslim and Christian. I think it started where instead of giving a present to the wedding couple and they were ending up with half a dozen kettles, they gave them the money to buy whatever they want.

The fit of the wedding dress must have plenty of movement to give a chance to the people to pin all of those hundreds and thousands of pounds on it! If it's skin tight, they can't do it.

The spring is the wedding season. In July and August everybody is away in Cyprus, and they stay for 4 or 5 or 6 weeks. If you had a wedding at that time of year, you'd be having it all by yourself.

We brought our own customs with us and we try to keep them. Weddings are a family affair and it's a chance to meet all your friends and family. The closeness of family is a very important factor in our life.

Matchmaking has died. In the old days that's how young people used to meet. Now the boys and girls meet outside at discos and restaurants and so on. There is always the chance the family won't approve of the choice but once the two people are of age, there is nothing you can do about it. It can cause friction, but you have to accept it. It's difficult being a parent. Always has been."

GREEN LANES, STOKE NEWINGTON —

In Stoke Newington, at the southern end of Green Lanes (a couple of miles down the road from Harringay), a small cluster of Turkish shops and cafés serve a specifically Turkish Cypriot community.

Shopping
Muzik Dunyasi, 58 Green Lanes, N16 (071-254 5337). Open from 10am to 8.30pm Monday to Sunday. A bit of everything: eyestones, jewellery, ornate clocks, Turkish books and a large selection of Turkish music on CD and cassette. Stocks a fascinating collection of the Turkish water-cooled smoking pipes which are known in Britain as hookahs, and in Turkey as nargiles.

Shopping (Food and Drink)
Ali Baba Delicatessen, 47 Newington Green, N16 (071-359 2338). Open from 9am to 9pm Monday to Sunday. Turkish Cypriot delicatessen.
Manor Farm Bakery, 108 Green Lanes, N16 (071-254 7907). Open from 7am to 8pm Monday to Saturday. Turkish Cypriot bakery and patisserie.

Eating Out
Cauli Balik Fish Restaurant, 131 Green Lanes, N16 (071-704 1003). Open from 12 noon to midnight Monday to Sunday. Restaurant specialising in Turkish fish dishes. Very ethnic with few non-Turkish customers.
Hodja Nasreddin, 53 Newington Green Road, N1 (071-227 7757). Open from 12 noon to 1.30am Monday to Sunday (except open until 4am Friday and Saturday). Turkish Cypriot restaurant.

'Inside Out'

Interview with Mehmet, early 30s, the manager of a Turkish Cypriot football team based in a village café in Green Lanes . . .

"The origin of these cafés go back to Cyprus. In the villages there, the café was the meeting place. The men left the women at home, came to the café and organised what the village needed, like if there was anyone that needed help, doing the farming and so on.

When the first generation came from Cyprus in the 50s from the village, they brought their home roots and did the same thing here. They formed a village association, and one of the first things they organised was to give the village association a home base in this café and what that's done is to keep their generation together.

Then over the years many of the village associations, they formed football clubs, and there are now twelve to fifteen clubs who play regularly on a Sunday. Also we have a united team that represents all the Turkish-Cypriots, and we play against the equivalent Greek side and we always beat them!

I go back to my village often, and it's a real relief. Here we live in a society that is very demanding, very fast. When you get back home and the door of the airplane opens, everything is so much slower. For example going to a restaurant, there I am eating away and all of a sudden the waiter comes over to me and looks at me, and I say to him, 'why are you looking at me?' and he says 'why are you rushing your food?' I say, 'I'm not rushing my food, I'm just eating'. So that just proves that when we are living here in London, its 100 mph, get through your meal and then go and do what you're supposed to be doing, whereas everything there is just a lot slower.

I came over here when I was six months old. When my parents' generation came from Cyprus they brought their rules with them, very strict. Like parents had to agree to marriages, and their children had to marry Turkish Cypriots or 9 out of 10 families wouldn't even speak to them. I think that's wrong. Yes, I would like my daughter to marry a Turkish Cypriot. Otherwise your views are different, your upbringing is different. I feel there are so many barriers to cross. But if she doesn't, I'll back her 100%. I'll give her all my support.

I think that we, the Turkish Cypriots, have really been forgotten. When if you ask the British public about Cyprus all they know is that it's Greek. Whenever there is a television programme, it's always the Greek-Cypriots that and the Greeks this. And even here we have an influx of Kurds coming over from Turkey and the emphasis is on them now. We've been here since the war and we've just been forgotten about. The Turkish Cypriots are here in London and I think more attention should be paid to us and our homeland."

OTHER PLACES TO VISIT ────────

The Church of All Saints, Pratt Street, Camden Town, NW1.

Most Greek Cypriots belong to the Greek Orthodox Church, one of the oldest of Christian churches. From a broad theological perspective, the Greek Orthodox Church is in many respects quite close to the High Anglican Church - though there are of course vast cultural differences.

During the early years of Cypriot immigration to Britain, the Greeks Cypriots worshipped at the Cathedral of Aghia Sophia (Divine Wisdom) in Moscow Road, W2. This was purpose-built in Byzantine style by mainland Greeks in 1878, and is still associated with that community. After the Second World War the cathedral became too small to hold the increasing number of Cypriot worshippers, and so the Cypriots took over the vacant *Church of All Saints* in Camden Town, which they opened for worship in 1948. If you want to go inside, phone 071-485 2149 to arrange a convenient time for a visit.

The interior of All Saints has been remodelled in a distinctively Greek Orthodox style. A large wooden iconostasis (icon stand) separates the sanctuary from the main body of the church. On the iconostasis, and dotted around the rest of the church, hang Orthodox icons - pictures of religious scenes painted in the traditional flat Byzantine style. The icon in the centre of the southern wall, which was painted in Asia Minor, dates from the 1730s. However, despite their apparent age, many of the other icons were painted only in the 1950s.

Tied on to the frames of some of these icons are taximata, representations of parts or of the whole of the human body which are usually made out of tin, aluminium or silver. They are attached here by worshippers in the belief that the icons act as channels of divine power, and that the saint depicted in the icon can intercede on behalf of the donor in medical or other matters. It was a dispute in the Orthodox Church about the role of icons, which were banned from churches between AD 730 and 843, that gave us the word iconoclast, from the Greek for image-breaker.

The Church of All Saints has witnessed some controversy in its own time . One of its priests, Kallinikos Macheriotis, was deported from Britain in 1956 on suspicion of having raised funds to aid EOKA's armed struggle in Cyprus against the British. One of the leaders of that struggle was Archbishop Makarios, the head of the Cypriot Church, who became President of Cyprus upon its independence in 1960. He conducted the service at All Saints on a number of occasions over the following years.

For the Orthodox Church, Easter is at least as important a festival as Christmas, and it continues to be celebrated as such by the Greek Cypriot community in Britain. On Good Friday evening a large embroidery which depicts Christ being placed in the tomb is taken from its glass case in All Saints and paraded through the neighbouring streets of Camden Town, accompanied by hundreds of singing worshippers. If you wish to observe these celebrations contact All Saints for details - and bear in mind that the Orthodox Church calculates the date of Easter in a different way from the Western churches, so it can fall on a different weekend.

Approaching the Easter period you will see olive branches on sale in Cypriot shops. These are left by worshippers in the church over the Easter period, then taken home and the leaves burnt for incense. Another Easter custom followed by Greek Cypriots is that of dyeing eggs, usually in the

Worshipper kissing an icon of Christ on entering the Church of All Saints, Camden Town.

colour red to symbolise the blood of Christ. Red-dyed eggs are given out to every member of the congregation at Easter services.

'Inside Out'

Interview with Archbishop Gregorios, who started his work in the Greek Orthodox church as an assistant priest at the Church of All Saints in 1960 . . .

"I was very pleased to be sent here to England. Here, I met many immigrants of different ages and with many problems. It was a challenge for me. In this country, the church was their refuge. They would come and get advice and ask the priest for assistance, we were invited to their homes to help them, because they were in a new country. They didn't know much of the language, they didn't know the customs or the city of London. They were insecure in many senses because they were strangers in a strange land. I used to go to many houses for their family problems, children's problems, and so on.

Camden has changed a lot. This used to be the centre of the Greek Orthodox community. People have moved since, but the church here remains very important for the community. It's a historical place, because it was the first to be established by the new immigrants.

Inside the church here at All Saints, you'll see icons, holy pictures. It is one of the special characteristics of the Orthodox church. Icons are very sacred objects, they are painted by people after prayer and fasting. Iconography as an art was established by the monks, by holy people, but now many young people and lay men and women, they paint icons because they want to continue this ancient tradition. The icon as such is a sacred object. We venerate it, we make the sign of the cross and we kiss the icon. It is a veneration and respect for the person who is depicted.

God is the first artist, so in our churches we have art in order to give to the faithful the sense of the creation, the sense of the oneness of God who created this magnificent world. Our art is part of our spirituality. The church is very important to the community. Worship unites the people and gives them a sense of belonging, and so I try hard to meet their expectations."

British Museum, Great Russell Street, WC1 (071-636 1555). Open from 10am to 5pm Monday to Saturday, 2.30pm to 6pm Sunday. Admission free. The British Museum contains few items from Cyprus itself but as much Greek antique sculpture, pottery and jewellery as most people would ever wish to see. Turkish antiquities are by contrast very poorly represented.

The Museum Gift Shop sells replicas of a selection of antiquities from the museum's collection. Many of these are Greek, including several representations of Aphrodite, the Greek goddess of beauty and love who is closely associated with Cyprus. Byzantine necklaces and earrings (c. AD 600) are the only available replicas of Cypriot origin.

Theatro Technis, 26 Crowndale Road, NW1 (081-387 6617). A Cypriot theatre. Professional and amateur productions of modern and ancient Greek plays in Greek and English, and of original plays about Cypriot life in

Britain. Also performances of Cypriot poetry, dance and music.

Porchester Spa, Queensway, W2 (071-792 2919). Open for women from 10am to 10pm Tuesday, Thursday and Friday, 10am to 6pm Sunday, for men from 10am to 10pm Monday Wednesday and Saturday, 6 to 10pm Sunday mixed sexes. The last ticket each day is sold two hours before closing time. Admission charge.

The spa is renowned for its Turkish baths, which have their origin in the hot baths that were brought to Turkey by the Romans. From these the Turks developed their own style of baths, which they spread across the Middle East in the 11th C. The Crusaders brought the idea back to Britain, and by the late 14th C Turkish baths were well-established in London. Since then their popularity in Britain has varied a great deal according to trends in fashion, public hygiene and sexual mores (in the 17th and 18th C they frequently doubled as high class brothels). There are few Turkish baths operating in London today, but in line with the present trend in health and fitness, public interest is on the increase again. Turkish baths are still popular in Turkey, though with the spread of indoor plumbing they are now used more for leisure than for purposes of cleanliness.

The Porchester Baths, opened in 1929, promise 'all the traditional virtues of its Islamic forebears - complete relaxation in the company of friends and a general toning up of the body chemistry'. Your skin is cleansed and muscles toned up through a combination of steam rooms, dry heat rooms, cold showers, plunges and massages. All you need to bring is your body, as towels are provided. The attendants can explain the procedure to first-timers. Two swimming pools are available to all and included in the price of the Turkish baths; gymnasium facilities and massages are extra.

SHOPPING

Zeno, 6 Denmark Street, WC2 (071-836 2522). Open from 9.30am to 6pm Monday to Friday, 9. 30am to 5pm Saturday. New and second-hand books about Greece and Cyprus in Greek and in English. Some antiquarian books. Also postcards, greeting cards, Greek newspapers and Greek language-learning material.

The Greek Shop, 6 Newburgh Street, W1 (071-437 1197). Open from 10.30am to 6pm Monday to Saturday. Greek arts and crafts. Patterned tiles, costume jewellery, sandals, woven shoulder bags, mats, plus reproduction antique busts, vases, plates and icons.

Pipes Music Gallery, 809-811 High Road , N17 (081-808 9214). Open from 9 30am to 5pm Monday to Saturday (closed Wednesday). A general music store that usually stocks the Greek musical instrument, the bouzouki.

See also **Harringay: Shopping,** *page 173;* **Stoke Newington: Shopping,** *page 175;* and **Other Places to Visit: British Museum - Gift Shop,** *page 179.*

FOOD AND DRINK

Many Londoners are disappointed by the food served up to them on Greek holidays. 'It isn't like this at home', they complain, and they are right;

virtually every 'Greek' restaurant in London serves not Greek but Greek Cypriot food, which has been far more influenced by Middle Eastern and Turkish cuisine. Thus pitta bread, hummous and sheftalia, which are common fare in Greek Cypriot restaurants in Britain, are little known in Greece itself.

There are some marginal differences between Greek Cypriot and Turkish Cypriot food, but the average diner will probably notice only the changes in the names of some of the dishes on the menu (since most of the Cypriot restaurants in London are run by Greek Cypriots I have followed their usage). A few mainland Greek and Turkish restaurants have been listed below for anyone who is interested in exploring how their cuisines differ from the Cypriot.

Kebabs are now as familiar to Londoners as curries, pizzas and hamburgers, and diners are no longer intimidated by menus that call for the pronunciation of taramasalata (fishroe dip), hummous (chickpea dip), moussaka (minced beef between layers of aubergines and other vegetables), tsatsiki (yoghurt with mint, cucumber and garlic), and sheftalia (minced lamb, beef or pork and parsley wrapped up in a skin of fat) . For an introduction to Cypriot food, order a *meze*, a selection of a wide variety of dishes.

Eating out Cypriot-style is often much more than a culinary experience . In an effort to increase trade, many restaurateurs provide kinds of entertainment that in Cyprus itself would only ever be found in night-clubs. Live music, Greek or Turkish, is quite common, and a dance floor is sometimes provided. The Middle Eastern tradition of belly-dancing (usually performed in Britain by pale-skinned Anglo-Saxons) is found in both Greek and Turkish Cypriot restaurants.

The smashing of plates is an old Greek tradition that forcefully expresses the feeling 'to hell with tomorrow, we live for today' . It is sometimes done in night-clubs as an emphatic kind of applause for a musical performance. Plate-smashing became commercialised in Greece during the tourist boom of 1960s, and it can be enjoyed in that rather unspontaneous kind of spirit in a number of Greek Cypriot restaurants in London. A word of warning however. The management in such restaurants will not be amused if you start flinging around the plates that you have just eaten from. Cheap, clean and easy-to-break plates are specially provided for this pastime and must be ordered from the waiter by the half dozen.

'Inside Out'

Interview with Tony, who manages a company which is a major manufacturer of Cypriot food, such as taramasalata and hummous . . .

"I got into this by accident. I came over in 1960 to study with the intention of going back to Cyprus to take over our family company's head office there. But we had a branch over here in England, which at the time imported Cypriot produce, and after a few months I liked England so much I decided to stay here and take over the branch here.

I liked England very much because I liked the people a lot. I found them very hospitable and very open-minded. And I could see there was a lot more opportunity to work in England, which is a much bigger country, than in going back to Cyprus, which is a small island really.

Our company started a chain of restaurants here and we decided to make our own food for them centrally in London so as to control the quality better. Then one of the supermarkets suggested that they were very interested to buy from us because they knew we were making good hummous and taramasalata for our own restaurants. We started selling to them and then other supermarkets followed because our quality was much better than anybody else in the market. Basically we became specialists in making Cypriot and Greek food in the UK and everybody respects us for our knowledge.

Cypriots generally speaking are very entrepreneurial people. In Cyprus most of them are self-employed and when they come to England or whereever else they go, they always try to start their own businesses. The first immigrants that came over could not speak English so the only thing they could do was washing up in restaurants. From washing up, they became chefs, then they learnt a bit of English and became waiters and then they developed to finally open their own restaurants.

In many people's minds, they think that all Cypriots are running fish and chip shops and kebab places. Bur our compatriots are flourishing in various ways. In the rag trade, everybody knows there are lots of Cypriots, they are very successful. They're into hotels, making shoes, and shipping lines of course. You name it you'll find Cypriots there really. Most Cypriots are very honest, hard working people, and it's this sheer perseverance and hard work that makes them successful. You just have to put a lot of hours in.

Greeks and Cypriots who come over on holiday here, they love our products, they say that our product is much better than what's made in Greece and Cyprus, because we use much better ingredients here. The other thing I have found is that in England, we use no preservatives, whereas in Greece and Cyprus unfortunately they use preservatives in their products, and that makes them not so tasty. And a lot of my friends who come from Greece and Cyprus, they buy our products from supermarkets in England and take it back to their own country."

EATING OUT: RESTAURANTS

Central and North London

The internment of Italians during the Second World War (see *Italian London*) created a vacuum in the catering trade into which the Cypriots eagerly moved. It was in Charlotte Street, which had been known for its Italian restaurants, that Cypriot restaurateurs first made their mark in London. There are still several Cypriot restaurants at the southern end of the street, where tables, chairs and people spill out on to the wide pavements in the summer, creating a lively, continental atmosphere.

Anemos Restaurant, 32 Charlotte Street, W1 (071-636 2289, 580 5907). Open from 12 noon to 3pm, 6 to 11.45pm (last orders) Monday to Saturday. Greek Cypriot and international cuisine. This is the last place you would want to go for a quiet tete-a-tete. The waiters are under strict instructions to make sure that customers enjoy themselves, and you will be encouraged on to the dance floor and into all kinds of tomfoolery. A professional magic show further enlivens the evening. Anemos is great for office parties and Christmas celebrations, but not for the easily embarrassed. Reservations essential. A buffet lunch is served Monday to Friday. Oh, and the food is quite good too. Moderately-priced.

Elyseé Restaurant, 13 Percy Street, W1 (071-636 4804, 580 3988). Open from 12 noon to 3pm, 7pm to 3.30am Monday to Friday, 7pm to 3.30am Saturday and Sunday. Greek Cypriot and international cuisine. Live music, dancing and belly dancers every night into the early hours. Plate-smashing at £10 per dozen. A roof garden is open in the summer. Expensive.

Maples Restaurant, 56 Maple Street, Wl (071-580 4819). Open from 12 noon to 3pm, 5.30 to 11pm Monday to Friday, 6 to 11pm Saturday. Greek Cypriot cuisine. Small, cosy, stylish. Moderately-priced.

Mega-Kalamaras, 76-78 Inverness Mews, W2 (071-727 9122/2564). Open from 7pm to midnight Monday to Saturday. *Micro-Kalamaras,* 66 Inverness Mews, W2 (071-727 5082). Open from 7pm to 11pm Monday to Saturday. Mainland Greek cuisine. Both restaurants are under the same management. Their menus are the same except that the smaller restaurant (Micro) is unlicensed, so you must bring your own wine. The larger restaurant (Mega) occasionally features live music. Kalamaras, incidentally, means scholar in Greek and is the name given by Cypriots to mainland Greeks. Expensive.

White Tower, 1 Percy Street, W1 (071-636 8191). Open from 12.30pm to 2.15pm, 6.30pm to 10.30pm Monday to Friday (except not for lunch Saturday). Long-established, luxurious Greek restaurant. Very expensive.

Cypriana, 11 Rathbone Street, W1 (071-636 1057). Open from 12 noon to 3pm, 5.30pm to 11.30pm Monday to Friday, 6pm to 11.30pm Saturday. Greek Cypriot restaurant. Moderately-priced.

Rodos, 59 St. Giles High Street, WC2 (071-836 3177). Open from 12 noon to 3pm, 6pm to midnight Monday to Saturday. Greek Cypriot. Moderately-priced.

Jimmy's, 23 Frith Street, W1 (071-437 9521). Open from 12.30pm to 3pm, 5.30pm to 11pm Monday to Saturday. Greek Cypriot. Moderately-priced.

Efes Kebab House, 80 Great Titchfield Street, W1 (071-636 1953). Open from 11.30am to midnight. Turkish restaurant. Moderately-priced.

Topaki, 25 Marylebone High Street, W1 (071-486 1872). Open from 12 noon to midnight. Turkish restaurant. Moderately-priced.

The City

Gallipoli, 7-8 Bishopsgate Churchyard, EC2 (071-588 1922/23). Open from 11.30am to 3pm, 6pm to 3am Monday to Friday, 6pm to 3am Saturday. Mainland Turkish and international cuisine. Belly dancers and cabaret twice nightly between 10.30pm and 1am. Dance floor, and live Turkish and English music.

The entrance to this underground restaurant looks like a whimsical Victorian oriental-style public convenience, but it was in fact built originally as the entrance to a Turkish baths. Much of the elaborate tiling and decoration from the baths was restored for the Gallipoli's opening in 1967, and for oriental-style decor in London the place cannot be beaten. Gracing the walls of the bar are photographs of some of the restaurant's better known visitors, such as Margaret Thatcher and Aristotle Onassis.

A notice at the bottom of the main stairs explains that the restaurant is named after 'the heroic campaign which brought the English and Turkish nations closer uniting them in an alliance of friendship'. This is a curious interpretation of history, for Gallipoli is the name of a First World War campaign in which the British were soundly hammered by the Turks. Could this be some kind of private joke by the proprietors - perhaps a reference to their prices? Expensive.

EATING OUT: SHOPPING

Faros Bakery, 219 Seven Sisters Road, N4 (071-272 7075). Open from 7.30am to 7pm Monday to Saturday, Sunday 10am to 5pm. Greek Cypriot bakery. Also stock Cypriot cheeses.

Athenian Grocers, 16a Moscow Road, W2 (071-229 6280). Open from 8.30am to 7pm Monday to Saturday. Greek Cypriot grocers. Also stocks wines.

See also **Harringay: Shopping,** *page 173* and **Stoke Newington: Shopping,** *page 175.*

PEOPLE

The pop singer George Michael, born Georgios Kyriacos Panayiotu, is by far and away the best-known British Cypriot. Born in Finchley in 1963, he made a number of very successful singles in the early 1980s in the pop duo 'Wham' with Andrew Ridgeley, before going solo. His most successful single was *Careless Whisper*, which was a massive international hit. In recent years he has been much more successful in the United States, and has been based there.

BLACK LONDON

HISTORY

There have been black people in Britain as far back as Roman times, when they served here in the Roman Army. Following the departure of the Romans in the 5th C, they were not to be visitors to these shores again until the mid-16th C, when the opening up of trade with West Africa led to the arrival of black servants and entertainers. The numbers involved were very small, but they disturbed Elizabeth I, who in 1601 issued a proclamation stating that she was 'highly discontented to understand the great numbers of negars and Blackamoores which (as she is informed) are crept into this realm'. She ordered the banishment of all black people from her kingdom, but the order was evidently not very effective, for they continued to live and work in Britain.

The first era of significant black settlement in Britain was from the mid-17th C to the late 18th C, spanning the period of Britain's greatest involvement in the slave trade. During that time manufactured goods were shipped from Britain to the west coast of Africa where they were exchanged for slaves, who were shipped across the Atlantic for sale to plantation owners. The ships were then filled with sugar, cotton and tobacco (the produce of slave labour on the plantations), and taken back to Britain. The 'triangular trade', as it was known, gave a substantial boost to the growth of Liverpool, Bristol and London, and was an important element in the development of the British industrial revolution.

Most of the black people who came to Britain in the 17th and 18th C were the slave-servants of returning colonial traders, plantation owners, army officers and Government officials. Living alongside these slaves in Britain were a smaller number of free blacks. Some of them were seamen from West Africa, others had previously been slaves and had either bought their freedom or run away from their owners in Britain or in the Americas. The majority worked as servants, seamen, labourers and craftsmen, though they were all too often reduced to beggary through lack of employment. In the London region the free black population lived mainly along the river front to the east of the city in Ratcliff and Limehouse.

The black population of Britain in the 18th C, which was predominantly male, is unlikely to have been more than 10,000 strong at any one time, and was probably much smaller than that during most of this period. The majority lived in London, where they maintained a lively social life if we can judge from a newspaper account of 1764 which described how black servants 'supped, drank, and entertained themselves with dancing and music, consisting of violins, French horns and other instruments, at a public-house in Fleet-street, till four in the morning. No whites were allowed to be present, for all the performers were black'.

The legal status of slavery in Britain was never clearly defined. In practice, slavery of whites was forbidden, and free blacks could not be enslaved, but black people who were brought as slaves to Britain were generally considered to remain bound to their owners. Although it was not a widespread practice, slaves were certainly bought and sold in Britain as is demonstrated in this newspaper advertisement from 1756:

Relaxing at the Notting Hill Carnival.

'To be sold, a Negro boy age about fourteen years old, warranted free from any distemper, and has had those fatal to that colour; has been used two years to all kinds of household work and to wait at tables; his price is £25 and would not be sold but the person he belongs to is leaving off business. Apply at the bar of George Coffee house in Chancery Lane, over the Gate.'

Slavery was disapproved of by many native Britons, particularly by the poor, who saw it as a crueller variation of the treatment they themselves suffered at the hands of the ruling classes. This opposition carried little weight on a legislative level but it did assist runaway slaves, whose bids for freedom regularly led to advertisements such as the following being placed in 18th C newspapers:

'Run away from his master about a Fortnight since, a lusty Negro boy, about 18 years of Age full of pock holes; had a silver collar about his neck engrav'd Capt. Thos. Mitchel's Negro, living in Griffith Street in Shadwell.'

However, if runaways were caught, they were usually shipped over to the invariably more barbaric cruelties of slavery in the Americas, and this was a powerful deterrent to any would-be runaway.

The beginning of the end for slavery in Britain came at a trial in 1772 when a ruling was made that a slave who had deserted his master could not be taken by force to be sold abroad. This verdict was heard in the courtroom by representatives of the black community and celebrated afterwards at a Westminster public house in a 'Ball of Blacks' which was attended by some 200 black people. From then on the legal enforcement of slavery became almost impossible, and by the 1790s most slaves had made themselves free simply by leaving their owners.

Having acquired their own freedom, British black people such as Olaudah Equiano (see *page 206)*, Ignatius Sancho and Ottobah Cugoano, played a significant role in the campaign to end slavery. Cugoano judiciously pricked consciences when he wrote of the British: 'Is it not strange to think, that they who ought to be considered as the most learned and civilised people in the world, that they should carry on a traffic of the most barbarous cruelty and injustice, and that many . . . are become so dissolute as to think slavery, robbery and murder no crime?' - *Thoughts and Sentiments on the Evil and Wicked Traffic of the Slavery and Commerce of The Human Species* (1787).

By the end of the 18th C the slave trade had declined greatly in economic importance to Britain, and British public opinion, most crucially amongst the ruling classes, was turning more firmly against slavery itself. In 1807 the British slave trade was abolished, and slavery was abolished throughout the British Empire in 1834.

The effective end of slavery in Britain in the late 18th C marked the end of black immigration for about a century - excepting only the small numbers of black loyalists who returned to Britain after fighting in the American War of Independence (1775-83) and the black seamen who settled here after service in the Napoleonic Wars (1792-1815).

It is not clear what happened to Britain's black population during the 19th C, except that it almost disappeared. One reason could be that the permanently resident black population in the 18th C was actually quite small, and that many of the black people who had lived in London were either young servants (who were forcibly returned to the West Indies when they became adolescents) or sailors (for whom the mortality rate while sailing abroad was very high). Furthermore, most of the black population was male, which undoubtedly led to intermarriage with white women and the gradual absorption of their descendants into the white population. However, there is no historical evidence so far of any significant mixed race community in early 19th C London, so the question of the real size of the black community in the 18th C remains a matter for debate.

Following the establishment of new shipping links with the Caribbean and West African in the 1880s, small black communities soon developed in the dock areas of many British ports, notably in Liverpool, Cardiff and London's Canning Town. Boosted by the arrival of black merchant seamen in the First World War, they have survived as Britain's oldest black communities.

Nevertheless, the forerunners of the modern era of black settlement were the Caribbeans, and to a lesser extent, the West Africans, who came to Britain during the Second World War. Here they worked in munitions factories, as merchant seamen, and in the armed forces (principally as flight mechanics in the RAF). Their numbers were fairly small, but through sending back knowledge of the opportunities in Britain to their home countries they paved the way for the mass immigration of the 1950s and early 1960s.

Immigrants came from all over the English-speaking Caribbean, with the Jamaicans forming the largest single group. Some were recruited directly from their home countries by the National Health Service, London Transport and British Railways. Immigrants also came, though in lesser numbers, from West Africa, principally from Nigeria and Ghana.

There has been little immigration from the Caribbean since the 1960s, but immigration from Africa picked up again in the late 1980s, as Somalians and Ethiopians fled from civil war in East Africa, and as West African immigration increased again. Today there are about 700,000 black people in Britain, of whom about 425,000 live in London, concentrated in South London in Lambeth and Lewisham and in North-East London in Hackney and Harringay. Africans now make up about one third of London's black population and are becoming an increasingly important and influential part of the black community.

'Inside Out'

Interview with Angela, mid-20s, British-born of Caribbean origin . . .

"If my daughter sees a red, gold and green flag, I hope she'll associate it with Jamaica or Africa or Dominica or whatever, and I just want her to know her roots and be proud of who she is and what she is. And when she grows up, I want her to be able to do some of the things that I didn't when I was young. Like her going places, no matter what. To do anything she wants, and just be really independent and successful.

What makes me most proud about being black is that black people are still so strong and have got a lot of dignity. It's a thing that's deep in the culture, and passed down by parents, that you've got to be strong. When I think of all the amazing things that have been done to black people and yet we've held together as a people and we don't look beaten down. We dress well, we look good. We've got pride. We've still got that dignity even though we've suffered a hell of a lot in our past."

BRIXTON

Britain's first group of post-war Caribbean immigrants arrived in London from Jamaica in 1948 on the liner *Empire Windrush*. Many of this pioneering group settled in Brixton, a once prosperous suburb that was then rapidly decaying into one of the city's poorest districts. Jamaicans were predominant amongst the many black people who settled in Brixton in the 1950s and 1960s, and this is reflected in the area's association with reggae and Rastafarianism (see **People: Selassie,** *page 211),* which are both of Jamaican origin.

Until the late 1980s, Brixton was London's most prominent black district and a symbol of black cultural and political self-assertion, acquiring national attention as a result of the anti-police riots by black youths in 1981 and 1985. Brixton today is less of a focus than it once was, and other areas of London have increased in importance for the black community. However, there is still quite a lot to see of interest in Brixton, and many black institutions and organisations are still based here.

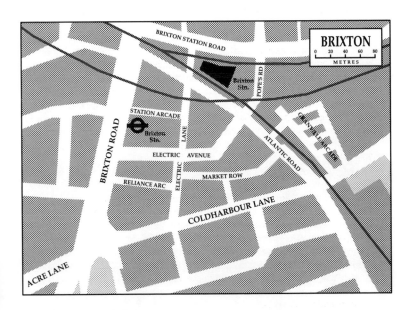

'Inside Out'

Interview with Loanna Morrison, gossip columnist on the black newspaper The Voice, whose offices are in Brixton . . .

"What's it like being a gossip columnist? Oh, you just get to have fun, you know, you go out partying every night and you get to eye up the men before anybody else sees them and make all the women jealous, and you get to talk to people a lot.

You get to mix with what is so-called black high society. Unlike the

Americans we don't really have a massive superstar high society part of the community here in Britain, but we do have a few people and everyone likes to mix and network.

It's not the same being a black gossip columnist as a white gossip columnist, because I hear too many things which I can't print. Even though I am a gossip columnist, I don't want to show people up in a bad light for the simple reason that I don't want to portray them to the white community in a bad way. So I don't do it. We have so few stars anyway, I don't want to give them any problems. So I go that much towards the edge, but not quite over it."

BRIXTON: SHOPPING

In its heyday in the late 19th C Brixton was the premier shopping centre in the whole of South London. When Electric Avenue was opened in 1888, it was one of the first shopping streets in London to be lit by electricity. Many people in their 20s and 30s will have heard of Electric Avenue through the lyrics of a chart single by the black singer Eddie Grant: 'We're going to rock down to/Electric Avenue'.

There has been a market in the tangle of narrow streets and arcades of Brixton town centre ever since the end of the 19th C. It is a general market, selling everything from second-hand clothes to fruit and vegetables. Stalls are located in Brixton Station Road, Pope's Road, Electric Avenue, Reliance Arcade, Station Arcade, Market Row and Granville Arcade. The market is closed on Sundays and Wednesday afternoons.

Shops and stalls which stock goods specifically for the black community are found in the greatest density in Granville Arcade. Look out for the following goods:

At the butchers: Caribbean specialities include goat's meat, cow's feet, salted pig's tails.

Fishmongers: Snappers, jackfish, flying fish, shark.

Greengrocers: Breadfruit, limes, mangoes, yams, green bananas, coconuts, plantains.

Grocers: Tins of ackee, breadfruit, and callaloo, bags of black-eyed beans and pounded yam, bottles of West Indian hot pepper sauce, loaves of the heavy Caribbean types of bread.

Record shops: Reggae/soul music.

Newsagents: The black British weekly newspapers *Caribbean Times, African Times* and *The Voice. The Voice* is orientated towards the younger, British-born black population; the others have a stronger slant towards news from their readers' countries of origin.

Granville Arcade

Access from Atlantic Road and Coldharbour Lane.

Jackie and Katie Fashion Wear, Second Avenue, 47 Granville Arcade, SW9 (no telephone). Open from 10am to 5pm Monday to Saturday (except to 1pm Wednesday). African-style clothes made to measure. Small selection of ready to-wear skirts, blouses and trousers.

The Wig Bazaar, Third Avenue, 57 Granville Arcade (071-733 3589). Open from 9am to 5pm Monday to Saturday (except to 1pm Wednesday). Black cosmetics, wigs and 'tie-ins' (additions to natural hair).

Nasseri Fabrics, Second Avenue, 35-36 Granville Arcade (071-274 5627). Open from 9.30 am to 5.30pm Monday to Saturday (except 1pm Wednesday). African fabrics sold by the yard or roll.

Robinsons, Third Avenue, 50/51 Granville Arcade (071-733 2405). Open from 9.30am to 5.30pm Monday to Saturday (except to 1pm Wednesday). Grocers and greengrocers which specialises in West African food. Spices, dried fish, bread, palm oil. A speciality is frozen Nigerian snails. Also stocks traditional West African teeth-cleaning sticks and Nigerian magazines and newspapers.

One Stop, Fourth Avenue, 72 Granville Arcade. Open from 9am to 5.30pm Monday to Saturday (except to 1pm Wednesday). Record shop. Reggae, soul, soca.

Arcade Bakeries, 2nd. Avenue, 1 Granville Arcade (071-733 3105). Open from 9am to 5.30pm Monday to Saturday (except to 1pm Wednesday). Caribbean breads, buns and patties.

Back Home Foods, 3rd. Avenue, 56 Granville Arcade (no telephone). Open from 8am to 5pm Monday to Saturday (except to 1pm Wednesday). Grocers and greengrocers. Specialities from Ghana and Sierra Leone.

Dagons Ltd., 1st. Avenue, 16 Granville Arcade (071-274 1665). Open from 7.30am to 5.30pm Monday to Saturday (except to 1pm Wednesday). Tropical fish including many Caribbean varieties.

Tina's Tropical Foods, 6th. Avenue, 90-91 Granville Arcade (no telephone). Open from 7.30am to 5.30pm Monday to Saturday (except to 1pm Wednesday). Greengrocers. African and Caribbean vegetables and fruits.

Elsewhere in Brixton

Red Records, 500 Brixton Road, SW9 (071-274 4476). Open from 9.30am to 8.30pm to Saturday, Sunday noon to 6pm. Record shop. Reggae, soul, jazz, African, dance and rave.

A-Z Connections, 21 Brixton Station Road, SW9 (071-738 6457). Open from 9.30am to 6.30pm Monday to Saturday. Imported clothing from Africa. Also African videos, music cassettes and handicrafts.

Afro Food Centre, 31 Electric Avenue, SW9 (071-274 4466). Open from 9am to 6pm Monday to Saturday. Grocers. Imported produce comes mainly from West Africa.

Franks, 33 Electric Avenue, SW9 (071-737 5073). Open from 9am to 6pm Monday to Saturday. Black cosmetics plus wigs and hair pieces.

Temple Gallery, 23 Brixton Station Road, SW9 (071-737 5332). Open from 9am to 6.30pm Monday to Friday (except closes at 4.30pm Wednesday, 6pm Saturday). Prints by black artists. Some exhibitions of original work by black artists.

Arts Crafts and Culture Shop, 54 Atlantic Road, SW9 (071-737 0970). Open from 9am to 6pm Monday to Saturday. Arts and crafts of Rastafarian interest.

Timbuktu Books, 378 Coldharbour Lane, SW9 (071-737 2770). Open from 10am to 6pm Monday to Saturday. Books of black interest. Some arts and crafts.

Index books, 10-12 Atlantic Road, SW9 (071-274 8342). Open from 10am to 6pm Monday to Saturday. General book shop, which specialises in politics. Good selection of literature of black interest.

BRIXTON: EATING OUT

Brixtonian Restaurant, 11 Dorrell Place SW9.

Dan Delights, 449 Coldharbour, SW9.

For further information see **Food and Drink: Restaurants,** *page 204.*

BRIXTON: PLACES TO VISIT

Black Cultural Archives Museum, 378 Coldharbour Lane, SW9 (071-738 4591). Open from 10am to 6pm Monday to Saturday. Admission free. Exhibitions on various aspects of black history. Archives may be inspected by appointment.

The Jamaican reggae musician *Bob Marley* (1945-81) never lived in Brixton but made frequent visits, giving live performances at local venues. A *plaque in Dexter Square*, off Railton Road, SW24, commemorates this 'national hero, poet and composer'. It was unveiled in 1987 by poet and reggae musician Linton Kwesi Johnson (see *Literature, page 214*).

A *plaque in the public gardens facing Brixton Library* commemorates the South African massacre of black people at *Sharpeville.* It reads: 'Sharpeville 21st March, 1960. They died so others may live'.

DALSTON ─────────────────────────────────

As the black presence in North-East London has increased, Dalston has become the focus of the black community in the area, and today Dalston is far livelier than Brixton. This is where you'll see all the latest black street fashion and hair styles, and where you'll find many of the trendiest black nightclubs. The main shopping streets are Kingsland High Street, E8, and Ridley Road, E8 (which has a large street market). On Saturdays in the summer, the centre of Dalston is packed, and the place buzzes with energy.

DALSTON: SHOPPING (incl. Food and Drink)

Trends Clothes Shop, 47 Ridley Road, E8 (071-254 5858). Open from 10am to 6pm Monday to Saturday. Specialises in clothes associated with the 'ragga' nightclub scene.

Emmannuel, 39A Ridley Road, E8 (no telephone). Open from 10am to 6pm Tuesday to Saturday. Specialises in Nigerian clothes, arts and crafts, herbal medicines.

Wentys, 41 Ridley Road, E8 (071-275 8928). Open from 9am to 6pm Monday to Saturday. Grocers. Unusual imported food from Jamaica includes bammies (made from cassava flour), gizzadas (coconut pastries) and cheese.

Joe's Shop, 166 Ridley Road E8 (071-254 5573). Open from 9am to 6pm Monday to Saturday. Basically a butchers, with goat meat always in stock, but also stocks salted fish and some fruit and vegetables.

The Business Record Store, 17 Kingsland High Street, E8 (071-249 3623). Open from 11am to 7pm Monday to Saturday (except open until 8pm Friday and Saturday). Soul imports, reggae and soca.

DALSTON: EATING OUT

West Indian Takeaway, 185 Sandringham Road, E8 (no telephone). Open from 10am to 6pm Monday to Saturday. Caribbean take-away. Curried goat meat and callaloo (similar to spinach) are usually on the menu.

Pamela's, 58 Dalston Lane, E8. Caribbean restaurant. See *page 203* for details.

THE NOTTING HILL CARNIVAL ———

The black community of Notting Hill has always been much smaller than that of Brixton (and is getting even smaller), but they have made sure of getting their share of the limelight through the creation of an African-Caribbean street festival which for the past fifteen years has been London's most popular public event. Held each year on August Bank Holiday Sunday and Monday, the Notting Hill Carnival is now the largest street festival in Europe, attracting up to half a million people over the two days.

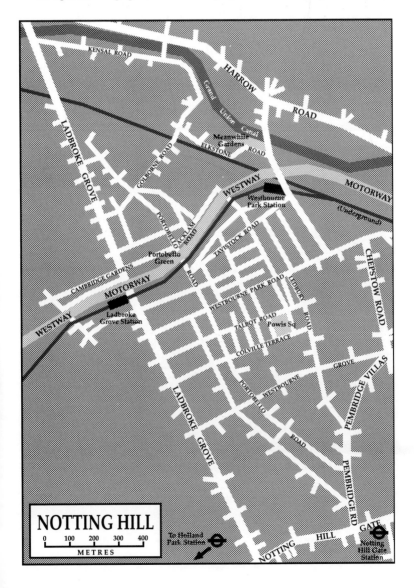

Notting Hill Carnival.

During the Carnival the whole area shown on the map is given over to music from sound systems and live bands playing soca, soul and reggae. Caribbean food is sold on street stalls, and bars have extended opening hours. Other stalls, especially down Portobello Road, sell African-Caribbean arts and crafts, clothes and literature.

Dozens of bands are featured each year. Some tour on open-backed lorries, but most play on stages in Powis Square, W11, Portobello Green (Cambridge Gardens, W10), and Meanwhile Gardens (Elkstone Road, W 10). The standard of music is high. The singer Eddie Grant and the band Aswad have both recorded very successful albums at the Carnival.

The costume parades are the Carnival's most outstanding feature. Each costumed group, which can consist of anything from 20 to 200 people, is kitted out in bright, beautiful and fanciful costumes which follow a theme of the group's own choice. Popular choices are African warriors, native Americans, Romans, butterflies and flowers. Each group usually features four principal figures, whose extravagant costumes extend outwards in all directions for an amazing distance with the assistance of wire and cane frames. The rest of the group are usually dressed in matching costumes of a comparatively simple nature. The costumed groups parade around the streets to music provided by accompanying steel bands.

The Notting Hill Carnival has its origins in a street party held on August Bank Holiday Monday in 1964 for the children of a local adventure playground. Steel bands provided the music, and food and drink was donated by local traders. The Carnival operated on a local basis until the early 1970s when it grew rapidly into the mass-participation event we know today.

When black people first moved into Notting Hill in the 1950s, it became a focus for Trinidadian immigrants. The Trinidadians made the Carnival their own, and they still run it today. Their influence is clearest in the costume parades and steel bands, both of which are central features of the centuries-old Carnival in Trinidad, an extravaganza of dance and music which envelops the island for the two days before Ash Wednesday.

The steel band is uniquely Trinidadian. A colonial prohibition on the use of drums on the island spawned a percussive tradition of playing pots, pans, bottles and anything else that came to hand. Out of this came the steel drum, which took its present form in the 1940s and 1950s when musicians learned to cut and hammer oil drums so that they could be precisely tuned to a wide range of tones. The steel bands grew up with calypso music, but today they usually play in the modern soca style.

A ready-made tradition in the form of the Trinidad Carnival gave the Notting Hill Carnival a powerful impetus, but probably the main reason why it made such spectacular strides in popularity was the near total lack of competition. London's indigenous mass participation festivals - such as Greenwich Fair, which once attracted crowds of 200,000 - were all closed down in the 18th C and 19th C because of the authorities' concern over the crime and rowdiness that invariably attended these events.

The Notting Hill Carnival risked a similar fate after anti-police riots by black youths in 1976, but despite subsequent pressure to 'tame' the carnival and take it off the streets, it has thankfully been allowed to continue in its raw form.

What's on and when. The Carnival starts late morning and continues into the early evening on both days. Sunday, which is when the children's

Notting Hill Carnival.

costume parades are held, is a quieter and more relaxed day, and some prefer it for that reason. Monday is the big day when the adult costumed groups, the steel bands and the sound systems are all judged by their performance 'on the road' for cash prizes.

Details of events can be obtained in the Carnival Programme (sold on the street and at local newsagents), in the London listings magazine *Time Out* or in the African-Caribbean press: the *Caribbean Times* and *The Voice.*

Access. The central area is closed to traffic during the Carnival, and finding parking space anywhere nearby is very difficult. You would be best advised to use public transport, which is well organised for the Carnival. The nearest underground stations are Royal Oak, Westbourne Park and Notting Hill Gate. Ladbroke Grove station is closed during the Carnival.

Safety. The crowds can become so dense that you will find yourself being forced to move in one particular direction whether you like it or not. Therefore if you have children, keep an eye on them or you may have to retrieve them from the Lost Kids Refuge (whose telephone number and address is given in the Carnival programme). Also bear in mind that a street festival as large and as crowded as the Notting Hill Carnival is a positive invitation to pickpockets and jewellery snatchers. The Carnival is much safer in this respect than it used to be, but it is sensible to carry nothing more than you strictly need.

'Inside Out'

Interview with Steve, British-born, in his twenties, at the Notting Hill Carnival. His family, who hail from St Lucia in the Caribbean, are long time residents of Notting Hill . . .

"I started out playing in steel bands when I was small, so I've been in the Carnival a long time. The Carnival has changed dramatically over the years. It's still fun, but it's more commercial, let's put it that way.

Over the Carnival weekend the family come to our house from all over . . . South London, North, East. The house gets packed with young and old family. Our cousins, they bring their girlfriends, they'll bring their friends. It's open house all Carnival. My old aunt is what, 97, and they'll be bringing her down so she can sit outside on a chair.

The Carnival cheers you. Everybody comes together, black and white, everybody joins together in the dancing, and has a few drinks. It's like Christmas and Carnival are the only times people are nice to each other. It's a fresh start each year, it gives you a feeling of oneness. You can do what you want, go around anywhere, and no-one's there to tell you what to do. People look forward to the carnival, really look forward to it with pride.

A lot of black people are losing where the music's coming from though. The music comes out of calypso and all the West Indians used to listen to it. There's a lot now who don't know it, never heard it before. We all grew up with calypso, soca, round here and it's a shame to lose it.

Calypso, soca, it relaxes you, funny enough. I have two calypso tapes I carry with me everywhere, and if I'm in a bad mood I put them on, singing my song as I walk down the road. It cheers you, that music."

OTHER PLACES TO VISIT ──────────

Museum of Mankind, 6 Burlington Gardens, W1 (071-437 2224). Open from 10am to 5pm Monday to Saturday, 2.30pm to 6pm Sunday. Admission free.
This is the Ethnographic Department of the British Museum, which owns, amongst much else, one of the world's finest collections of African art. The Museum of Mankind presents changing exhibitions which illustrate a variety of non-Western societies and cultures, ancient and contemporary. At any one time it is likely that there will be an exhibition on an African theme.
Book and Gift Shop. Small stock of books on African art, culture and society. Also provides replicas of a selection of objects held by the British Museum, such as the bronze head of a Benin Queen Mother from 16th C Nigeria, a snip at £100.
The Commonwealth Institute, Kensington High Street, W8 (071-603 4535). Open from 10am to 5.30pm Monday to Saturday, 2pm to 5pm Sunday. Admission free.
The Commonwealth Institute was opened in 1962 as the primary cultural centre of the Commonwealth, and association of nations that emerged out of the disintegration of the British Empire. Its purpose is to express the cultures of the countries of the Commonwealth and to educate the people of Britain about the Commonwealth, about half of whose members are from African and Caribbean countries.
The Main Galleries contain permanent exhibitions on various Commonwealth countries and there are also changing exhibitions on various themes, which are often of black interest.
The Institute hosts seasons of films, music, dance and drama. Details are available in their free monthly leaflets.
Harriet Tubman Centre, Exhibition Centre, 136-142 Lower Clapton Road, Hackney E5 (985 6449). Contains a permanent exhibition of 'black achievement in culture and civilisation'.
Africa Centre, 38 King Street, WC2 (071-836 1973). Open for general activities from 9.30am to 5.20pm Monday to Friday. 'A cultural centre and meeting place for everyone interested in Africa', the Africa Centre was opened in November 1964 by President Kenneth Kaunda of Zambia, one month after he had led his country to independence. The Centre houses a restaurant, a bookshop, a craft shop and an exhibition gallery. Music and drama performances, poetry readings, film screenings, lectures and evening classes of African interest are held on the premises. Members are sent details of all forthcoming events.
Africraft, Ground Floor (071-240 6098). Open from 10am to 7pm Monday to Saturday, 11am to 6pm Sunday. African arts and crafts.
Visual Arts Gallery, First Floor. Exhibition by artists on African themes.
Africa Bookcentre, Second Floor (071-240 6649). Open from 9.30am to 5.30pm Monday to Friday (except sometimes closed between 1 and 2pm), Saturday 11am to 5pm. English language books from and about Africa and

the Caribbean, plus black British literature.
Calabash Restaurant, Basement Floor. See *page 202* for details.
The Black-Art Gallery, 225 Seven Sisters Road, N4 (071-263 1918). Open from 10am to 6pm Tuesday to Friday, 10am to 7pm Saturday. Changing exhibitions by black artists. A small selection of sculpture, jewellery, clothes, posters and post cards is on sale in the reception area.
Westbourne Gallery, 331 Portobello Road W10 (081-960 1867). Open from 10am to 6pm Monday to Friday. Changing exhibitions of contemporary black art from Africa, the Americas, the Caribbean and Asia. There is also a permanent collection of work upstairs.
Talawa at the Cochrane Theatre, Southampton Row, W1 (071-242 7040). Black theatre venue.
A statue of the black South African *Nelson Mandela* stands on the walkway on the west side of the Royal Festival Hall, SE1. Mandela was imprisoned in South Africa in 1962 as a result of his activities against apartheid. For Mandela, as it says on the statue, 'The struggle is my life'. The statue was unveiled in 1985 by Oliver Tambo, the President of the African National Congress, an organisation which was then outlawed in South Africa. Nelson Mandela was finally released on 11 November, 1990, and became the President of the ANC.
See also **Brixton:** *Black Cultural Archive Museum, Bob Marley Memorial* and *Sharpeville Memorial, page 192.*

SHOPPING

Record Shops
Stern's African Record Centre, 116 Whitfield Street, W1 (071-387 5550). Open from 10.30am to 6.30pm Monday to Saturday. African music specialists.
Spindler Records, 78 Craven Park Road, NW10 (081-965 8292). Open from 10am to 8pm Monday to Saturday. Specialists in soca. Also stocks reggae, 'soft soul' ballads, gospel, African, cadence, calypso, steel band, soul and rhythm and blues.
City Sounds, 8 Procter Street, WC1(071-405 5454). Open from 9.30am to 6pm Monday to Saturday. Soul, jazz, dance, American soul imports.
Daddy Kool, 9 Berwick W1(071-437 3535). Open from 10am to 6.30pm Monday to Friday, 10am to 7pm Saturday. Reggae music, including early reggae styles of ska and rocksteady. Jamaican imports.
Rock On, 3 Kentish Town Road, NW1(071-485 6469). Open from 10.30am to 6pm Monday to Friday, 10am to 6.30pm Saturday, 11am to 6pm Sunday. Specialises in music from the 1950s and 1960s . Excellent coverage of black American music of the period: jazz, soul, rock and roll, and rhythm and blues.
Ray's Jazz Shop, 180 Shaftesbury Avenue, WC2 (071-240 3969). Open from 10am to 6.30pm Monday to Saturday. Covers whole range of jazz from the 1920s to the 1980s. Also stocks books about jazz, videos of jazz performances, and jazz magazines.
James Asman, 23a New Row, St Martins Lane, WC2 (071-2401380). Open from 10am to 6pm Monday to Saturday. Trad jazz, blues and nostalgia.
Hawkeye Record Store, 2 Craven Park Road, NW10 (081-961 0866). Open from 10am to 7pm Monday to Saturday. Soul, reggae and soca.

Peckings Record Shop, 42 Askew Road, W12 (081-749 4517). Open from 9.30am to 5.30pm Monday to Wednesday. 9.30am to 1pm Thursday. Friday and Saturday 9.30am to 7pm. Soul, reggae and soca.

Quaff Records, 4 Berwick Street, W1 (071-287 0705). Open from 10.30am to 7.30pm Monday to Saturday. Dance music.

Dub Vendor Record Shack, 155a Ladbroke Grove, W10 (071-969 3375). Open from 9.30am to 6.30pm Monday to Saturday. Reggae and soul.

Wyld Pytch, 51 Lexington Street, W1 (071-434 3472). Open from 11am to 7pm Monday to Saturday, Sunday 12 noon to 5pm. Reggae, soul, jazz, rap and house.

Unity, 47 Beak Street, W1 (071-494 0830, 734 2746). Open from 10am to 7pm Monday to Saturday. Soul, rap, jazz, hard-core and house.

Starlight Records, 17 Craven Park Road, NW10 (081-965 5039). Open from 9am to 6pm Monday to Saturday. Imports, reggae, soca, soul and some jazz.

See also **Brixton: Shopping,** *page 191;* and **Dalston: Shopping,** *page 192.*

Books, Arts and Crafts, Fashion

Walter Rodney Bookshop, 5A Chignell Place, W13 (579 4920). Open from 10am to 6pm Monday to Saturday. Third world books, good stock of black interest.

New Beacon Bookshop, 76 Stroud Green Road, N4 (272 4889). Open from 10.30am to 6pm Tuesday to Saturday. Radical bookshop which specialises in African-Caribbean literature. Wide range of children's books, plus magazines and newspapers from Africa, the Caribbean and Britain. Organises the bi-annual Book Fair of Radical Black and Third World Books.

Headstart Books n'Crafts, 25 West Green Road, N15 (081-802 2838). Open from 9.30am to 6pm Monday to Friday, 9.30am to 7pm Saturday. Books, arts and crafts, some clothing.

Suli Suli, Unit 1, 235 Portobello Road, W11 (071-243 3130). Open from 10.30am to 6pm. African arts and crafts.

British Commonwealth Trading Centre, 16-18 High Street, NW10 (081-961 0283). Open from 9.30am to 6pm Monday to Friday, 9.30am to 1pm Saturday. Imports from Commonwealth countries including African arts and crafts.

Yermanja, 7 Stroud Green Road, N4 (071-281 8668). Open from 10.30am to 8pm Monday to Saturday. African clothes, arts and crafts, from a black British perspective.

See also **Brixton: Shopping,** *page 190;* and **Dalston: Shopping,** *page 192.*

'Inside Out'

Interview with Junior, mid-20s of Caribbean origin, who runs Yermanja, a shop selling African clothes and other goods . . .

"I love the clothes, I love the culture. Besides it being a business, it was started up so that others could get to know that Africans have fashion, their own way of dressing, that we have a culture, a literature, a history of our own for a long time. It's a learning experience. My aim was to show, especially, to Caribbean children, and my generation, that they don't have to be ashamed to wear

African clothes. The clothes aren't funny or weird, they're normal. Before we were wearing Western clothes, we were wearing these. It's a stepping stone to knowing their roots. Once they know, then they can go forward.

America has played a big influence in this. People see it on TV in the shows. They see the rappers wearing the garments, so they're interested straight away. They want to know where to get it from. Now you see me walking down the street and someone's going to accost me and say, where'd you get that from?

I feel undressed if I'm not in African clothes. Sometimes I wear Western clothes and people treat me differently. I like the way people approach me when I'm wearing African clothes.

I think London's the right place to do it as well, because in London you can get away with wearing what you want to some extent, as opposed to say Kingston or one of the other Caribbean capitals."

African Fabrics

The centre of London's trade in African fabrics is in Middlesex Street, E1. The bold-patterned and bright-coloured designs are mainly of West African origin, though the cotton, lace and velvet fabrics themselves are invariably manufactured in Europe, particularly Holland and Switzerland. Many of the buyers in London are visitors from West Africa who shop here because of the competitive prices and the superior quality of the fabrics.

Raynes Textiles, 66 Middlesex Street, El (071-247 3502). Open from 9am to 6pm Monday to Friday, 9am to 2pm Sunday.

Good Luck Textiles, 68 Middlesex Street (071-247 8987). Open from 9am to 6pm Monday to Friday (except early closing Friday in winter), 8.30am to 2pm Sunday.

Dans Textiles, 14 Gravel Lane, El (071-247 4681). Open from 9.30am to 5.30pm Monday to Friday, 9am to 2pm Sunday. Situated just off Middlesex Street.

Eko Fabrics, 75 Middlesex Street, E1 (071-247 4681). Open from 9.30am to 5.30pm Monday to Friday, 9am to 2pm Sunday.

Hello Dolly, 89 Middlesex Street (071-377 0814). Open from 9.30am to 5.30pm Sunday to Friday (closes 3pm Sunday).

Middlesex Textiles, 93 Middlesex Street (071-247 2991). Open from 9am to 5.30pm Monday to Friday (except early closing Friday in winter), 8.30am to 2pm Sunday.

Benny's Textile Corner, 1 Stoke Newington Road, N16 (071-254 7998). Open from 9.30am to 6pm Monday, Tuesday, Wednesday and Friday, 9.30am to 2pm Sunday and Thursday.

Vogue Embroideries, 31 Middlesex Street, E1 (071-377 0814). Open from 9.30am to 5.30pm Monday to Friday, 9am to 3.30pm Sunday.

FOOD AND DRINK

Caribbean food reflects the mixture of peoples who have settled in the region. It draws on African, Indian, Chinese, British, Spanish and French cuisine, in addition to that of the original inhabitants, the Carib Indians. Caribbean food has received surprisingly little attention in London considering the popularity of other ethnic cuisines, but it certainly has the potential to break through to a much wider market.

Look out for the following Caribbean dishes:

Ackee and saltfish. Flakes of salted cod fish mixed with ackee, a yellow fruit used as a vegetable that looks rather like scrambled egg when cooked.

Crab and callaloo soup. Callaloo is a spinach-like vegetable.

Curried goat. Although the Asian population of the Caribbean is concentrated in Guyana and Trinidad, their taste for curries and rice has spread right across the region. Goat is a lean, good quality meat, which is fairly cheap in the Caribbean but expensive in Britain, so portions here tend to be small.

Rice and peas. Small brown beans are known as peas in the Caribbean. Rice and peas is made with coconut milk and pepper or chilli.

Pepperpot. A hot stew made with cassareep juice and a variety of meats such as ox-tails, pig's trotters and pig's tails.

Fruit and vegetables. The yam and the dasheen are both brown root vegetables which taste rather like potatoes. The plantain looks like a large, thick banana, but it is not edible raw. It is often eaten in chip form. 'Green banana' is just an ordinary banana prior to ripening. It also has to be cooked before it can be eaten.

Drink. With your meal you should try one of the many varieties of rum for which the Caribbean has long been famous. The region's soft drinks also deserve attention. Sorrel, mango and sour sop juices are made from fruits, mauby from tree bark and sarsaparilla from dried roots. Soft drinks are sometimes combined with milk and spices to make non-alcoholic cocktails.

African cuisine has become more widely available in London over the last few years, as the African population has increased. It shares many ingredients with Caribbean cuisine, but the dishes are prepared very differently.

Restaurants

The Humming Bird Restaurant, 84 Stroud Green Road, N4 (071-263 9690). Open from 12 noon to 12 midnight Monday to Saturday, 2pm to 10pm Sundays. Take-away service, same hours. Caribbean (Trinidadian) and European food, some vegetarian dishes. A spacious restaurant with a relaxed atmosphere. Moderately-priced.

Peewees West Indian Restaurant, 96 Stroud Green Road, N4 (071-263 4004). Open from 6 to 11pm Monday, 12 to 3 and 6 to 11pm Tuesday to Saturday (except to 12 midnight Saturday), 5 to 10pm Sunday. Take-away service, same hours. Caribbean (Trinidadian) food. Cosy and cheerful. Features a good selection of non-alcoholic cocktails - try their house special 'soul juice', which is made from tropical fruit juices, condensed milk, fresh milk, cinnamon and nutmeg. Moderately-priced.

Afric-Carib, 1 Strand Green Road, N4 (071-263 7440). Open from 11.30am to midnight Monday to Sunday, 12 noon to 11.30pm Sunday. Cuisine combines Nigerian and Caribbean dishes. Take-away service.

Calabash Restaurant, basement floor, Africa Centre, 38 King Street, WC2 (071-836 1976). Open from 12.30 to 3pm, 6 to 11.30pm Monday to Friday, 6 to 11pm Saturday. African food. Don't be put off by the entrance, which might give you the impression that you are intruding upon a private club. The restaurant is bright, friendly and informal inside, with African batiks and wooden carvings adorning the walls. Taped African music plays in the background. The short menu aims to cover all of African cuisine, so it changes frequently. Typical dishes include Nigerian Egusi (beefstew, melon seeds, spinach and dried shrimps) and Dioumbi, a lamb/orka stew from the Ivory Coast. Moderately-priced.

El-Dorado, 210 Church Road, NW10 (081-451 0883). Open from 1pm to 11pm Monday to Thursday, 1pm to midnight Friday to Sunday. Caribbean food concentrating on the popular dishes - saltfish with ackee, rice and peas, jerk chicken.

Caribbean Restaurant, 47 Broad Lane, N15 (081-885 5908). Open from 12 noon to 1am Monday to Friday, 2pm to 1am Saturday, 5pm to midnight Sunday. Caribbean food.

Le Caribe, 20 Northwold Road, N16 (071-241 0011). Open from 6pm to midnight Tuesday to Sunday. Caribbean food, vegetarians catered for.

A Taste of Africa, 50 Brixton Road, SW9 (081-587 0343). Open from 12 noon to midnight Monday to Saturday, 5pm to midnight Sunday. Caribbean and African food. There is an 'African Evening' on the last Friday of the month with music and costumes.

Hauma Restaurant, 86 Mountgrove Road, N5 (071-354 1255). Open from 2.30pm to 11.30pm Monday to Friday, 3.30pm to 11.30pm Saturday. Ghanaian restaurant.

Pamela's, 58 Dalston Lane, E8 (071-923 2244). Open from 6.30pm to 10.30pm Tuesday to Thursday, 6.30pm to 11.30pm Friday to Sunday. Interesting up-market variations on standard Caribbean fare, e.g. saltfish and ackee is served within a puff-pastry shell and accompanied by a wine sauce.

Smokey Joe's Diner, 131 Wandsworth High Street, SW18 (081-871 1785). Open from 12 noon to 3pm, 6pm to 10pm Monday to Saturday 3.30pm to 10pm Sunday. Caribbean café. The menu varies, but usually includes jerk chicken. Bring your own wine.

'Inside Out'

Interview with 'Smokey', proprietor and cook at 'Smokey Joe's' Caribbean diner in Wandsworth . . .

"My name's really Charlie, but they call me Smokey because I used to smoke charboiled corn over an open wooden fire in the open markets. We started out on the streets, and found that our cooking was different, and thought it was about time we became respectable, so we opened up here.

We're not a restaurant, we're a back street dive, a real little diner. It's more or less like being home from home, because some of my regulars they give a hand in serving other customers, they wash up, they walk through the kitchen and walk out.

My personal favourite is braised oxtail. We're going back roots there, man. And jerk chicken. We still cook ours over wood. That's why our jerk chicken is so famous in London. People come from all over, man.

Most of our customers who come in even say you're too cheap Smokey, you deserve better, Smokey. But our philosophy here is it's not the place to be entertained, it's not the place to hang around in. We get you in, we get you out, we get your money. We close when we feel like, but when we have a boring crowd, we get rid of them quick. But sometimes the place bubbles man, you know, even last night we were bubbling till 2 o'clock, you know.

One of the things about this job is there's plenty of freebies. I've been everywhere. I've been to Ascot, I've been to Paris. I can't make out why people invite me. I've been to fantastic parties. I mix with everybody, man. I have a good time."

Plantation Inn, 337-339 High Road, Leytonstone, E11 (081-558 6210). Open from 6pm to midnight Tuesday to Saturday. Caribbean food.

African Cuisine, 24 Blackstock Road, N4 (071-226 6521). Open from 10am to 11.30pm Monday to Sunday. Nigerian restaurant.

African Pot, 236 Harlesden High Street, NW10 (081-453 0453). Open from 10am to 11.30pm Monday to Sunday. West African restaurant specialises in Ghanaian dishes.

Brixtonian Restaurant, 11 Dorrell Place, SW9 (081-978 8870). Open from 12 noon to 3.30pm and 7pm to 11pm Tuesday to Saturday. Smart Caribbean restaurant with cocktail bar that stocks 150 different rums, some extremely rare.

Dan Delights, 449 Coldharbour Lane SW9 (071-737 6412). Open from 7am to 11pm Monday to Saturday (except closes at 6pm Friday and Saturday). Caribbean snack bar/take-away.

Shopping

The best places to buy African and Caribbean food in London are Brixton market (see *page 190*), Ridley Road market (see *page 192*) and Shepherd's Bush Market, Uxbridge Road, W12.

Blue Mountain Peak, 4 Craven Park Road, NW10 (081-965 3859). Open from 7.30am to 6pm Monday to Saturday. Caribbean fruit and vegetables.

Craven Park Stores, 19 Craven Park Road, NW10 (081-965 1503). Open from 8am to 6pm Monday to Saturday. This grocers stocks many varieties of Caribbean and African fish, in addition to the popular dried, salted cod. Goat meat is also available.

Bedford Fisheries, 75 Golborne Road, W10 (081-960 3100). Open from 7.30am to 6.30pm Monday to Saturday. Fishmongers with large stock of Caribbean and African fish.

North London Emporium, 43 Strand Green Road, N4 (071-263 3779). Open from 8.30am to 7.30pm Monday to Thursday, 7am to 9pm Friday and Saturday, 9am to 7pm Sunday. African fruit, vegetables, black cosmetics.

Continental Food Store, 167 Shepherd's Bush Market, W12 (081-743 1191). Open from 9.30am to 5.30pm Friday to Wednesday, 9am to 1.30pm Thursday. Much of the stock is imported from the Indian sub-continent, Africa and the Caribbean.

MUSIC

Modern popular music has its origins in America, where the rhythms and music brought by black people from Africa mixed with the music of the European settlers. Out of this fusion has come ragtime, gospel, blues, jazz, rock and roll, soul and reggae, a dynamic progression in which black musicians have always been firmly in the forefront.

Black people in Britain first began to have an impact on British music in the late 70s, initially as soul musicians playing in a firmly American style, and then in popularising reggae in Britain. However, while white groups such as The Police used reggae rhythms with great commercial success, chart success for black British reggae artists was relatively limited. The London based reggae artist Linton Kwesi-Johnson recorded several albums in this period which were notable for their perceptive lyrics commenting on the black British experience.

The American soul influence dominated most black music in Britain until the mid-1980s, although a distinct British style was evident in a lighter, more 'poppy' type of soul, such as that played by the bands Imagination and Five Star. However, since then there has been an explosion of black musical talent in Britain, and black musicians have become an increasingly important force in British popular music.

Black musicians have been particularly notable on the dance music scene, but artists such as Sade, Joan Armatrading, Seal, Terence Trent D'Arby and Soul II Soul have worked in a variety of styles that have been both enormously popular in the music charts, and very influential across the whole music scene.

Until the late 1980s, London had no legal radio stations specialising in black music, and a number of pirate radio stations moved in to fill the gap. Responding to the pressure, principally by those who wanted to listen to black music, the government responded by permitting a number of new stations to operate in London. 'Choice FM' is now the principal station for black music.

If one looks across British culture today, and asks where Britain's ethnic groups are having the most impact, then the black influence on British music is probably the most remarkable.

See also **Shopping: Record Shops,** *page 199.*

'Inside Out'

Interview with West African drummer, Steve, in his 30s, who busks at London Bridge Station . . .

"I've been working at London Bridge for a few years, and I always have a good contact with people. I think they love it, they really love it. Most of the people who give money are women, because they feel the drums more. Some of them come to me and say, yes, you make me feel better today when I hear your drum, I feel good now. When the man beats the drum, the woman will move her body in the same way, and feel the vibes. Women can feel the drum because the drum is mystic, it's something mystic.

When I was young, I lived in a village on the Ivory Coast. In Africa we don't have so much electricity, but we have the moonlight that God gave us and it's free, and it shines well enough so we can even find a penny on the floor. In the night we met to play the drums and sing songs. Girls, boys, everybody met, and we stayed there late. In Europe they have guitars or they have a keyboard. We have the drum, so everybody is used to it. Everything is changing now, because people like to travel to the city and do the same as they do there, so the drums have disappeared a bit, but sometimes we do a revival.

As an African, I really care about Africa. We, the new generation, have to unite to help each other. That was the word of Haile Selassie, when he was in Addis Ababa when he got all the governments of Africa together. I believe the people who control Africa now, they don't understand what we - the new generation - understand now about unity."

PEOPLE

Olaudah Equiano was the first widely recognised spokesman for Britain's black community. Born in Nigeria c 1745, he was kidnapped by slave traders at the age of about ten and shipped across the Atlantic. In his memoirs, *The Interesting Narrative of the Life of Olaudah Equiano or Gustavas Vassa the African* (1789), Equiano describes the hold of the ship as 'a scene of horror almost inconceivable' . Two slaves who were chained together jumped over the side of the ship in a suicide pact. Many others died of disease. Equiano himself was flogged for refusing to eat.

After short periods of slavery in the West Indies and North America, Equiano was sold to a British naval officer, Lieutenant Michael Pascal, who took him to Britain. On his arrival at Falmouth, Cornwall, in 1757, Equiano noted 'the particular slenderness of their women, which I did not first like, and I thought that they were not so modest and shamefaced as the African women'.

After a couple of years at sea with Lieutenant Pascal, Equiano made his first visit to London, where he was cared for by two sisters he called the 'Miss Guerins', who were relatives of Pascal's. They sent Equiano to school, and when he asked to be baptised, persuaded Pascal to give his consent. The baptism took place at St Margaret's Church, St Margaret's Street, SW1, which has been the 'national church for the use of the House of Commons' since 1621 and boasts many other interesting historical associations.

Equiano was soon back at sea with Pascal and saw action against the French with General Wolfe in Canada and with Admiral Boscawen in the Mediterranean. At the end of these campaigns Equiano's ship was ordered back to London, and in December 1761 it anchored off Deptford.

Equiano, who had been advised by a number of people that his master could not forcibly detain him, was planning to declare himself a free man. Unhappily, Pascal somehow learned of Equiano's intentions and resolved to sell him there and then to a ship bound for the West Indies. Equiano was forced aboard a rowing boat and taken from ship to ship as Pascal tried to find a buyer. Equiano recorded:

'The boat's crew, who pulled against their will, became quite faint different times, and would have gone ashore; but he would not let them. Some of them strove then to cheer me, and told me he could not sell me, and that they would stand by me, which revived me a little . . . but just as we had got a little below Gravesend, we came alongside of a ship which was going away on the next tide for the West Indies; her name was the *Charming Sally*, Captain James Doran, and my master went on board and agreed with him for me; and in a little time I was sent for into the cabin. When I came there Captain Doran asked me if I knew him; I answered that I did not;

"Then", said he, "you are now my slave".'

Equiano was shipped to Montserrat in the West Indies, where he was resold and put to work as a shipping clerk and navigator. His owner was a liberal man by the standards of the day, and Equiano was allowed to trade on his own account in order to raise money to buy his freedom. Eventually, in 1766, at the age of 21, he became a free man.

In March 1767 Equiano's 'longing eyes' were 'gratified with a sight of London after having been absent from it above four years'. He called on the 'Miss Guerins' and with their help was apprenticed to a hairdresser at premises in Coventry-Court, Haymarket, SW1. However, dissatisfied with his wages, Equiano was soon back at sea, and over the next 20 years travelled widely as a merchant seaman, using London as his base. Amongst his many voyages were trips to the Arctic, where his ship was trapped in ice for 11 days, and to the Caribbean, where he was kidnapped back into slavery but managed to make a quick escape.

In 1774, while Equiano was working on a ship that was fitting out in the Thames, a black cook was kidnapped from it by his former owner, a Mr Kirkpatrick. Equiano determined to rescue the cook, and armed with a writ of habeus corpus and accompanied by a tipstaff, made his way to Kirkpatrick's house in St Paul's Churchyard, EC4. Before approaching the house itself, Equiano whitened his face in order to survey the scene without arousing suspicion, and through this deception enabled the tipstaff to serve the writ. Although Kirkpatrick was brought before a judge, he was allowed to go free on bail, and the lawyer whom Equiano engaged to fight the case proved useless. Despite all of Equiano's efforts, the cook was transported back to the West Indies, where he died in slavery on St Kitts.

In 1786 Equiano was appointed to work on a Government-backed scheme which aimed to resettle destitute London blacks to Sierra Leone on the West African coast. Following his exposure of corruption in the provision of supplies, Equiano was dismissed from the project as a 'troublemaker'. In the event, the resettlement scheme turned out to be a disaster for most of those who went on it.

Equiano's memoirs were published in 1789, and as a best-seller the book made an important contribution to the debate on the abolition of slavery. In the following years he spent much of his time touring Britain to speak against slavery at public meetings, where he also sold copies of his book.

In 1788, when a Bill was put forward to regulate overcrowding on slave ships, Equiano was consulted by its proposers during its successful passage through Parliament. He also listened to the debates in the chamber and was introduced to the Prime Minister, William Pitt. A white abolitionist of the time credited Equiano as 'a principal instrument' in the introduction in 1791 of a Bill for the abolition of the slave trade. The Bill failed, but public opinion was changing and abolition eventually came in 1807. Sadly, Equiano did not live to see it. He died in London on 31 April 1797.

William Davidson was born in Kingston, Jamaica, in 1786, the son of a black woman and the island's white Attorney-General. As a teenager he was sent to Edinburgh to complete his education, and after a varied career which included being press ganged into the navy and work as an articled clerk in Liverpool, Davidson eventually settled in London as a cabinet-maker.

Following the end of the Napoleonic Wars in 1815, Britain entered a period of intense political ferment. Davidson suffered along with many others from the high unemployment of the time, and at one point was forced to pawn his tools and beg on the streets. In the wake of the brutal killings by the military of peaceful demonstrators in the Peterloo Massacre at Manchester in 1819, a group of radicals gathered around Arthur Thistlewood, a veteran of the French revolution, to plan armed action against the Government. Amongst them was Davidson, who became one of the senior figures in the conspiracy.

Thistlewood's men thought they saw their chance when a newspaper announced that the entire Government cabinet would be dining in a house in Grosvenor Square, SW1, on 23 February 1820. The conspirators planned to storm the house and kill them all, hoping to spark a nation-wide insurrection.

On the evening of 23 February, 25 men assembled in the loft of 1a Cato Street, W1 (marked by a plaque), where the group stored its weapons. They were preparing to leave for Grosvenor Square when police and soldiers stormed the premises. Davidson, who was the sentry, fought back with a pistol and a sword, but was overpowered. Thistlewood escaped, only to be captured the next day. It later emerged that one of the conspirators, George Edwards, had been a Government informer.

Thistlewood, Davidson and three others were tried on a charge of high treason at the Old Bailey Sessions House, Old Bailey, EC4 (the Central Criminal Court now stands on the site). In the dock Davidson defended the rights of Englishmen to take up arms against tyrannical governments. His only regret, he said, was 'that I have a large family of small children, and when I think of that, it unmans me'. He concluded: 'I hope my death may prove useful to my country - For still England I call thee so - and I trust that those by whom I shall be condemned, may lay down their lives with as clear a conscience'.

All five men were sentenced to death, and their execution set for Monday 1 May, 1820, outside Newgate Prison (formerly in Newgate Street, EC1). The authorities were mindful of public sympathy for the conspirators, and worried about a rescue attempt, so security was tight. Soldiers were placed in the surrounding streets and artillery positioned on Blackfriar's Bridge, EC4.

A huge crowd assembled to watch the executions. On the scaffold, Davidson prayed, bowed to the crowd, and called out 'God bless you all! Good-bye'. After he was hanged a masked man cut off his head and held it up to the crowd with the words: 'This is the head of William Davidson, a traitor'. Most of the crowd reacted angrily to the beheadings, and some people vomited or fainted in shock. These were the last public beheadings to be carried out in England. The men's wives were refused the bodies, which were buried in lime inside Newgate Prison.

William Cuffay was a prominent London leader of the Chartists, a mid-19th C movement which advocated democratic political reform. Born in Chatham, Kent, in 1788, Cuffay was a tailor by trade, though because of his political activities he often found it difficult to obtain work.

Cuffay was a leading figure in the organisation of the celebrated Chartist rally on Kennington Common in 1848 *(see page 160)*. Later that year Cuffay was arrested and charged with planning an insurrection in London. He denied the charge, and stated in the dock: 'As I certainly have been an important character in the Chartist movement, I laid myself out for something of this sort from the first. I know that a great many men of good moral character are now suffering in prison only for advocating the cause of the Charter; but, however, I do not despair of its being carried out yet. There may be many victims. I am not anxious for martyrdom, but I do feel that . . . I have the fortitude to endure any punishment your lordship can inflict upon me'.

Cuffay was exiled to Tasmania, where he was joined by his wife in 1853. Pardoned in 1856, he stayed on in Tasmania, where he continued to campaign for political reform. He died in poverty in a Tasmanian workhouse in 1870.

Mary Seacole, 'the black Florence Nightingale', cared for sick and wounded British soldiers during the Crimean War (1854-6). Born Mary Grant in 1805 in Kingston, Jamaica, her mother was a free black who ran a boarding house which catered for sick army officers. Her father was a Scottish soldier.

Of her childhood Mary wrote: 'I was never weary of tracing upon an old map the route to England; and never followed with my gaze the stately ships homeward bound [i.e. to England] without longing to be in them'. As a young woman she spent three years in London, though she recorded that her most vivid memories of the visit were 'the efforts of the London street-boys to poke fun at my and my companion's complexion'.

Until late middle-age Mary worked as a hotelier and storekeeper in various parts of the Caribbean and Central America. On her mother's death she had taken over the family's boarding house in Kingston, where she practised the medical skills that she had learnt from her mother. Mary's ability was such that in 1853 she was appointed to oversee nursing arrangements in a military camp in Jamaica during an epidemic of yellow fever.

On her return to Britain in 1854 Mary resolved to serve as a nurse in the Crimea, where many of the soldiers she had known in Jamaica were being sent to fight. At that time it was becoming clear that cholera, malaria and dysentery were a far greater risk to life than the enemy, and the lack of proper medical attention for the troops became a national scandal. Although Mary had considerable practical experience in dealing with such diseases, and testimonials from doctors to that effect, none of the organisations to which she applied in London were prepared to take her on.

Mary was uncharacteristically despondent as she walked home after her last application had been rejected:

'The disappointment seemed a cruel one. I was so conscious of the unselfishness of the motives which induced me to leave England - so certain of the service I could render among the sick soldiery, and yet I found it so difficult to convince others of these facts. Doubts and suspicions arose in my heart . . . Did these ladies shrink from accepting my aid because my blood flowed beneath a somewhat duskier skin than theirs? Tears streamed down my foolish cheeks, as I stood in the fast thinning streets; tears of grief that any should doubt my motives - that Heaven should deny me the opportunity that I sought. Then I stood still, and looking upward through and through the dark clouds that shadowed London, prayed aloud for help. I dare say that I was a strange sight to the few passers-by, who hastened homeward through the gloom and mist of that wintry night.'

Mary soon recovered her usual good spirits, and acting on the motto 'God helps those who help themselves', made her own way to the Crimea, where she opened up a shop to sell provisions to the military and a hotel where officers could convalesce. However, in her nursing activities Mary went far beyond commercial considerations, and indeed in contrast to the official army nurses, who worked in the relative safety of the wards, she nursed men out in the fields. An observer of the time noted: '. . . during the time of battle, and in the time of fearful distress, [she] personally spared no pains and no exertion to visit the field of woe and minister with her own hands such things as could comfort, or alleviate the sufferings of those around her, freely giving to such as could not pay, and to many whose eyes were closing in death, from whom payment could never be expected'. Mary's good work was noted by *The Times'* war correspondent William Russell, whose despatches made her a household name in Britain.

The abrupt end of the war in March 1856 left Mary with a worthless hotel and a huge amount of unsaleable stock on her hands. At the age of 51, she returned impoverished to live in lodgings in Tavistock Street, WC2. She had not been forgotten by the troops however, and in August *The Times* noted that her appearance at an official guards dinner 'awakened the most rapturous enthusiasm. The soldiers not only cheered her, but chaired her around the garden'.

In December the magazine *Punch* published a poem in Mary's honour that included these lines:

She gave her aid to all who prayed,
To hungry, and sick, and cold:
Open hand and heart alike ready to part
Kind words, and acts, and gold.

After settling into lodgings in Soho Square, W1, Mary wrote her autobiography *Wonderful Adventures of Mrs Seacole in Many Lands* (1857, and Falling Wall Press 1984). In the introduction to this lively and very readable book, William Russell writes: 'I trust that England will not forget one who nursed her sick, who sought out her wounded to aid and succour them, and who performed the last offices for some of her illustrious dead'.

After the publication of *Wonderful Adventures,* a musical benefit was arranged for Mary at the Surrey Gardens Music Hall (since demolished, its site is now partly covered by Penton Place, SE17). About 1000 singers and musicians participated, and they played to capacity audiences of 10,000 for four nights. Unfortunately, the company which ran the music hall went bankrupt shortly afterwards and Mary received very little money from the event.

Mary did however recover her fortunes in the last 20 years of her life, which she spent shuttling between London and Kingston, Jamaica. She died in London in May 1881 and was buried in St Mary's Roman Catholic Cemetery, Harrow Road, NW10. Her grave was restored and reconsecrated in 1973.

Samuel Coleridge-Taylor was born in Theobald's Road, WC1, in August 1875. He entered the Royal College of Music at the age of 15 and went on to become a classical composer of international repute. His incorporation of elements of traditional black music into the European concert tradition was his greatest musical innovation. *Hiawatha's Wedding Feast* (1898) was his most popular work, but although it earned large sums of money for its publishers, little came to Coleridge-Taylor, who had to earn his living through teaching and conducting. He died at the early age of 37.

Marcus Garvey was a pioneering advocate of black pride, African culture, and independent black political and cultural organisation. Born in Jamaica in 1887, he came to London in 1912, where he worked on the magazine *Africa Times and Orient Review* and studied African history and literature.

It was in London that Garvey first saw himself as a potential black leader: 'I asked myself "Where is the black man's Government?" "Where is his King and his kingdom?" "Where is his President, his country, and his ambassador, his army, his navy, his men of big affairs?" I could not find them, and then I declared "I will help to make them" . . . I saw before me then . . . a new world of black men, not peons, serfs, dogs and slaves, but a nation of sturdy men making their impress upon civilisation and causing a new light to dawn upon the human race. I could not remain in London any more'. - *Philosophy and Opinions of Marcus Garvey* (1923 and 1925).

In July 1914 Garvey returned to Jamaica, where he founded the Universal Negro Improvement Association. Following its move to the United States in 1916, the UINA grew at a phenomenal rate. At its peak in the early 1920s it had millions of followers, and was spreading its message of black self-assertion around the globe. Yet Garvey's plans for a black-run shipping line and for the resettlement of black people in Africa ended in utter failure, and he was imprisoned in the United States on a charge of fraud.

In 1927, after serving almost three years in jail, Garvey was deported to Jamaica, where he continued his activities despite persistent harassment from the colonial authorities. By the time he moved back to London in 1935, Garvey was an isolated figure, cold-shouldered by many black activists who thought he was out of touch with political developments. He died penniless in West Kensington in 1940. Buried in London, his remains were disinterred in 1964 and reburied in Jamaica.

Garvey was a powerful, flamboyant and controversial character, and his rise and fall was a phenomenon in itself. His speeches and writings have had an enormous influence, particularly on the development of Rastafarianism and on the black power movement in the United States. Many of his pithy statements are still in currency, as for example: 'Africa for the Africans', 'I shall teach the black man to see beauty in himself', and 'A people without the knowledge of their past history, origin and culture, is like a tree without roots'.

In October 1930 the Crown Prince Ras Tafari (born 1892) was crowned Emperor of Ethiopia, Africa's oldest independent state. On his coronation he took the name *Haile Selassie,* which means Might of the Trinity.

In 1936 Selassie was forced to leave Ethiopia after its invasion by the Italians, and was carried into exile in Britain by a British cruiser. On his arrival at Waterloo Station, SE1, he was greeted by cheering crowds of British sympathisers, including representatives from the black community. After suffering the humiliation of defeat, Selassie was greatly moved and encouraged by this show of support: 'At the railway station in London the British public gave Us a great welcome. . .The people assembled there demonstrated to Us their participation in our grief, and We admired the tenderness and kindness of the British people'.

After a trip to Geneva, where he denounced the Italian invasion in a famous address to the League of Nations, Selassie settled in a house on the outskirts of Bath in Somerset and waited for a chance to return to Ethiopia. It came in 1940 when Italy declared war on Britain, and by the following year Selassie was back on his throne after British and Ethiopian forces had driven the Italians out of the country.

In post-war Africa Selassie was a prominent campaigner against colonialism, and played a leading role in the formation of the Organisation of African Unity. He ruled Ethiopia until 1974, when he was deposed by a military junta and put under palace arrest. According to the junta Selassie died from natural causes on 27 August 1975.

The black religious movement that became known as Rastafarianism grew up in Jamaica in the 1930s. It has no centralised creed, and beliefs vary widely between different sects, but most Rastafarians agree on the following points:

- Emperor Haile Selassie is the Black Messiah. (Rastafarians support the idea of the Black Messiah with prophecies from the Bible. Selassie denied all such claims made on his behalf.)

- The necessity of the return of black people to Africa spiritually or physically.

- The necessity of the redemption and rise of black people internationally in cultural, political, spiritual and economic affairs.

Rastafarians characteristically wear long plaited or matted hair called dreadlocks, and clothing which bears the Ethiopian colours of red, green and gold. Marijuana is smoked as a sacred herb, the consumption of pork is forbidden and a distinctive vocabulary is used which features such words as natty, skank, dread, dub, Babylon and Jah.

Although there have been Rastafarians in London since the 1950s, it was not until the 1970s, and in particular through the influence of reggae artists like Bob Marley, that they made a significant impact here. Many British blacks adopted the outward trappings and cultural perspectives of Rastafarianism in that period but only a very tiny minority took on its religious commitments.

Paul Robeson, who was born in the United States in 1898, was a man of many talents. A lawyer, athlete, actor and singer, if he had been white he would have become an 'All-American hero'. However, as a black civil rights activist with left-wing views, his fate was to be very different.

Robeson first came to Britain in 1922 as an actor in a touring play called *Voodoo.* He returned in 1928 to star in the stage musical *Show Boat* at the Drury Lane Theatre, Catherine Street, WC2, in which he performed *Old Man River,* the song with which his name will always be linked. After the musical completed its run, Robeson decided to settle in London and became a familiar face on the West End stage. One of his most successful performances was in 1930 when he starred opposite Peggy Aschcroft in Othello at the Savoy Theatre, Savoy Court, WC2.

Robeson also starred in six British films, including Song of Freedom (1936) in which he plays a London-born docker who rises to fame as an opera singer before returning to Africa in search of his ancestors, and *The Proud Valley* (1940) in which he plays an unemployed seaman who is befriended by a Welsh mining community and joins them in their struggles.

However it was not Robeson's acting abilities but his exceptional bass baritone voice that made him an international star, and in the 1930s and 1940s he was one of the world's top concert attractions.

Robeson returned to the United States in 1939. In his autobiography *Here I Stand* (1958) he wrote that his stay in Britain had taught him that 'The essential character of a nation is determined not by the upper classes, but by the common people, and the common people of all nations are truly brothers and sisters in the great family of mankind'.

Robeson's promotion of left-wing politics and black civil rights led to the cancellation of his passport by the American Government in 1950. Confined to the United States, organised boycotts made it virtually impossible for him to get work, and details of his athletic achievements were even removed from sports' record books.

After a prolonged international campaign, Robeson's passport was restored in 1957, and in 1958 he returned to Britain. At a concert staged in St Paul's Cathedral he sang to an audience of 5000 inside and 5000 listening outside. After many travels Robeson returned to the United States in 1963, where he lived quietly until his death in 1976.

LITERATURE

Prose

To Sir, With Love by E R Braithwaite (1959). A black teacher, born in Guyana, wins the hearts and minds of an unruly bunch of kids in an East End school in the late 1940s. *To Sir, With Love* was made into a successful British film starring Sidney Poitier in *1967.* *Recommended.

Second Class Citizen by Buchi Emecheta (1975). An ambitious young Nigerian woman leaves a good job in Lagos to join her husband, who is studying in London. Britain, 'the land of her dreams', proves rather different from her imaginings, and her lazy, chauvinistic husband doesn't make life any easier. *Recommended.

In the Ditch, Buchi Emecheta (1972). A sequel to *Second Class Citizen,* though not so engaging. The Nigerian woman has separated from her husband and is having to cope with the day to day tribulations of looking after five small children on a decaying housing estate in North London.

Gwendolen, Buchi Emecheta (1989). On the one hand this is a familiar story of cultural adjustment as a Jamaican family move to Britain in the 1960s; on the other hand it is also a sensitive and tragic story about a young girl who is the victim of two incestuous relationships, both arising out of the circumstances of her family's migration.

Come Home Malcolm Heartland by Andrew Salkey (1976). After living in London for 20 years a black intellectual decides to return to his native Jamaica. As he prepares to leave, and agonises over his decision and its implications, he is befriended by a group of black political activists whose interest in him is far from innocent.

The Final Passage by Caryl Phillips (1985). The first half of the story takes place on a small Caribbean island and outlines the background to the emigration of a young couple to Britain. Despite their hopes, the couple's troubled marriage does not receive a new lease of life through the move to London.

The Emigrants by George Lamming (1954). This novel follows a group of West Indian immigrants of varying backgrounds on their voyage to London and through their subsequent experiences and disillusionments. There are many interesting observations, but it is written in a mannered, modernistic style that can be heavy going.

Samuel Selvon is a Trinidadian of Asian origin who has written about Afro-Caribbean life in London in the comic trilogy *The Lonely Londoners* (1956), *Moses Ascending* (1975) and *Moses Migrating* (1983). The central character is a Trinidadian immigrant called Moses, a likeable if sometimes rather foolish man with a weakness for social pretension.

The Lonely Londoners gives a panoramic view of the experiences of

Caribbean immigrants in London. In *Moses Ascending,* Moses becomes the landlord of a run-down property in Shepherd's Bush after having spent years living in dingy rented lodgings. He thinks his problems are over, but he has reckoned without some of his tenants - a black power organisation, illegal immigrants from Pakistan and his own white 'Man Friday'. *Recommended. In *Moses Migrating,* Moses decides to revisit his birthplace after an absence of many years and ends up taking part in the Trinidad Carnival dressed as Britannia.

Blues Dance by Amos Saba Saakana (1985). Set in the 1970's, it tells the story of Michael, a black teenager living in London. Disturbed by racism at school, he drops out after conflict with his parents, and he drifts into petty crime and a Rastafarian subculture. After exploring black history and culture, he goes back into education, and eventually to university. A forthright and frank depiction of how frustration and alienation can become channelled into violence and crime.

Waiting In The Twilight by Joan Riley (1987). A crippled old woman who cleans council offices in South London looks back on the sad story of her life in England. She was abandoned by her unfaithful husband after her arrival in London in the 1950's and then lost her hard-won home in Brixton when it was compulsorily purchased by the council for redevelopment. Finally she reflects on the unfortunate events in 1950s Jamaica that set her off on this unhappy path in life.

Romance by Joan Riley (1988). A lively family drama set in South London. Overweight Verona lives with her elder sister Desiree, who's married to John, a lapsed black activist. Tension rises when Verona starts a secret relationship with a white man and Desiree's wish to continue her education is met with hostility from John. On top of all this comes the arrival of John's elderly grandparents from Jamaica . . . *Recommended.

Poetry

The poetic tradition is very strong among black British writers of Caribbean origin.

Voices of the Living and the Dead, Dread Beat an' Blood, Inglan is a Bitch, are all collections of poems by Linton Kwesi Johnson, who makes extensive use of Jamaican dialect (patois). Johnson's work is one expression of the way in which Jamaican patois has become an important element in black identity in London. Many British-born blacks who do not have a real command of patois will still nevertheless use particular words with a strong Jamaican pronunciation, even if their own parents did not come from Jamaica. Reggae music has had an important influence in maintaining patois in the British-born generation. *Recommended.

News For Babylon, edited by James Berry (1984). An anthology of 'West-Indian-British' poetry, including work by Linton Kwesi Johnson, Benjamin Zephaniah, Andrew Salkey, Samuel Selvon and James Berry.

ARAB LONDON

HISTORY

The Arab-speaking world stretches from Morocco in the west to Iraq in the east and takes in about 190 million people.

Arabs first came to Britain in the late 19th C. Trade with the Ottoman Empire was opening up and Syrian-Lebanese businessmen came to trade in England, many opening offices in Manchester. Yemenite seamen working on ships that passed through Aden also settled in the ports of Cardiff and South Shields.

The establishment of South Yemen as a British protectorate in 1905 consolidated its links with Britain, and there was a steady trickle of Yemenite immigration through to the 1980s, by which time Yemenite communities had been established in Cardiff, Sheffield, Liverpool, South Shields, and in particular, Birmingham. Small numbers also settled in London.

The next major phase of Arab immigration started in the 1950s and was focused very much on London, but it was not until the oil boom of the 1970s that Arabs became a significant community in London. It was then that oil money brought a large, mainly non-resident population of Gulf Arabs to London. They came to the capital because of its position as a financial centre, because it was English-speaking, and because of its already cosmopolitan culture. For the most part they stayed in London only over the summer, when the English weather is at its best and their own countries at their hottest.

The influx of Gulf Arabs coincided with the outbreak of the Lebanese civil war. At that time Beirut was the major newspaper centre in the Arab world, and the industry soon relocated to London, with the help of Gulf money. London has been the major Arab newspaper centre ever since.

Gulf Arabs also drew in other Arabs to Britain to provide services for them. The Lebanese opened restaurants, the Moroccans worked in the restaurants, the Egyptians opened up video shops and other businesses. Even today much employment for Arabs in London is provided directly or indirectly by Gulf money.

The 'Arab community' in London today is very fragmented. The largest resident communities are Egyptian, Moroccan and Iraqi, but there are many other small national groups. Some Arabs are professionals who have come to Britain for economic reasons, some are refugees and political exiles (particularly the Iraqis), and some are low-paid migrants working in hotels and catering (particularly the Moroccans). Most are Muslims, but there are significant numbers of Christians from Egypt, Iraq and the Lebanon.

It is difficult to say exactly what the size of the Arab population of Britain is, as statistics have not been properly compiled. A government report in 1987 gave an estimate of 75,000 Arabs in the UK and 30,000 in London, but this is probably an underestimate and a figure of 50,000 Arabs in London is probably more accurate.

Most Arabs live in the City of Westminster or the borough of Kensington and Chelsea, and the southern end of Edgware Road, W2, and Queensway, W2, in Bayswater have become noticeable Arab business and cultural centres.

'Inside Out'

Interview with Ibrahim, an Egyptian journalist . . .

"London is the publishing centre of the Arab world. You have five major newspapers here and about a hundred other publications - weekly magazines, monthlies etc. They use the most advanced technology to print. Using a satellite computer link they send the finished paper or magazine to printing centres in the Middle East and across the world so that it is printed in every place on the same day. There's no Arab 'Fleet Street' in London though, the journalists are scattered across the city.

I came here in 1984 to do a Ph.D. in economics at Durham University, but I couldn't continue as a full-time student, so I came down to London where I was recruited as an economic reporter by a Saudi newspaper. Today I work as a freelance for several papers, specialising in economic news and in transferring news about the Western world to the Arab world.

I visit Cairo at least every couple of months. I belong to the Arab community here but you cannot forget you are Egyptian. People in London forget that the Gulf Arabs are not the only Arab people. It's because when they see Gulf Arabs wearing traditional clothes, they say, 'oh they're Arabs', but if they're Egyptians or Lebanese wearing western clothes, they don't notice them. Anyway, most Gulf Arabs come here only in the summer when it's the hottest in the Gulf and when their kids have their school holidays. They go everywhere to escape the heat - Cairo, Tunis, Morocco, Geneva, Paris, London."

SHOPPING

Fota Video. 15-17 Edgware Road, W2 (071-724 1221). Open from 9am to 11pm Monday to Sunday. An Egyptian-owned shop that principally sells Hi-Fi equipment, but also stocks Arabic magazines and books, mostly from Egypt.

Sam Stores, 37 Edgware Road, W2 (071-723 4673). Open from 9.30am to 10pm Monday to Sunday (open from 10am Sunday). Newspapers and magazines in Arabic.

Kingscraft, 62 Edgware Road, W2 (071-402 9201). Open from 10.30am to 10.30pm Monday to Sunday. Arabic videos, music cassettes and jewellery.

Eman's News U.K., 123 Queensway, W2 (071-727 6122). Open from 7am to midnight Monday to Sunday. Newspapers, books and magazines in many languages, including a large Arabic selection.

Al Saqi Books, 26 Westbourne Grove, W2 (071-229 8543). Open from 10am to 7pm Monday to Saturday. Books in Arabic or on Arabic subjects.

Al Hoda, 76-78 Charing Cross Road, WC2 (071-240 8381). Open from 10am to 6pm Monday to Saturday. Books on Islam and the Islamic world, mainly in English.

Arthur Probsthain, 41 Great Russell Street, WC1 (071-636 1096). Open from 9am to 5.30pm Monday to Friday, 11am to 4pm Saturday. Books on Islam and the Islamic world, mainly in English.

Moroccan Bazaar, 16 D'Arblay Street, W1 (071-439 4014). Open from 11am to 6pm Monday to Friday. Moroccan arts and crafts including kaftans, brassware, jewellery and tagines (earthenware casseroles for cooking Moroccan stews).

Al Kashkool Bookshop, 56 Knightsbridge, SW1 (071-235 4240). Open from 10am to 8pm Monday to Saturday. Books in English and Arabic on Arab subjects.

Muslim Book Shop, 233 Seven Sisters Road, N4 (071-272 5170). Open from 10am to 6pm Monday to Saturday. 11am to 4pm Sunday. Books in Arabic and English on Islam and the Islamic world.

Egyptian Touch, 76 Goldhawk Road, W12 (081-749 8790). Open from 10am to 6pm Monday to Saturday. Egyptian arts and crafts including carpets, lamps and sculpture. Strong emphasis on Ancient Egypt.

FOOD AND DRINK

Most Arabic food sold and served in London's shops and restaurants is Lebanese, which is regarded as the haute cuisine of the Middle East and is not dissimilar to Cypriot cuisine. Most Lebanese restaurants offer similar food, served amidst similar, usually rather glitzy surroundings. There is always a lengthy list of appetizers (meze), hot and cold, but the main courses rarely stray too far from grilled meats or fish.

The other type of Arab food found in London is the cuisine of the North African countries of Morocco, Algeria and Tunisia, which is quite distinct from that of the Middle East.

Couscous, found in all three countries, is steamed semolina served with meat, vegetables and sauce. Other specialities are *tajines* (a type of meat pie) and *brik à l'oeuf* (a triangular *filo* pastry envelope stuffed with raw egg, chopped onion, parsley and sometimes fish).

Restaurants

Maroush 1, 21 Edgware Road, W2 (071-262 1090). Open from 12 noon to 2am Monday to Sunday. One of a group of restaurants, Maroush 1 specialises in Lebanese cuisine. There is a snack bar on the ground floor, but the restaurant on the lower floor has a more ambitious menu - with live music nightly.

Ranoush Juice, 43 Edgware Road, W2 (071-723 5929). Open from 9am to 2am Monday to Friday. Snack bar and take-away. As the name implies, the speciality here is fruit juices - all made from fresh fruits. There is also a Lebanese take-away menu. Probably the smartest take-away of any type in London.

The Lebanese Restaurant, 60 Edgware Road, W2. (071-262 9585/723 9130). Open from 12 noon to midnight Monday to Sunday. In addition to standard Lebanese fare, couscous and some French main courses are available. Medium price range.

Halal, 118 Edgware Road, W2 (071-723 2248). Open from 11am to 1am Monday to Sunday. Lebanese café/take-away. Good value for money.

Al Omaraa, 27 Queensway, W2 (071-221 8045/229 9898). Open from 12 noon to midnight, Monday to Saturday. Meze is the speciality of this small Lebanese restaurant, and there is a vegetarian selection.

Abohammad Restaurant, 102 Queensway, W2 (071-727 0830). Open from

11am to 1am Monday to Sunday. There is a café/snack bar in the entrance; the main restaurant lies below. Lebanese.

Bab Marrakech, 91 Golborne Road, W10 (no telephone). Open from 8.30am to 8 .30pm Monday to Sunday. Morrocan café. Mint tea and Morrocan cakes.

Phoenecia, 11-13 Abingdon Road, W8 (071-937 0808). Open from 12.15pm to midnight Monday to Sunday. Up-market Lebanese restaurant.

Le Petit Prince, 5 Holmes Road, NW5 (071-267 0752). Open from 12 noon to 2.30pm, 7pm to 11.30pm Monday to Sunday (except closed for lunch Sunday). Owned by a Frenchman, but specialising in North African food, this café/restaurant includes couscous and merquez (meat balls) on its menu. There are also vegetarian dishes.

Al Basha, 222 Kensington High Street, W8 (O71-938 1794). Open from 12 noon to midnight Monday to Sunday. A very smart Lebanese restaurant, which boasts a small terrace overlooking Holland Park for summer dining.

Ali Baba, 32 Ivor Place, NW1 (071-723 5805/723 7474). Open from 12 noon to midnight Monday to Sunday. Egyptian restaurant.

Adam's Café, 77 Askew Road, W12 (081-743 0572). Open from 7.30am to 10.30pm Monday to Saturday (no credit cards). This extraordinary establishment leads a double life; by day it is a café, serving eggs and bacon etc. but a transformation takes place in the evening. Table clothes are laid, the breakfast counter disguised, the walls decorated and it becomes a Tunisian restaurant. The menu varies, but couscous can be depended on. So highly regarded is the Tunisian patron/chef that Adam's Café made the 1992 Good Food Guide. Bring your own wine and make a reservation as there are not many tables.

Baalbek, 18 Hogarth Place, W1 (071-373 7199). Open from 6 to 11pm Monday to Saturday. A medium priced Lebanese restaurant.

Maroush, 62 Seymour Street, W1 (071-724 5024). Open from 12 noon to 1am Monday to Sunday. Lebanese restaurant.

La Reash Cous Cous House, 23-24 Compton Street, W1 (071-439 1062/437 2366). Open from 12 noon to midnight Monday to Sunday. Moroccan restaurant, but also includes some Lebanese dishes.

The Tageen, 12 Upper St. Martins Lane, WC2 (071-836 7272). Open from Monday to Saturday 12 noon to 12.30pm, 6.30pm to 11pm (except closed for lunch Saturday). A smart Moroccan restaurant.

Al Hamra, 31-33 Shepherds Market, W1 (071-493 6934). Open from 1pm to midnight Monday to Saturday. A very smart Lebanese restaurant.

Fakhreldine, 85 Piccadilly, W1 (071-493 3244). Open from 12 noon to midnight Monday to Sunday. Lebanese, very smart and very expensive.

The Olive Tree, 11 Wardour Street, W1 (071-734 0808). Open from 12 noon to 11pm Monday to Sunday. This restaurant is hard to classify as the Jewish patron was born in Baghdad and includes hot salt beef on his otherwise Arabic menu. Half the dishes are vegetarian, but kebabs and couscous also make an appearance. Moderately priced.

Alrafidain Restaurant, 72 Dalling Road, W6 (081-748 8791). Open from 6pm to 12 midnight, Monday to Sunday. Iraqi restaurant/café.

Food Shops

Lords Arabic Food, 18-20 Queensway, W2 (071-727 3139). Open from 8am to 11pm. Monday to Sunday (except opens at 9am Sunday). Middle Eastern sweets.

Green Valley, 36 Upper Berkeley Street, W1 (071-402 7385). Open from 9.30am to 9pm Monday to Saturday, 10am to 5pm Sunday. Middle Eastern sweets and pastries.

L'Etoile Sousse, 79 Golbourne Road, W10 (081-960 9769). Open from 8am to 8pm Monday to Saturday. Moroccan bakery.

OTHER PLACES TO VISIT

British Museum, Great Russell Street, WC1 (071-636 1555). Open from 10am to 5pm Monday to Saturday, 2.30 to 6pm Sunday. Admission free. The John Addis Islamic Gallery holds a large collection of antiquities from Arab and other Islamic countries and cultures, including ceramics, metalwork, paintings and woodwork from earliest times up to the present day. The Museum also features extensive collections of antiquities from pre-Islamic Middle Eastern cultures.

Victoria and Albert Museum, Cromwell Road, SW7 (071-589 6371). Open from 12 noon to 5.50pm Monday, 10am to 5.50pm Tuesday to Sunday. The Islamic Gallery features antiquities from Arab and other Islamic countries from the 7th to the 19th C, with particular emphasis on pottery, textiles and metalwork. Islamic antiquities can also be found elsewhere within the ceramic, textile and metalwork collection.

A SELECT BIBLIOGRAPHY

Unless stated otherwise the following titles were published in London.

Titles mentioned in text

L Wagner *London Saunterings* (Allen & Unwin, 1928). Sun Yat Sen *Kidnapped in London* (Arrowsmith, Bristol, 1897). Timothy Mo *Sour Sweet* (Deutsch, 1982). James D Hunt *Gandhi in London* (Promilla, New Delhi, 1978). Kamala Markandaya *The Nowhere Man* (Allen Lane, 1973). Hassif Kreishi *The Buddha of Suburbia* (1990). Ravinder Randhawa *A Wicked Old Woman* (The Women's Press, 1987). Farhana Sheikh *The Red Box* (The Women's Press, 1991). Atima Srivastava *Transmission* (Serpent's Tail, 1992). Farrukh Dhondy *East End at Your Feet* (Macmillan, 1976). Jerzy Peterkiewicz *Future to Let* (Heinemann, 1958). Peppino Leoni *I Shall Die on the Carpet* (Frewin, 1966). George Sims (ed) *Living London* (Cassell, 1902). M Green (ed) *Casanova: In London* (Mayflower, 1969). Wolf Mankowitz *A Kid for Two Farthings (Deutsch,* 1953). Arnold Wesker *Chicken Soup with Barley* (from *The Wesker Trilogy,* Cape, 1960). Emmanuel Litvinoff *Journey Through A Small Planet* (Joseph, 1972). Harry Blacker *Just Like it Was: Memoirs of the Mittel East (Vallentine,* 1974). Israel Zangwill *Children of the Ghetto* (Heinemann, 1892). Joe Jacobs *Out of the Ghetto* (Simon, 1978). Chaim Bermant *The Jews* (Weidenfeld & Nicolson, 1977). Gerda Charles *The Crossing Point* (Eyre and Spottiswoode, 1960). Sidney Lightman (ed) *The Jewish Travel Guide* (Jewish Chronicle Publications, 1985). Gustav Dore and Blanchard Jerrold *London* (Grant and Co, 1872). Donall MacAmhlaigh *An Irish Navvy* (Routledge, 1964). Tim Pat Coogan *The IRA* (Pall Mall Press, 1970, 2nd edition Fontana, 1980). Edna O'Brien *Girls in their Married Bliss* (Cape, 1964). Brendan Ward *Builders Chancers and Crack* (Allen, 1985). Ottobah Cugoano *Thoughts and Sentiments on the Evil and Wicked Trafficof the Slavery and Commerce of the Human Species* (1787). Olaudah Equiano *The Interesting Narrative of the Life of Olaudah Equiano or Gustavas Vassa the African* (1789). Paul Edwards (ed) *Equiano's Travels* (Heinemann, 1967). Mary Seacole *Wonderful Adventures of Mrs Seacole in Many Lands (1857,* and Falling Wall Press, 1984). Amy Garvey (ed) *Philosophy and Opinions of Marcus Garvey* (Universal Publishing House, New York, 2 volumes, 1923 and 1925). E R Braithwaite *To Sir, With Love* (The Bodley Head, 1959). Buchi Emecheta *Second Class Citizen* (Allison and Busby, 1975), *In the Ditch* (Barrie and Jenkins, 1972), *Adah's Story* (Allison and Busby, 1983). Andrew Salkey *Come Home, Malcolm Heartland* (Hutchinson, 1976). Caryl Phillips *The Final Passage (Faber and Faber,* 1985). George Lamming *The Emigrants* (Allison and Busby, 1954). Samuel Selvon *The Lonely Londoners* (Alan Wingate, 1956), *Moses Ascending* (David-Poynter, 1975), *Moses Migrating* (Longman, 1983).

Titles not mentioned in text

Ng Kwee Choo *The Chinese in London* (Oxford University Press, 1968). D Jones *Chinese in Britain* (from the magazine *New Community,* Commission for Racial Equality, 1979). M Dummett (chairman) *Southall 23 April 1979: the Report of the Unoffcial Committee of Enquiry* (National Countil of Civil Liberties, 1980). K Vadgama India in Britain (Royce, 1984). J Watson (ed) *Between Two Cultures* (Blackwell, 1977). C Kumar and M Puri *Mahatma Gandhi: His Life and Influence* (Heinemann, 1982). J Zubrycki *Polish Immigrants in Britain* (Martinus Nijhoff, The Hague, 1956). Z Najder (ed) *Conrad's Polish Background* (Oxford University Press, 1964). *U Marin Italiani in Gran Bretagna* (Centro Studi Emigrazione, Rome, 1975). R Palmer *Immigrants ignored: An Appraisal of the Italians in Britain* (thesis, no date given). Gerald Croner (ed) *England* (Keter, Jerusalem, 1978). Aubrey Newman (ed) *The Jewish East End 1840-1939* (Jewish Historical Society of England, 1981). Cecil Roth *A History of the Jews in England* (Clarendon Press, Oxford, 1964). Cecil Roth (ed) *The Concise Jewish Encyclopedia* (New American Library, New York, 1980). K O'Connor *The Irish in Britain* (Sigdwick and Jackson, 1972). L H Leese *Exile of Erin: Irish Migrants in Victorian London* (Manchester University Press, 1979). H Bolan *A Dictionary of Irish Biography* (Gill and Macmillan, Dublin, 1978). R Hogan (ed) *The Macmillan Dictionary of Irish Literature.* P Fryer *Staying Power* (Pluto *Press,* 1984). F Shyllon *Black People in Britain 1555-1833* (Oxford University Press, 1977). E Scobie *Black Brittania* (Johnson, Chicago, 1972). *The Brixton Disorders 10-12 April 1981: Report of an Inquiry by the Rt Hon The Lord Scarman* (HMSO, 1981). C Dakers *The Blue Plaque Guide to London* (Macmillan, 1981). S Rossier (ed) *Blue Guide: London* (Benn, 1978). D Stephenson *Bookshops of London* (Lascelles, 1984). A Byron *London Statues* (Constable, 1981). Lindsey Bareham *A Guide to London's Ethnic Restaurants* (Pan, 1989). Linda Zeff *Jewish London* (Piatkus, 1986). Jorgen Nielsen *Muslims in Western Europe* (Edinburgh University Press, 1992). *Arabs in Britain: Concerns and Prospects* (Riad El-Rayyes Books, 1991).

ACKNOWLEDGEMENTS

My many thanks to Christopher Turner for all his work on updating the book for this second edition, and to Marion Bowman and Carlton TV for their permission to use photos and interviews from the series 'Dilly Down Town' in this book. Many of the interviews featured in the 'Inside Out' sections in this book were made by Dilly Braimoh, the presenter on 'Dilly Down Town', so my thanks too to him and to all the production team on the series.

Thanks are also due to Aamer Hussein, Christiane Keane, Erica Wagner, Andrew Leddy, Lucy Pilkington, Adriana Luba, Nick Axarlis, Rickie Burman, David Jacobs, Maureen Hartigan, Gaik See Chow, Prabhu Guptara, Pino Maestri, Jim Pines, Rose Shillito, Kazimierz Wieliczko, Edward Hotspur Johnson and Bill Fishman.

INDEX